"Urban resettlement, a silent phenomenon in the Global South, is given real light and insightful analyses. The destruction, production, and re-production of urban spaces underlie the process of urbanisation and urban development in the Global South yet given less attention in both theory and practice. This is certainly a captivating and a must-read book for both urban practitioners and theorists."

George Owusu, *Professor of Urban Geography, Institute of Statistical, Social & Economic Research (ISSER) and Dean, School of Social Sciences, University of Ghana, Ghana*

"Envisioning urban resettlement as an ambiguous, poorly conceptualised yet prevalent urban condition, this critical, fresh and timely edited collection draws together scholarship working to centre the diverse lived experiences of those who are resettled. Global in its reach, and thick with empirical insights, the book advances understanding of the complexities and contradictions of legal, political, economic and subjective facets of resettlement. Claiming the significance of a critical politics of the urban, the book's subtle and informed analyses speak directly to planning and housing policy and offer a valuable resource for urban researchers."

Paula Meth, *Reader & Director of Student Experience, Department of Urban Studies and Planning, University of Sheffield, UK*

"A very important intervention, that critically conceptualises the idea of urban resettlement, in order to understand the dual, ambivalent and dialectic process of displacement and relocation in all its complexities. Grounded in the lived experiences of city dwellers, richly woven and careful ethnographies account for the liminal conditions that resettled dwellers experience, their home- and place-making capacities. At the same time, this book offers a cutting-edge political analysis of the governing of everyday life, the production of unequal subjectivities and identities in the Global South, bringing together a truly international collective of researchers and fostering theory-generating connections between variegated sites. A precious, insightful read."

Myriam Houssay-Holzschuch, *Professor, Institut d'Urbanisme et de Géographie Alpine, Université Grenoble Alpes, France*

"Urban Resettlements in the Global South is an engaging collection of 'lived experiences' of people and places going through often traumatic displacement and relocation induced by urban development projects. It goes far beyond conventionally prescriptive studies on getting resettlement right or critical literature on resettlement as a coercive mechanism. This book establishes a fresh insight into intricacies of resettlement through empirically-rich case studies on lifeworlds of resettled people as major weavers of urban fabrics across continents. It urges readers to think through meanings of uprootedness and continuous rebuilding of lives in our rapidly urbanising world."

Kei Otsuki, *Associate Professor in International Development Studies, Utrecht University, The Netherlands*

URBAN RESETTLEMENTS IN THE GLOBAL SOUTH

Urban Resettlements in the Global South provides new perspectives on resettlement through an urban studies lens. To date, resettlement has been theorised through development studies and refugee studies, but urban resettlement is also a major dimension of urban development in the Global South and may help to rethink contemporary urban dynamics between spectacular new town developments and rising incidences of eviction and displacement. Conceptualising resettlement as a binding notion between production/regeneration and destruction/demolition of urban space helps to illuminate interdependencies and to underline significant ambiguities within affected people's perspectives towards resettlement projects. This volume will offer an interesting selection of ten different case studies with rich empirical data from Latin America, North and Sub-Saharan Africa, and Asia, focused on each stage of resettlement (before, during, after relocation) through different timescales. By offering a frame for analysing and rethinking resettlement within urban studies, it will support any scholar or expert dealing with resettlement, displacement, and housing in an urban context, seeking to improve housing and planning policies in and for the city.

Raffael Beier is a Postdoctoral Research Fellow at the department of International Planning Studies at TU Dortmund University, Germany. During the time of co-editing and writing, he was working as the coordinator of the PhD programme in International Development Studies at the Institute of Development Research and Development Policy at Ruhr University Bochum and was further associated with the Centre for Built Environment Studies (CUBES) at the University of the Witwatersrand, Johannesburg, South Africa. Currently, he is leading a research project on dropout and post-resettlement mobilities in state-led affordable housing projects, funded by the German Research Foundation (DFG).

Amandine Spire is Assistant Professor in Geography at the Centre for Social Sciences Studies on Africa, America, and Asia (CESSMA) of the University of Paris, where she researches migration and urban issues and leads courses on urban and social geography. Her current research focuses on power relations and city dwellers' subjectivities in cities in the Global South, particularly in Lomé (Togo) and Accra (Ghana). From 2014 to 2019, she led a research program on the right to the city in the Global South and she focused her research on the relocation and urban resettlement of city dwellers in Africa.

Marie Bridonneau is an Assistant Professor in Geography at the University of Paris-Nanterre and a member of the LAVUE research unit. She has also been the director of the French Centre for Ethiopian Studies in Addis Ababa (Ethiopia) since September 2018. Her research deals with urban dynamics (involuntary displacements, small towns, urban peripheries) and politics of cultural heritage in Ethiopia and Eritrea.

URBAN RESETTLEMENTS IN THE GLOBAL SOUTH

Lived Experiences of Housing and Infrastructure between Displacement and Relocation

Edited by Raffael Beier, Amandine Spire and Marie Bridonneau

Routledge
Taylor & Francis Group
NEW YORK AND LONDON

First published 2022
by Routledge
605 Third Avenue, New York, NY 10158

and by Routledge
2 Park Square, Milton Park, Abingdon, Oxon OX14 4RN

Routledge is an imprint of the Taylor & Francis Group, an informa business

British Library Cataloguing-in-Publication Data
A catalogue record for this book is available from the British Library

Library of Congress Cataloging-in-Publication Data
Names: Beier, Raffael, editor.
Title: Urban resettlements in the Global South : lived experiences of housing and infrastructure between displacement and relocation / edited by Raffael Beier, Amandine Spire and Marie Bridonneau.
Description: Abingdon, Oxon ; New York, NY : Routledge, 2021. |
Includes bibliographical references and index.
Identifiers: LCCN 2021008945 (print) | LCCN 2021008946 (ebook) |
ISBN 9780367644444 (hbk) | ISBN 9780367644437 (pbk) | ISBN 9781003124559 (ebk)
Subjects: LCSH: Urban poor--Housing--Developing countries. | Relocation (Housing)--Developing countries. | Urbanization--Developing countries. |
Land settlement--Developing countries.
Classification: LCC HD7287.95 .U58 2021 (print) | LCC HD7287.95 (ebook) | DDC 363.5/83--dc23
LC record available at https://lccn.loc.gov/2021008945
LC ebook record available at https://lccn.loc.gov/2021008946

ISBN: 978-0-367-64444-4 (hbk)
ISBN: 978-0-367-64443-7 (pbk)
ISBN: 978-1-003-12455-9 (ebk)

DOI: 10.4324/9781003124559

Typeset in Bembo
by Taylor & Francis Books

CONTENTS

FIGURES

TABLES

CONTRIBUTORS

Toktam Ashnaiy is a joint PhD candidate in Urban Planning and Development Studies at Iran University of Science and Technology (IUST), Tehran, Iran, and at the International Institute of Social Studies (ISS), part of Erasmus University Rotterdam (EUR), The Netherlands. She holds a master's degree in Regional Development Studies from IUST. Her main research interest is the critical and radical assessment of the urban informal settlements by applying a post-development approach. Working on peri-urban areas, spatial development, and everyday life methodologies are some of her other experiences and interests in academic and professional settings.

Raffael Beier is a Postdoctoral Research Fellow at the department of International Planning Studies at TU Dortmund University, Germany. During the time of co-editing and writing, he was working as the coordinator of the PhD programme in International Development Studies at the Institute of Development Research and Development Policy at Ruhr University Bochum and was further associated with the Centre for Built Environment Studies (CUBES) at the University of the Witwatersrand, Johannesburg, South Africa. Currently, he is leading a research project on dropout and post-resettlement mobilities in state-led affordable housing projects, funded by the German Research Foundation (DFG).

Erhard Berner is Associate Professor of Development Sociology at the International Institute of Social Studies (ISS), The Hague, the Netherlands, and a Visiting Associate Professor at the University of the Witwatersrand, Johannesburg, South Africa. He has done extensive research on urban poverty and community responses in several countries in Africa, South, and Southeast Asia and published a book and numerous articles on the subject. He has also served as a consultant to UN-Habitat, international and Dutch NGOs and government institutions in the fields of urban poverty, housing, basic services, and small enterprise promotion. Current research focuses on urban governance, informal housing, microenterprises, and poverty alleviation. Teaching experience includes Ateneo de Manila University, Tribhuvan University in Kathmandu, University of Namibia in Windhoek, and Nsamizi Institute in Mpigi, Uganda

Marie Bridonneau is an Assistant Professor in Geography at the University of Paris-Nanterre and a member of the LAVUE research unit. She has also been the director of the French Centre for Ethiopian Studies in Addis Ababa (Ethiopia) since September 2018. Her research deals with urban dynamics (involuntary displacements, small towns, urban peripheries) and politics of cultural heritage in Ethiopia and Eritrea.

Corentin Chanet holds a Master's in Anthropology (ULB, 2014) and a Master's in Sociology (ULB, 2015) from the Université Libre de Bruxelles. Currently finishing a PhD thesis at the Laboratoire d'Anthropologie des Mondes Contemporains (LAMC-ULB), his research focus on mining-induced urban resettlement and social stratification in Ghana. Aside from his doctoral research, he has also been active in the fields of philosophy of mind and artificial intelligence.

María Alejandra Ciuffolini is a Professor of Contemporary Political Theory and Juridic Sociology at the Universidad Nacional de Córdoba (UNC), Argentina. At the UNC, she is a full researcher and a member of the Social Council of the Social Science Faculty, which is dedicated to science transfer and dissemination. She obtained a PhD in Social Sciences from the University of Buenos Aires (UBA). Since 2004, she has been the director of the "El Llano en Llamas" research team that led this study. Currently, she is running research projects on the forms of government and power of neoliberalism in Argentina and in Latin America. In addition, she is the lead editor of the academic journal *Crítica y Resistencias.*

Candela de la Vega is a Professor of Contemporary Political Theory at the Universidad Nacional de Córdoba (UNC), Argentina, and the Universidad Católica de Córdoba (UCC), Argentina. She works as a Postdoctoral Fellow at the Consejo Nacional de Investigaciones Científicas y Técnicas (National Scientific and Technical Research Council Argentina – CONICET). She obtained a PhD in Social Sciences from the University of Buenos Aires (UBA). Since 2004, she has been a member of "El llano en llamas" research team, dedicated to the study of contemporary social conflicts and political struggles in Latin America, where she coordinates the research line in environmental and territorial conflicts. Regarding science transfer, for more than 10 years she has been running dissemination projects oriented to convey research results that may be useful for local marginalised communities in order to improve both their life conditions and citizen practices.

Véronique Dupont is a senior research fellow in urban studies at the Institut de Recherche pour le Développement (IRD) – French National Research Institute for Sustainable Development, in the CESSMA research unit – the Centre for Social Sciences Studies on Africa, America and Asia, University of Paris. She is also associated with the Centre for Indian and South Asian Studies, Paris and is a Senior Visiting Fellow at the Centre for Policy Research, Delhi. She was joint director of CESSMA from 2014 to 2018 and the director of the Centre for Social Sciences and Humanities (CSH) in Delhi from 2003 to 2007. Her research focuses on the socio-spatial transformations of Indian metropolises. She is particularly interested in the interrelations between urban policies and residential and coping strategies of the populations in informal settlements.

Kira Erwin is an urban sociologist and Senior Researcher at the Urban Futures Centre at the Durban University of Technology in Durban, South Africa. Her research and publications focus largely on race, racialisation, racism, and anti-racism work within the urban context. Her current projects explore issues of migration, gender, and inclusion and how recipients of state delivered housing construct narratives of home and belonging. Her projects make use of creative participatory methods, and she collaborates with colleagues in various creative fields to produce forms of public storytelling that extend research beyond the walls of academia.

M.M. Shankare Gowda is an independent social science researcher based in Delhi. He holds a PhD in political sciences and was a Postdoctoral Fellow of the Indian Council of Social Sciences Research from 2009 to 2012. He has been associated with the Centre for Policy Research, Delhi. Earlier, he was associated with the Centre for Social Sciences and Humanities (CSH) in Delhi. His areas of interest include identity politics, government and politics, party systems, and local and urban governance in India. He has conducted extensive field research in Delhi as well as in several states in India.

Juliana Hernández Bertone is a researcher at the Universidad Católica de Córdoba (UCC), Argentina. She holds a PhD in Political Science from the Universidad Nacional de Córdoba (UNC), Argentina, and also holds a PhD in Humans Rights from the University of Deusto (UD), Spain. She was a Postdoctoral Fellow of the UNESCO Chairs program at the UD. Since 2004, she has been a member of "El llano en llamas" research team, dedicated to the study of contemporary social conflicts and political struggles in Latin America, where she coordinates the research line in housing policies and social conflicts. Currently, she is conducting research projects on the intersection between feminism, democracy, and citizenship. In addition, she is a member of the editorial board of the academic journal *Crítica y Resistencias.*

Marie Huchzermeyer is a Professor in the School of Architecture and Planning at the University of the Witwatersrand in Johannesburg, South Africa, where she currently convenes the Master's in Urban Studies. She is affiliated to the Centre for Urbanism and Built Environment Studies (CUBES) in the School, and is a Principle Investigator of the German-funded Wits-TUB-UNILAG Urban Lab, which has its focus on sustainable development goals with critical engagement with the urban context on the African continent. Her research interests are in housing and informal settlement policy, private rental housing, housing rights, urban policy, and the right to the city. She has published extensively, with her studies spanning South Africa, Brazil, Kenya, and Germany.

Sílvia Jorge is an architect. She graduated from the Lisbon School of Architecture, University of Lisbon (2007) with a Master's degree in Architecture and Rehabilitation of Urban Centres (2009) and a PhD in Urban Planning (2017). Since 2008, she has been a member of the Urban Socio-Territorial and Local Intervention Study Group (Gestual) of the Research Centre for Architecture, Urbanism, and Design (CIAUD), where she has been focusing mainly on Portuguese and Mozambican urban contexts. Sílvia has also collaborated with other research centres, such as the Centre for Studies and Development of Habitat at Eduardo Mondlane University, Maputo, and the Centre for African Studies, at the University Institute of Lisbon, as well as with non-governmental organisations.

Vanessa Melo is an architect. She graduated from the Lisbon School of Architecture, University of Lisbon (1998) with a master's degree in Planning and Sustainable Construction (2008) and a PhD in Urban Planning (2015). Since 2009, she has been a member of the Urban Socio-Territorial and Local Intervention Study Group (Gestual) of the Research Centre for Architecture, Urbanism, and Design (CIAUD), where she works on themes related to urban space production and housing in Southern Africa. For two years, she was also a Postdoctoral Fellow at the University of the Witwatersrand, in Johannesburg, where she was involved in a research project about urban transformations related to the growth of the middle class.

Sogen Moodley is an urban planner with over 21 years of local government experience at the eThekwini Municipality, Durban, South Africa. He has extensive experience in urban strategic planning and City-to-City (C2C) learning through his former position as Technical Chair of the Urban Strategic Planning Committee and the Learning Forum of the international United Cities and Local Governments (UCLG). He led the Durban strategic planning process for 10 years before conceptualising and managing the Municipal Institute of Learning (www.mile.org.za), a knowledge management initiative that promoted knowledge networks and supported local governments in the global South for nine years. In September 2017, he transitioned into the world of academia, joining the Durban University of Technology (DUT), where he is currently a Research Associate at the Urban Futures Centre (UFC).

Francesca Pilo' is Assistant Professor in Spatial Planning at Utrecht University. Her research primarily focuses on the political role of infrastructure in the production of cities and in mediating the relationship between the citizens and institutional actors, particularly in the Global South. Her current research concerns the governance of urban infrastructure and the interplay of urban services, citizenship, informal urbanisation, and urban energy transitions predominantly in Rio de Janeiro (Brazil) and Kingston (Jamaica). Prior to joining Utrecht University, she held positions at the Université libre de Bruxelles, Paris Diderot University, and the University of Amsterdam.

Amandine Spire is Assistant Professor in Geography at the Centre for Social Sciences Studies on Africa, America, and Asia (CESSMA) of the University of Paris, where she researches migration and urban issues and leads courses on urban and social geography. Her current research focuses on power relations and city dwellers' subjectivities in cities in the Global South, particularly in Lomé (Togo) and Accra (Ghana). From 2014 to 2019, she led a research program on the right tothe city in the Global South and she focused her research on the relocation and urban resettlement of city dwellers in Africa.

ACKNOWLEDGEMENTS

The idea for this book was born during a small but inspiring panel on urban resettlements at the 7th European Conference on African Studies (ECAS) in Basel in 2017. One-and-a-half years later, in February 2019, the four presenters and panel organisers finally came together at the University of Paris to substantiate the idea for a collective edited volume. After this starting point, the book project further developed during another stimulating panel at the 8th ECAS conference in Edinburgh in June 2019, which allowed us to meet with other contributors in person. We would not have expected this to be one of the last times we met each other in person. Thus, we are extremely grateful to Corentin Chanet, who started this endeavour with us and who influenced it from the very first moment in Basel. Moreover, we would like to thank ECAS conference organisers in both Basel and Edinburgh for offering us a platform to meet in person, to discuss, and to develop the initial ideas of this book.

This book wouldn't have been possible without the support and contribution of a series of persons and institutions. We are first of all very grateful to all reviewers who agreed to read and comment on the individual chapters during special and extremely challenging times. Their constructive feedback has helped to further strengthen the individual chapters as well as the entire book: Genet Alem, Nadine Appelhans, Johanna Brugman Alvarez, Eva Camelli, Tanya Chaudhary, Valérie Clerc, Agnès Deboulet, Irit Eguavoen, Hassan Elmouelhi, Matthias Gebauer, Christoph Haferburg, Myriam Houssay-Holzschuch, Hossein Imani Jajarmi, Gerhard Kienast, Amit Kumar, Paula Meth, Laura Montedoro, Alan Morris, Kei Otsuki, Stefano Portelli, Sophie Schramm, Gilbert Siame, Julia Tabbita, and Jeanne Vivet.

We are immensely grateful to Marie Huchzermeyer who spent much of her time discussing the consistency of the entire book and who pushed us to clarify our own red line of arguments. We thank her for agreeing to write an outlook essay for the end of the book, which wraps up the volume's ideas by connecting them to the most recent developments in light of the COVID-19 pandemic.

We want to acknowledge Lize Swartz, who worked to improve some of the book's chapters by providing much more than just English-language assistance for non-native speakers. We really appreciate her enthusiastic professionalism and her extremely useful recommendations.

We would like to express a final thank to the CESSMA research unit (University of Paris), its direction, and Thanusiya Nadanalingam. They made it possible for Lize Swartz to work on the editing of certain chapters. We really thank them for the follow-up and for the financial support, which was very valuable for finalizing this book.

Raffael Beier, Amandine Spire, and Marie Bridonneau

1

INTRODUCTION

Positioning "Urban Resettlement" in the Global Urban South

Raffael Beier, Amandine Spire, Marie Bridonneau and Corentin Chanet

Urban development in the Global South has gained momentum in light of global trends such as rapid urbanisation, mounting global competition among cities for increasingly mobile capital, a New Urban Agenda, and a Sustainable Development Goal (SDG) directed at building sustainable cities. Cities in Africa, Asia, and Latin America are undergoing unprecedented transformations. In various countries, political and economic elites escape congested and unsafe megacities towards private enclaves and even entirely new capital cities (Carmody and Owusu 2016; Grant 2015; van Noorloos and Kloosterboer 2018; Shatkin 2008). At the same time, new skyscrapers, waterfronts, large-scale infrastructure, and other flagship architecture are reshaping the inner cities of emerging metropoles such as Beirut, Cape Town, Mumbai, and Addis Ababa. Both trends reveal an attempt to move away from the negative image of the megacity by propagating new representations of cities linked to modernity, development, and hubs for national wealth (Côté-Roy and Moser 2019; Robinson 2002; Roy and Ong 2011; Watson 2014). These practices of neoliberal city-making and worlding place pressure on slum dwellers, street traders, and other urban dwellers that supposedly embody elitist conceptions of urban congestion and backwardness (Huchzermeyer 2011; Parnell and Pieterse 2010; Roever and Skinner 2016; Roy 2014; Spire and Choplin 2018). Consequently, new satellite cities and large-scale housing developments at the cities' peripheries have been accommodating a growing population that struggles to (re-) access modernised, central urban spaces (Buckley, Kallergis, and Wainer 2016; Croese, Cirolia, and Graham 2016; Turok 2016).

Against this backdrop of rapid and fundamental urban transformation, displacement and planned relocation have become significant features of urban development and planning in cities of the Global South. On the one hand, inner-city beautification and redevelopment, slum clearance and top-down

DOI: 10.4324/9781003124559-1

"upgrading", infrastructure construction and modernisation, disaster-prevention, and market-driven evictions have occurred somewhat simultaneously, all of them requiring poor residents to leave their urban dwellings – at least temporarily. On the other hand, one observes the construction of new cities and dormitory towns and the provision of state-subsidised housing, as well as the development of new infrastructure, sites-and-services schemes, temporary shelters, and high-rise apartment buildings that come to replace informal settlements. All of them mark beginnings, opportunities, and challenges for urban dwellers in a new spatial setting – even if it is in the same location.

Apart from ongoing forced evictions without alternatives (Brickell, Fernández Arrigoitia, and Vasudevan 2017; du Plessis 2005), both actions – the destruction and production of living spaces – are increasingly being linked directly to each other (cf. Meth et al. 2020; Shannon et al. 2018). Incremental in-situ upgrading as well as the renovation of existing urban structures hold little appeal to an aspiring political, business, and urban planning elite that tends to ignore residents' everyday urban practices and aspirations. Striving for their version of elitist "modernity", they prefer building and developing from scratch, supporting large-scale rehousing and subsidy schemes that move people within cities (Buckley, Kallergis, and Wainer 2016; Côté-Roy and Moser 2019; Croese, Cirolia, and Graham 2016). As such, the urban lives of many low-income dwellers in rapidly transforming and growing cities are becoming increasingly disrupted, subject to constrained movements, and, hence, shaped by interdependent experiences of both displacement *and* relocation (cf. Bhan and Shivanand 2013; de Wet 2008; Doshi 2013; Fernández Arrigoitia 2017).

Following this, the aim of this book is to link displacement and planned relocation from an analytical perspective. Focusing on lived experiences, this book will diverge from displacement and relocation as two different and successive parts of the same process. Instead, we suggest analysing displacement, relocation, and reinstallation *together* through a focus on lived experiences that reveal the inextricability of these processes. These three dimensions contained in the notion of resettlement invite us to adopt a mid- or long-term perspective to the study of urban resettlement, leading us to analyse the production and destruction of urban space as connected, often overlapping, and diverse lived experiences (Figure 1.1). Hence, it allows us to stress post-displacement perspectives still underrepresented in urban studies (Wang 2020). In doing so, the book stresses the term "urban resettlement" by referring to the interwoven processes of displacement, planned relocation, and reinstallation that occur for multiple reasons *within* metropolitan areas. Notwithstanding the existence of urban resettlement within the Global North, this book is particularly interested in revealing new dynamics of rapid urban transformation in emerging cities in the Global South.

Displacement and Relocation: Two Related Concepts for Understanding Resettlement

The terms "displacement" and "resettlement" have been defined and applied in different ways across disciplines and linguistic contexts. Relatively distinct

FIGURE 1.1 Graphic representation of urban resettlement as a lived experience of both the destruction and production of space.
Source: Authors' own figure.

understandings exist in the context of forced migration studies, where displacement is seen as caused by "armed conflict, situations of generalised violence, violations of human rights, or natural or human-made disasters" (UN 1998, paragraph 2). Internally displaced persons flee for reasons similar to those driving refugees from their countries but do not cross state borders. They are thus forcibly displaced within their own countries. In the same context, resettlement refers to the state-planned relocation of forcibly displaced persons to a place differing from the one in which they temporarily settle. While the use of violence or force is frequent in urban resettlements, too, such strictly conflict-related definitions bound to the nation state seem too narrow to explain intra-urban displacements and resettlements that occur for various reasons in more or less coercive settings, processes, and events, while being related to increasingly market-driven urban policies. This motivates our desire to explore the dynamics of both exclusion and (selective) inclusion produced by displacement and resettlement in the name of urban development.

Another differentiated understanding of the two terms has emerged alongside large development projects, often dams or mines, that have forced a large number of people to leave their productive land for the "greater good for greater numbers" (Cernea 1997, 1579). So-called "development-caused forced displacement and resettlement" (DFDR) largely occurred within World Bank-funded projects and urged the Bank to develop operational manuals and policy guidelines to limit the negative effects of involuntary resettlement (Cernea and Maldonado 2018). Following the World Bank's (2001) Operational Policy 4.12 on Involuntary Resettlement, the term displacement is here seen to relate to "all those people who lose land or the right to use land" (World Bank 2004, 5), causing a loss of shelter, assets, or access to assets and income sources, or means of livelihood (World Bank 2001, paragraph 3a). Hence, because of the associated risks of impoverishment for so-called project-affected persons (Cernea 1997; Cernea and Maldonado 2018), the World Bank proclaims that "involuntary resettlement should be avoided where feasible" (World Bank 2001, paragraph 2a). For "unavoidable" DFDR projects led by public authorities and/or private-sector actors, environmental and social standards need to be guaranteed.

However, the Bank's notion of "resettlement" is twofold, to some extent overlapping with "displacement", but in any case, going beyond mere physical relocation. First, resettlement "covers all direct economic and social losses resulting from land taking and restriction of access, *together* with the consequent compensatory and remedial measures" (World Bank 2004, 5, emphasis added). Second, according to the World Bank's (2015) Resettlement Fact Sheet, "involuntary resettlement refers to two distinct but related processes", which are "displacement" and – again – "resettlement". The latter is defined as "the process by which those adversely affected are assisted in their efforts to improve, or at least to restore, their incomes and living standards". Thus, the English term "resettlement" within DFDR is to a certain extent ambiguous and may refer both to a process of involuntary relocation *including* displacement (fr: *relogement*) and the assisted practice of reconstruction *after* displacement and at a different location (fr: *réinstallation* or *replacement*).

Yet, one may distinguish four basic characteristics of a DFDR-based understanding of displacement and resettlement. The first is its rural origin. DFDR literature has emerged in the context of the construction of large dams and other big development projects that have destroyed rural livelihoods and caused the resettlement of a mostly rural population. Hence, a related understanding of resettlement is biased towards the *reconstruction* of rural livelihoods and poses challenges for its application in urban contexts (Herath, Lakshman, and Ekanayake 2017; Patel, Sliuzas, and Mathur 2015). The second is the strong acknowledgement of multiple risks of impoverishment (Cernea 1997; Cernea and Maldonado 2018), often disregarded by policy makers and private developers in the context of urban resettlement (Koenig 2018). The third is the notion of involuntarily resettled, project-affected persons. However, for the same project, some may feel forcibly evicted, while others are inclined to move to new, better-quality, and socially accepted housing (Anand and Rademacher 2011; Beier 2019; Doshi 2013). The last is a focus on policy improvement – whether of private or public actors. Seeing resettlement as a consequence of an unavoidable development project, the objective of DFDR literature is to understand and propose "solutions to the problems caused by resettlement" (Rogers and Wilmsen 2020, 259), even if resettlement is seen as a "solution" for the problems caused by displacement. Hence, these four basic characteristics of a DFDR-related definition of resettlement pose challenges to a more urban, people-centred, and nuanced understanding of resettlement that incorporates overlapping notions of displacement, relocation, and reinstallation.

Moreover, beyond the World Bank's definition of resettlement, the very same term may have different connotations when referring to national and local politics. In Ethiopia, for example, *sefera* (see Chapter 9) are nationally known as public policies implemented in the twentieth century at different scales for territorial integration and spatial rebalancing through displacement *and* new settlements. Despite international intervention, resettlements here echo national and local politics – with their own meanings and words in Ethiopian languages (Pankhurst and Piguet 2009). In South Africa, the term is strongly associated with Apartheid policies of racial segregation and the forced relocation of the Black population to so-called rural homelands. In francophone West Africa, the word *déguerpissement* is still used to refer to forced evictions and urban displacement and, in some cases, relocation to a new settlement (Blot and Spire 2014). Here, it refers to an authoritarian expulsion of precarious city dwellers during and after the colonial period (Coquery-Vidrovitch 2006). The oldest known use of the term could be the *déguerpissement* of the shantytown of Medina in Dakar and the driving of residents to the dunes of Pikine where no services were available during this colonial period (Dorier-Apprill 2001).

Despite multiple and to some extent ambiguous definitions and histories of resettlement, there seems to be agreement that resettlement and displacement are interconnected. While displacement is generally referred to as a loss of place, resettlement may describe the subsequent and related process of space production. Deboulet and Lafaye (2018) note, "there is no rehousing [*relogement*] without prior dehousing [*délogement*], or, in other words, without the obligation of leaving one's house" (156, translated). Likewise, Rogers and Wilmsen (2020) state, "displacement is always a feature of resettlement, even if resettlement does not always follow displacement" (269). Our understanding of resettlement put forward in this book builds on these conceptions, stressing the interconnectedness of displacement and resettlement.

Seeing Urban Resettlement as Variegated Lived Experiences

Following these reflections, we opt for a more general definition of resettlement as "a distinctive form of mobility in that why, where, and how people move are determined by authorities ahead of displacement" (Rogers and Wilmsen 2020, 256). Hence, we consider resettlement to be a particular political moment that reflects both a loss of place through displacement and a gain of place through the attempted planned relocation of people. This political dimension of resettlement will be long-term and will influence the way in which the city is lived and understood by resettled people. This basic understanding allows for diverse, people-centred notions of resettlement situated between destruction, loss, and threat on the one hand, and production, gain, and chance on the other. As such, we agree with Rogers and Wilmsen (2020) on an understanding of resettlement that is more in line with the French notion of *relogement*, including both displacement *and* relocation. In this book, resettlement should not be limited to the assisted practice of reinstallation *after* displacement (*réinstallation/replacement*) – a notion clearly rooted in rural DFDR studies. Instead, the notion of urban resettlement should stress the interdependence of destruction and production, as well as the in-betweenness of place many resettled people are experiencing. To be clear, seeing resettlement as *relogement* (rehousing) means displacement may occur without resettlement, but resettlement always requires a certain degree of displacement that influences the practices and conditions of settling for a long time (Deboulet and

Lafaye 2018, 156; Fernández Arrigoitia 2017, 72; Rogers and Wilmsen 2020, 269). If displacement is not followed by resettlement, people may move to dispersed urban locations, become homeless, or move back to rural areas. If displacement is followed by resettlement, people are supposed to move to designated places, where they are allowed to build and sometimes assisted in building their own houses or where they move into already-constructed houses or flats. Nevertheless, resettlement does not necessarily mean the end of (constrained) mobilities. Depending on the mode of implementation or the resettlement location, people may decide to or are forced to rent out or sell their new plot of land or housing unit. They may then move to a cheaper place or may move back to a more central area with better access to their workplace (Bridonneau 2018; Charlton 2018a).

Across disciplines, the term displacement is related more to notions of "destruction" and to "leaving a place" (Elliott-Cooper, Hubbard, and Lees 2020; Wang 2020), while resettlement tends to be associated with "production" and "arriving/settling at a new place". What we would like to stress is that these processes do not take place independently. The same mobility may be experienced by resettled people in very different and often ambiguous ways. For example, for one person who has a strong attachment to the place he/she is forced to leave, the same process of resettlement may feel more like a "loss", while for another, happy to leave the site because of poor living conditions, the process is rather perceived as a "gain". Again, others struggle to decide between "gain" or "loss", carefully balancing positive and negative aspects within the very same process (Anand and Rademacher 2011; Beier and Strava 2020; Bhan and Shivanand 2013; Hammar 2017; Spire, Bridonneau, and Philifert 2017). From a more material perspective, a process of resettlement entails physical destruction but also the creation of new infrastructure and built environments (Shannon et al. 2018). Thus, it is exactly this heterogenous simultaneity of destruction and production, these "in-between" places (old vs. new sites) and times (memories vs. aspirations) that we would like to stress with the book's notion of urban resettlement as reflecting diverse lived experiences. In-between places and times are shaped through interconnected processes: settling at a new site while some neighbours, relatives, and friends remain at the old one; carrying on working at the old and sleeping at the new site; keeping and reconstructing memories while trying to make a new home. In other words, we argue that people do not experience displacement and resettlement as separate, but rather as interconnected processes, shaped to an extent both by destruction and production taking place at the same time (Figure 1.1).

Related to this, we argue that many urban resettlements challenge a clear-cut categorisation of residential mobility as either "voluntary" (linked to new job opportunities, family changes, better housing, etc.) or "forced" (linked to conflicts, economic difficulties, gentrification, etc.) (cf. de Wet 2008). Urban resettlement takes place in more or less coercive settings, not only depending on project implementation, but also on people's perspectives and livelihoods. When focusing on people's lived experiences within the entire resettlement process over time, voluntary action and force are often experienced together, differing according to individual preferences, social status, financial resources, project implementation, and time (cf. Beier 2019;

Doshi 2013; Hammar 2017). Throughout this book, we observe that resettlement leaves affected people with limited choices. However, in most of the cases presented in this book, except for those studied by Dupont and Gowda (Chapter 2) and Jorge and Melo (Chapter 8), it is not only about forced evictions. Rather, authorities, associations, private companies, and even neighbours may pressure or convince dwellers to "accept" relocation, making it difficult to assess the degree of voluntariness and underlying force (Chapters 3, 4, 6, and 9). Thus, instead of simplifying or generalising, it seems more appropriate to interrogate the constraints *and* opportunities that resettlement presents – of both destruction and production – over time and for each individual case. These constraints and opportunities are both the result of a balance of power between urban authorities and city dwellers and a process of acceptance or resistance by the city dwellers themselves.

With this differentiated and people-centred conceptualisation of urban resettlement as a lived experience – combining both destruction and production, force and self-determination – this book responds to a growing number of scholars who have stressed a lack of scholarly focus on subjectivities and agency in resettlement, displacement, and housing research (Anand and Rademacher 2011; Doshi 2013; Dupont et al. 2015; Fernández Arrigoitia 2017; Hammar 2017; Lemanski, Charlton, and Meth 2017; Ramakrishnan 2014; Wang 2020). They have called for more nuanced, people-centred analyses of displacement, resettlement, and new housing, highlighting complexities, ambiguities, and differences. As such, Herath, Lakshman, and Ekanayake (2017, 574) emphasise heterogeneity within displaced and resettled communities: "Needs and aspirations of displaced people differ and their sense of wellbeing also differs". This heterogeneity further translates into diverse perspectives of displacement and resettlement, which urges planning authorities and scholars to move beyond the classification of effects as either "all positive" or "all negative". Instead of keeping such rigid *a priori* categorisations of resettlements, a relative approach to resettlement in terms of practices, perception, and appropriation is required. As Dwivedi (1999, 73) writes, "binary conceptions can be inadequate for understanding people's experiences of displacement-resettlement problems. People confront displacement and resettlement as simultaneous and shifting realities". Thus, resettlement and displacement may produce multiple realities that are simultaneously both positive and negative (Anand and Rademacher 2011; Charlton and Meth 2017; Doshi 2013; Wang 2020). Echoing Bhan and Shivanand (2013) resettlement has been a "double-edged moment for the poor – it is certainly a moment of violence and eviction, but it is also a moment of possibility where the process of resettlement offers the tenuous hope of legality and tenure security" (54). Similar voices are present in Hammar's (2017) work on the resettlement of informal settlement communities in Bulawayo, Zimbabwe: "Despite the looming worries about distance from town, the loss of income, the lack of infrastructure and services, [...] excitement about future possibilities was palpable" (91).

Following this logic, it is necessary to reject wholly positive or negative *a priori* notions of resettlement by acknowledging that affected residents often have very nuanced, heterogeneous, and evolving perceptions and experiences of resettlement before, during, and after actual relocation. Such experiences are difficult to grasp in an analytical way if sticking to concepts such as "displacement", which have an ultimately negative connotation (Meth et al. 2020). We argue that to ensure openness towards people's heterogeneous, sometimes even contradicting perspectives, critical empirical research should stress a rather impartial understanding of "urban resettlement". Unlike concepts such as "displacement" or "eviction" with a negative connotation or others such as "affordable" or "adequate" housing with a positive connotation, using the concept "urban resettlement" leaves scope for people's own interpretations. Likewise, implicit assumptions are of relevance with regards to political subject-making within resettlement projects, where terms such as "project-affected persons" or "beneficiaries" imply certain expectations vis-à-vis the attitudes and behaviours of designated persons (Charlton 2018b). The failure of actual behaviour to correspond to these expectations may lead to disappointment and a lack of comprehension among leading stakeholders (Anand and Rademacher 2011). Thus, being open and acknowledging heterogeneity are crucial for a holistic, people-centred understanding of urban resettlement as a lived experience.

Urban Resettlement: Setting the Scene

As mentioned above, in Anglo-Saxon research, the concept of "resettlement" has primarily referred to rural contexts of DFDR (Herath Lakshman, and Ekanayake 2017, 555; Koenig 2006, 2018; Patel, Sliuzas, and Mathur 2015, 233). This may be explained by the World Bank's strong role in developing the concept of resettlement in relation to the development projects it funds in rural areas, especially large dams. The rural bias exists despite the World Bank mentioning the construction of urban infrastructure and new towns as potential causes of displacement and resettlement (Koenig 2018). A recent, state-of-the-art article on resettlement has primarily built on examples of displacement and resettlement in rural areas (Rogers and Wilmsen 2020), notwithstanding large-scale, rural-to-urban resettlement in China that is intended to foster top-down urbanisation as a state project (Gomersall 2018; Wilmsen 2018). Following this, housing and urban studies often avoid using the term "resettlement", as it is a supposedly "rural" concept. Instead, urban studies have focused on gentrification, eviction, and relocation and less on re-*settling* and the process of "living" in a new location. This may explain why the relatively recent second edition of the Encyclopaedia of Housing does not include a chapter on resettlement (Smith 2012). Likewise, the *Routledge Handbook on Cities of the Global South* does not feature resettlement in a prominent way (Parnell and Oldfield 2014).

This being said, a relatively small number of scholarly works have adapted the DFDR framework to urban contexts. In contrast to rural DFDR projects, these authors emphasise the lower relevance of the productivity of land for the restoration of people's livelihoods, as well as problems related to the contested tenure status of urban residents affected by displacement and resettlement (Diwakar and Peter 2016; Herath, Lakshman, and Ekanayake 2017; Patel, Sliuzas, and Mathur 2015, Spire, Bridonneau, and Philifert 2017, Steel, van Noorloos, and Otsuki 2019). Others have used the term resettlement to stress dynamic attitudes towards housing for the urban poor (Beier 2019; Nikuze et al. 2019). Again others – similar to our notion of urban resettlement as diverse lived experiences – have used the notion of resettlement to emphasise multiple subjective realities with regards to state housing (Anand and Rademacher 2011; Beier and Strava 2020; Bhan and Shivanand 2013; Doshi 2013; Dupont et al. 2015; Ramakrishnan 2014). However, in many other studies, "resettlement" appears less in a conceptual way and more as a term designating physical relocation.

Besides, aspects of resettlement are discussed under diverse different terms and concepts within scholarship concerned with urban development and (informal) housing. As mentioned earlier, various forms of urban redevelopment and transformation may include resettlement. However, despite all heterogeneity, those most affected are the urban poor and residents living in auto-constructed, informal housing. Reasons for displacement and resettlement include: the improvement and construction of infrastructure (Anand 2006; Carolini 2017; Graham 2018; Shannon et al. 2018; Chapter 3; Chapter 8), disaster prevention measures (Karaman 2014; Kita 2017; Chapter 8), housing programmes (Bhan 2013; Bridonneau, 2018; Gastrow 2020; Rubin and Charlton 2019; Chapter 7; Chapter 4) and slum clearance and upgrading (Choplin and Dessie 2017; Ghertner 2012; Huchzermeyer 2010; Patel, Sliuzas, and Mathur 2015; Roy 2014; Schramm 2017; Chapter 5; Chapter 2; Chapter 6), as well as inner-city redevelopment, tourism, and modernisation policies (Berry-Chikhaoui 2010, Bhan 2009; Broudehoux 2007; Steinbrink 2013; van Blerk 2011; Chapter 9).

These reasons often determine the dominant analytical perspective. For some, the focus is more on aspects of displacement and, hence, on the fate of individuals and communities *prior* to or *during* relocation or during their mobility (cf. Wang 2020). For others, the focus is more on their situation *after* relocation (i.e., housing programmes). Following the aim of this edited volume, the advantage of using the term "urban resettlement" is to combine both perspectives and to discuss the destruction of urban space in relation to its production. Notwithstanding the numerous reasons, justifications, and processes behind resettlement in the above-mentioned urban contexts, people share the dynamic experience of a changing place of residency. These projects, whether intentionally or not, impose new spatial and residential realities on people, forcing them to adapt – even if they move on a rather voluntary basis. Thus, all these projects and programmes produce lived experiences of resettlement with emotions kept in between the destruction and production of place, no matter whether resettlement is a future project (see Chapter 5 and Chapter 7) or whether it occurred decades ago (see Chapter 8).

Through these lived realities of a changing place, each individual makes sense of resettlement by comparing past, current, and future housing, and its multiple functions (Figure 1.2). Hence, whether people are in favour of or opposed to resettlement may not only depend on the nature of the project and the process of implementation, but also on people's subjective demands, experiences of, and aspirations towards housing and its different functions. Whereas for some, emotional attachment to the previous place of residence is the most significant factor influencing their experience, for others it is the increased social status resulting

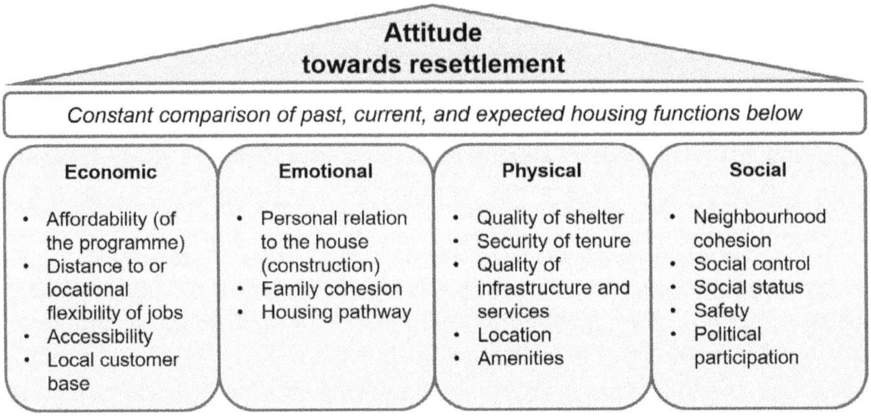

FIGURE 1.2 The formation of different attitudes towards resettlement.
Source: Authors' own graph.

from their move out of a stigmatised place. This is not to ignore that, of course, some projects may rather produce feelings of displacement (see Chapter 2 and Chapter 9) in contrast to others, where people are more in favour of moving (see Chapter 6). However, heterogeneity and complexity still matter and lead to multiple subjective and evolving realities beyond black (all negative) and white (all positive). As Figure 1.2 shows, positive and negative aspects of a changing living environment may co-exist. Furthermore, they are very likely to differ within the very same community. Questions of compensation would add even more complexity (see Chapter 3). Thus, it needs to be acknowledged that affected residents have very nuanced and heterogeneous attitudes towards resettlement (cf. Anand and Rademacher 2011; Charlton and Meth 2017; Doshi 2013).

Urban Resettlement: New Housing and Infrastructure

In the following section, we focus on issues that cut across and appear in the book's different chapters and that structure the remainder of the book. The first issue that cuts across is new built environments. Often, urban resettlement occurs in the context of housing programmes aiming to replace auto-constructed housing with formal housing. Here, housing is framed by urban authorities as beneficial, turning people into "beneficiaries" of resettlement projects while ignoring the potential adverse effects of resettlement. Koenig (2018, 90f) notes that many resettlement projects in urban areas are treated as mere housing programmes, assuming the reconstitution of jobs and urban livelihoods as unproblematic. However, even if people move on a seemingly voluntary basis, adverse effects of resettlement, such as the severing of social ties and challenges in accessing urban job markets, abound (Beier 2019; Hammar 2017; Charlton and Meth 2017; Planel and Bridonneau 2017). Most of the book's case studies underline insufficient transportation options and the adverse effects of this on resettled dwellers at the new sites. Hence, like Koenig (2018), we argue that it is useful to treat housing programmes as resettlement projects in order to stress their potentially adverse effects on people's livelihoods and everyday lives. Thus, the concept of urban resettlement refers to empirical housing research that analyses people's livelihoods and everyday realities related to a comprehensive understanding of housing that sees it as stretching far beyond merely four walls and a roof (Figure 1.2).

However, much of the literature dealing with housing in the Global South has primarily been concerned with housing policy techniques (for example Berner 2002; Bredenoord and Lindert 2014; Buckley, Kallergis, and Wainer 2016; Payne 2014; Satterthwaite 2009; van Gelder 2010; van Noorloos et al. 2020), and housing policy failure (Baken and Linden 1993; Berner 2016; Werlin 1999). While providing policy recommendations for improving policies to produce new, supposedly better housing, a central concern of this literature seems to be the issue of affordability of both adequate land and housing. Consequently, detailed analyses of people's living practices and conditions within communities targeted by housing programs are less visible (for exceptions, see Hammar 2017; Meth and Buthelezi 2017). In contrast, other literature takes a more critical perspective, focusing on housing markets (Durand-Lasserve 2006; Goodfellow 2017; Gruffydd Jones 2012; Rolnik 2019) and demolition policies fighting inadequate housing (Bhan 2013; Bogaert 2018; Ghertner 2012; Huchzermeyer 2011; du Plessis 2005; Roy 2014), as well as resistance to evictions and displacement (Bayat 2000; Dupont et al. 2015; Huchzermeyer 2009; Mitlin 2018). By assuming more macro or meso perspectives stressing the political and economic logics behind the loss and destruction of housing, this body of research hardly addresses individual subjectivities towards housing. Furthermore, post-displacement perspectives and the empirical analysis of the actual effects of displacement and relocation for the evicted people often play a minor role (Fernández Arrigoitia 2017; Meth et al. 2020; Wang 2020). Thus, most literature on housing in the Global South tends to focus either on the production of new housing or the destruction of existing, often auto-constructed housing.

The chapters in this volume subsequently look at new housing by acknowledging dynamic, people-centred perspectives of changing residential environments. By stressing heterogeneous subjectivities hovering between the threats of displacement and the opportunities that new housing provides, the authors stress that housing is a personal concept that means more than just shelter. Choosing a pre-displacement perspective, Chapter 7, by Toktam Ashnaiy and Erhard Berner, contrasts people-led homemaking practices in Tehran's informal settlement Mianabad with the standardised dwellings provided through the national housing and resettlement programme *Mehr*. Although both are peripherally located, residents' everyday lives in Mianabad stand in sharp contrast to the mainstream urban life enforced through the Mehr programme. The powerful accounts of Mianabad's residents highlight the subjectivities behind housing demands, as well as the advantages of incremental housing that tend to be ignored within developmentalist housing schemes. Such discrepancies between home and shelter are also obvious in Chapter 5, by Sogen Moodley and

Kira Erwin, which focuses on social networks in relation to homemaking and risk in two neighbourhoods in Durban. The authors contrast social disruptions and mistrust as a result of resettlement in an "orderly", planned new housing project with the established and protective social relations of a densely populated informal settlement.

Moodley and Erwin also zoom in on the role of local planning authorities that struggle to implement an in-situ upgrading of housing in a way that is sensitive to social networks. The social complexities and constant changes within informal settlements present a challenge to technical planning driven by quantitative targets. As such, the authors warn of a growing gap between the ideals and pressures of technical planning and people's narratives of home, bound to certain places and social networks. Raffael Beier's Chapter 6 adds that, despite the advantages of people-led, informal homemaking, socially respected, putative "formal" housing still entices many dwellers to accept resettlement. Focusing on shantytown resettlement in Casablanca, Morocco, he shows how the changing built environment has led to inner conflicts among many resettled people. While appreciating improved shelter quality, they tend to miss former social networks, locations, and everyday practices of homemaking. As such, their new housing situations can hardly be understood as either "better" or "worse", urging us to consider concepts such as "shelter" and "home" as highly subjective.

Urban Resettlement: New Political Realities

Besides new housing, urban resettlement functions as a political tool, used to implement a new, planned order that may contrast with the supposed disorder of auto-constructed neighbourhoods (Beier 2021; Ghertner 2012; Huchzermeyer 2009). These new spatial orders may come with altered political recognition, fostering new political realities as well as the enhanced integration of resettled residents into formal market systems (Gastrow 2017; Morange, Pilo', and Spire 2018; Roy 2014). As such, we argue that urban resettlement contributes to a transformation of the relationship between city dwellers, private actors, and state agents at different scales and through the re-enactment of socio-political hierarchies and power relations. Following di Nunzio's (2017) work on the political dimension of daily life and that of Boudreau, Boucher, and Liguori (2009) on the political dimension of urban experiences, we see resettlement not merely as a public housing policy (focusing on "shelter"), but as an operation that transforms "homes" and city dwellers' relationships with the state. These micropolitics shape experiences of urban resettlement in different ways. Social differentiation also takes place when only some subsets of populations generally marginalised by public actions are recognised and moved to new urban settings linked to different rights and duties (Beier 2021; Gastrow 2017; Morange, Pilo', and Spire 2018; Otsuki 2019). This opens up a new avenue for questioning intertwined issues of sensemaking about citizenship and "the urban contract" – what Doshi (2013) calls the "politics of evicted people".

All of the chapters of the book testify to the selective nature of resettlement programs and to the exclusions produced. As urban resettlement takes place across diverse neoliberal contexts, the right to be resettled relies on selective processes that often disenfranchise and exclude city dwellers unable to demonstrate a "proper" urban identity (Anand and Rademacher 2011; Doshi 2013). Several authors of the book, especially Dupont and Godwa (Chapter 2), Hernandez Bertone, de la Vega, and Ciuffolini (Chapter 4), and Spire and Pilo' (Chapter 3) investigate these selective processes in connection with the kind of political recognition induced. In Delhi (Chapter 2), the resettlement process produces a differentiated treatment of evicted people by the local state (the Delhi Development Authority) and by the private developer in charge of the allocation of plots for "the winners" resettled in the transit camp. The authors invite us to understand the option of the camp as a specific place to discipline and control selected resettled people and, hence, to make them "more governable".

In this era of neoliberal urban policies, focusing on resettlement programmes thus offers the possibility of investigating the modes of production of socio-spatial orders (Huchzermeyer 2016; Roy 2014), which include the propagation of new urban norms through individualisation processes and the growth of the increasingly market-driven value of land (Spire, Bridonneau, and Philifert 2017; Steel, van Noorloos, and Otsuki 2019). In this perspective, Juliana Hernández Bertone, Candela de la Vega, and María Alejandra Ciuffolini (Chapter 4) explore urban resettlement in its relation to political subjectivities in the case of Córdoba in Argentina. They question how the resettlement affects rights and the social integration of displaced people through the "*Mi Casa, Mi Vida*" ("My House, My Life") programme. The state policies treat slum dwellers as beneficiaries and not as citizens, but also as poor and those who do not consume enough, i.e., "minimum consumers". In Lomé in Togo, write Amandine Spire and Francesa Pilo' (Chapter 3), the authorities introduced a pilot resettlement program relying on a contract between the state and resettled persons that transformed poor dwellers into "landlords" on the outskirts of the city. As in Delhi, the distribution of basic services for city dwellers in the city of Djagblé is reorganised through strong, novel social controls that contribute to defining new norms in everyday urban lives.

Using the notion of governmentality, with some precautions, we can, as a result, elaborate on how people reshape their relationship with the state *through* resettlement processes. The resettlement could even create a new political urban condition that may resemble Sigona's (2015) notion of "campzenship". For Véronique Dupont and M.M. Shankare Gowda (Chapter 2), this is defined in Kathputli Colony, a resettlement site in Delhi, by strong control of the developer's personnel of "its" resettled population. The specific relocation to the transient resettlement site is very relevant for the political transformation triggered by the creation of a "state of exception" that stems from the temporary nature and uncertainty associated with resettlement. Spire and Pilo' (Chapter 3) also insist on the limits of resettlement operations for an uncertain political inclusion of city dwellers. As temporary and uncertain as it may be, the Djagblé resettlement in Lomé offers us the possibility to unravel techniques and logics of governance formed both by authorities and by city dwellers themselves to reorder urban space and increase the market-driven value of their land or houses. Several chapters of the book capture resettlement as part of a deeper neoliberal mechanism that generalises the extension of market rationalities to political and social relationships (see, for example, Chapter 4 by Hernández Bertone, de la Vega, and Ciuffolini, and Chapter 3 by Spire and Pilo'). For these authors, even if some minor form of political inclusion is enabled through resettlement, the programs still serve as an effective device oriented at creating competition, markets and consumers where they did not exist before or in different configurations. These uncertain new political realities evolve over time and according to the representations the actors of resettlement make of time.

Urban Resettlement: Temporal Scales and Long-term Analyses

Finally, assessing city dwellers' experiences of both displacement and planned relocation requires a focus on various time scales (cf. Meth et al. 2020). A long-term perspective should allow us to consider three major steps that make up urban resettlement experiences: (1) reacting to rumours and formal announcements (a time of fear and hope); (2) experiencing project implementation (a time of moving); and (3) dealing with spatial normalisation (a time of adaptation and reconstruction). Our point is not to reduce the resettlement experience to the immediate experience of displacement/relocation, but to include long-term practices and perceptions (see Figure 1.1 and Figure 1.2). These may include urban dwellers living with the fear of "looming" resettlement for years, as well as resettled citizens living with memories of a lost place, or even displaced people who never reached the relocation site. It should also bring to our attention the multiple (constrained) residential mobilities that a first resettlement can enable (cf. Lelévrier 2013; Navez-Bouchanine and Dansereau 2002; Watt 2018). From an even broader perspective, resettlement narratives are embedded in previous resettlement memories, which will foster both dwellers' practices and perceptions of upcoming and ongoing resettlement (cf. de Wet 2008).

In postmodern urban contexts, local governments may use "urban nostalgia" (Gervais-Lambony 2012) to construct images of the past and to build heritage neighbourhoods and touristic areas (Didier 2018). However, grounded memories rarely inform urban policy making. In some more authoritarian or post-socialist local contexts, public policies often driven by private developers tend to simply erase old neighbourhoods on behalf of development and modernisation, with no consideration for past and existing urbanity (Berry-Chikhaoui 2010; Bhan 2009; Huchzermeyer 2010). Both pay little attention to ordinary citizens' urban memories. In-depth research attempts to capture those memories of lost places (Chapter 5). Often, dwellers' memories construct a quite rigid distinction between central/demolished areas associated with tradition and community and peripheral/reinstallation settlements linked to modernity and individualism. However, at the same time, perceptions are likely to be uncertain, meandering between a missing, lost urbanity and aspirations to urban modernity.

Following this, several chapters of this book embrace long-term observations, bringing together two resettlement processes that occurred at two different times over the past two decades (Chapter 8) or one single resettlement that was implemented over the course of five years and empirically observed for ten years (Chapter 9). Addressing resettlement at different time scales underscores the complexity of the reconstruction process that moves far beyond the phase of relocation. As Silvia Jorge and Vanessa Melo (Chapter 8) write, it takes time to replace a *habitat* and an even longer time to move from occupation to *inhabiting*. The authors highlight that only time allows for the appropriation of new places of settlement. In southern towns or cities experiencing rapid urban growth, peripheral settlements can easily be integrated within the urban tissue within five or ten years, and this can possibly change perceptions of living in a resettlement area. Long-term analyses can also reveal gaps between expectations, hopes, and fears prior to resettlement and realities afterwards. Chapter 9, by Marie Bridonneau, reminds us how profound the memories of a lost place and former lives can be and how relations to spaces can be severed, even ten years after relocation happened. Time does not erase memories but rebuilds them and turns them into nostalgia despite the construction of a new and original social space. In her chapter, Bridonneau relates the painful memories, nostalgia, and difficulties associated with building community life in a "new" neighbourhood. As Chapter 8 and Chapter 9 also show, resettlement is increasingly rooted in urban experiences, where people do live with the idea of possible resettlement and with the memories of past resettlements.

In brief, these two chapters, shaped by long-term empirical observations, address significant methodological questions, with two dilemmas highlighted here. First, the issue of staying or going as a researcher after relocation is considered. This is a major dilemma in urban resettlement studies that prompts us to ask the question: how can we assess such kinds of urban policies and their true outcomes without understanding whether people remain/leave/come back and where they go if they go? Longitudinal studies are key to addressing this issue. Second, bridging the gap between project discourses and material implementations remains an issue in resettlement studies. Long-term investigations put into perspective immediate appropriations or the rejection of a resettlement project. Continued observations blur several dichotomies related to resettlement (before/after, destruction/production, old neighbourhood/new settlement, etc.) and prevent researchers from overlooking in-depth urban politics.

To conclude, this introduction attempted to position the term "urban resettlement" within urban studies and related literature on housing in the Global South. The individual chapters follow the introductory conceptualisation of urban resettlement as a lived experience while dealing with diverse urban contexts ranging from Tehran to Lomé and Córdoba. Moreover, they have emerged in different linguistic regions and in diverse theoretical and disciplinary approaches, which has further strengthened the inclusivity and relevance of this volume. The remainder of the book is divided into three parts, which are similar to the last three sections of the introduction. They focus on new political realities, the differences between home and shelter, and long-term perspectives as central analytical dimensions of urban resettlement. However, these should not be considered as the only themes that cut across chapters. In her concluding outlook in Chapter 10, Marie Huchzermeyer wraps up the volume by linking its fruitful discussions on resettlement to the concept of "un-homing" and the uncertainties and interruptions prompted by the COVID-19 pandemic. As such, she writes about new incentives for displacement and resettlement in light of the COVID-19 pandemic in South Africa. Finally, she calls for more empirical research on the diversities of home (re-)making and the disrupted and interrupted lived experiences of urban citizens.

References

Anand, N. 2006. "Disconnecting experience: making world-class roads in Mumbai." *Economic and Political Weekly* 41 (31): 3422–3429.

Anand, N., and A. Rademacher. 2011. "Housing in the urban age: inequality and aspiration in Mumbai." *Antipode* 43 (5): 1748–1772.

Baken, R.J., and J. van der Linden. 1993. "'Getting the incentives right': banking on the formal private sector: a critique of World Bank thinking on low-income housing delivery in third world cities." *Third World Planning Review* 15 (1): 1–27.

Bayat, A. 2000. "From 'dangerous classes' to 'quiet rebels': politics of the urban subaltern in the Global South." *International Sociology* 15 (3): 533–557.

Beier, R. 2019. *From the City to the Desert: Analysing Shantytown Resettlement in Casablanca, Morocco, from Residents' Perspectives*. Berlin: Logos.

Beier, R. 2021. "From visible informality to splintered informalities – reflections on the production of 'formality' in a Moroccan housing programme." *International Journal of Urban and Regional Research* (online first).

Beier, R., and C. Strava. 2020. "Losing or gaining home? Experiences of resettlement from Casablanca's slums." In *The Everyday Life of Urban Inequality: Ethnographic Case Studies of Global Cities*, edited by A. Storey, M. Sheehan, and J. Bodoh-Creed, 3–22. Lanham: Lexington Books.

Berner, E. 2002. "Learning from informal markets: innovative approaches to land and housing provision." In *Development and Cities: Essays from Development in Practice*, edited by D.G. Westendorff, and D. Eade, 226–247. Oxford: Oxfam GB.

Berner, E. 2016. "Housing disablement: market failures, haphazard policies and the global proliferation of slums." In *Local Governance, Economic Development and Institutions*, edited by G.M. Gomez and P. Knorringa, 98–117. Basingstoke: Palgrave MacMillan.

Berry-Chikhaoui, I. 2010. "Major urban projects and the people affected: the case of Casablanca's Avenue Royale." *Built Environment* 36 (2): 216–229.

Bhan, G. 2009. "'This is no longer the city I once knew': evictions, the urban poor and the right to the city in millennial Delhi." *Environment and Urbanization* 21 (1): 127–142.

Bhan, G. 2013. "Planned illegalities: housing and the 'failure' of planning in Delhi: 1947–2010." *Economic & Political Weekly* 48 (24): 53–63.

Bhan, G., and S. Shivanand. 2013. "(Un)settling the city: analysing displacement in Delhi from 1990 to 2007." *Economic & Political Weekly* 48 (13): 54–61.

Blot, J., and A. Spire. 2014. "Déguerpissements et conflits autour des légitimités citadines dans les villes du Sud." *L'Espace Politique* 22 (online).

Bogaert, K. 2018. *Globalized Authoritarianism: Megaprojects, Slums, and Class Relations in Urban Morocco*. Minneapolis: University of Minnesota Press.

Boudreau, J.A., N. Boucher, and M. Liguori. 2009. "Taking the bus daily and demonstrating on Sunday: reflections on the formation of political subjectivity in an urban world." *City* 13 (2–3): 336–346.

Bredenoord, J., and P. van Lindert. 2014. "Backing the self-builders: assisted self-help housing as a sustainable housing provision strategy." In *Affordable Housing in the Urban Global South: Seeking Sustainable Solutions*, edited by J. Bredenoord, P. van Lindert, and P. Smets, 55–72. Abingdon: Routledge.

Brickell K, M. Fernández Arrigoitia, and A. Vasudevan. 2017. "Geographies of forced eviction: dispossession, violence, resistance." In *Geographies of Forced Eviction*, edited by K. Brickell, M. Fernández Arrigoitia, and A. Vasudevan, 1–23. London: Palgrave Macmillan.

Bridonneau, M. 2018. "Vers la fin de l'illusion développementale en ville? Défiances silencieuses dans les sites de condominium en ville." *L'Espace Politique* 35 (online).

Broudehoux, A.M. 2007. "Spectacular Beijing: the conspicuous construction of an Olympic Metropolis." *Journal of Urban Affairs* 29 (4): 383–399.

Buckley, R.M., A. Kallergis, and L. Wainer. 2016. "The emergence of large-scale housing programs: beyond a public finance perspective." *Habitat International* 54 (3): 199–209.

Carmody, P., and F. Owusu. 2016. "Neoliberalism, urbanization and change in Africa: the political economy of heterotopias." *Journal of African Development* 18 (1): 61–73.

Carolini, G.Y. 2017. "Sisyphean dilemmas of development: contrasting urban infrastructure and fiscal policy trends in Maputo, Mozambique." *International Journal of Urban and Regional Research* 41 (1): 126–144.

Cernea, M.M. 1997. "The risks and reconstruction model for resettling displaced populations." *World Development* 25 (10): 1569–1587.

Cernea, M.M., and J.K. Maldonado. 2018. "Challenging the prevailing paradigm of displacement and resettlement: its evolution, and constructive ways of improving it." In *Challenging the Prevailing Paradigm of Displacement and Resettlement: Risks, Impoverishment, Legacies, Solutions*, edited by M.M. Cernea, and J.K. Maldonado, 1–42. Abingdon: Routledge.

Charlton, S. 2018a. "Spanning the spectrum: infrastructural experiences in South Africa's state housing programme." *International Development Planning Review* 40 (2): 97–120.

Charlton, S. 2018b. "Confounded but complacent: accounting for how the state sees responses to its housing intervention in Johannesburg." *The Journal of Development Studies* 54 (12): 2168–2185.

Charlton, S., and P. Meth. 2017. "Lived experiences of state housing in Johannesburg and Durban." *Transformation: Critical Perspectives on Southern Africa* 93: 91–115.

Choplin, A., and E. Dessie. 2017. "Titling the desert: land formalization and tenure (in) security in Nouakchott (Mauritania)." *Habitat International* 64: 49–58.

Coquery-Vidrovitch, C. 2006. "De la ville en Afrique noire." *Annales. Histoire, Sciences Sociales* 61 (5): 1087–1119.

Côté-Roy, L., and S. Moser. 2019. "Does Africa not deserve shiny new cities? The power of seductive rhetoric around new cities in Africa." *Urban Studies* 56 (12): 2391–2407.

Croese, S., L.R. Cirolia, and N. Graham. 2016. "Towards Habitat III: confronting the disjuncture between global policy and local practice on Africa's 'challenge of slums'." *Habitat International* 53: 237–242.

De Wet, C. 2008. "Reconsidering displacement in Southern Africa." *Anthropology Southern Africa* 31 (3–4): 114–122.

Deboulet, A., and C. Lafaye. 2018. "La rénovation urbaine, entre délogement et relogement: les effets sociaux de l'éviction." *L'Année Sociologique* 68: 155–183.

Didier, S. 2018. "Droit de mémoire, droit à la ville. Essai sur le cas sud-africain." *Géographie et cultures* 105: 135–151.

Di Nunzio, M. 2017. "Marginality as a politics of limited entitlements: street life and the dilemma of inclusion in urban Ethiopia." *American Ethnologist* 44 (1): 91–103.

Diwakar, D.G., and V. Peter. 2016. "Resettlement of urban poor in Chennai, Tamil Nadu: concerns in R&R policy and urban housing programme." *Journal of Land and Rural Studies* 4 (1): 97–110.

Dorier-Apprill, E., ed. 2001. *Vocabulaire de la Ville: Notions et Références*. Paris: Éditions du Temps.

Doshi, S. 2013. "The politics of the evicted: redevelopment, subjectivity, and difference in Mumbai's slum frontier." *Antipode* 45 (4): 844–865.

Du Plessis, J. 2005. "The growing problem of forced evictions and the crucial importance of community-based, locally appropriate alternatives." *Environment and Urbanization* 17 (1): 123–134.

Dupont, V., D. Jordhus-Lier, E. Braathen, and C. Sutherland. 2015. "Modalities of social mobilisation in substandard settlements." In *The Politics of Slums in the Global South*, edited by V. Dupont, D. Jordhus-Lier, C. Sutherland, and E. Braathen, 181–209. Abingdon: Routledge.

Durand-Lasserve, A. 2006. "Market-driven evictions and displacements: implications for the perpetuation of informal settlements in developing cities." In *Informal Settlements: A Perpetual Challenge?*, edited by M. Huchzermeyer, and A. Karam, 207–227. Cape Town: UCT Press.

Dwivedi, R. 1999. "Displacement, risks and resistance: local perceptions and actions in the Sardar Sarovar." *Development and Change* 30 (1): 43–78.

Elliott-Cooper, A., P. Hubbard, and L. Lees. 2020. "Moving beyond Marcuse: gentrification, displacement and the violence of un-homing." *Progress in Human Geography* 44 (3): 492–509.

Fernández Arrigoitia, M. 2017. "Unsettling resettlements: community, belonging and livelihood in Rio de Janeiro's Minha Casa Minha Vida." In *Geographies of Forced Eviction*, edited by K. Brickell, M. Fernández Arrigoitia, and A. Vasudevan, 71–96. London: Palgrave Macmillan.

Gastrow, C. 2017. "Cement citizens: housing, demolition and political belonging in Luanda, Angola." *Citizenship Studies* 21 (2): 224–239.

Gastrow, C. 2020. "Housing middle-classness: formality and the making of distinction in Luanda." *Africa* 90 (3), 509–528.

Gervais-Lambony, P. 2012. "Nostalgies citadines en Afrique du Sud." *EspacesTemps.net*. Accessed 8 October, 2020. https://www.espacestemps.net/en/articles/nostalgies-citadines-en-afrique-sud/

Ghertner, D.A. 2012. "Nuisance talk and the propriety of property: middle-class discourses of a slum-free Delhi." *Antipode* 44 (4): 1161–1187.

Gomersall, K. 2018. "Resettlement practice and the pathway to the urban ideal." *Geoforum* 96: 51–60.

Goodfellow, T. 2017. "Urban fortunes and skeleton cityscapes: real estate and late urbanization in Kigali and Addis Ababa." *International Journal of Urban and Regional Research* 41 (5): 786–803.

Graham, S. 2018. "Elite avenues: flyovers, freeways and the politics of urban mobility." *City* 22 (4): 527–550.

Grant, R. 2015. "Sustainable African urban futures: stocktaking and critical reflection on proposed urban projects." *American Behavioral Scientist* 59 (3): 294–310.

Gruffydd Jones, B. 2012. "'Bankable slums': the global politics of slum upgrading." *Third World Quarterly* 33 (5): 769–789.

Hammar, A. 2017. "Urban displacement and resettlement in Zimbabwe: the paradoxes of propertied citizenship." *African Studies Review* 60 (3): 81–104.

Herath, D., R.W.D. Lakshman, and A. Ekanayake. 2017. "Urban resettlement in Colombo from a wellbeing perspective: does development-forced resettlement lead to improved wellbeing?" *Journal of Refugee Studies* 30 (4): 554–579.

Huchzermeyer, M. 2009. "The struggle for in situ upgrading of informal settlements: a reflection on cases in Gauteng." *Development Southern Africa* 26 (1): 59–73.
Huchzermeyer, M. 2010. "Pounding at the tip of the iceberg: the dominant politics of informal settlement eradication in South Africa." *Politikon* 37 (1): 129–148.
Huchzermeyer, M. 2011. *Cities With 'Slums': From Informal Settlement Eradication to a Right to the City in Africa.* Cape Town: UCT Press.
Huchzermeyer, M. 2016. "Informal settlements at the intersection between urban planning and rights: advances through judicialisation in the South African case." In *Rethinking Precarious Neighbourhoods*, edited by A. Deboulet, 195–210. Paris: Agence Française de Développement.
Karaman, O. 2014. "Resisting urban renewal in Istanbul." *Urban Geography* 35 (2): 290–310.
Kita, S.M. 2017. "Urban vulnerability, disaster risk reduction and resettlement in Mzuzu City, Malawi." *International Journal of Disaster Risk Reduction* 22: 158–166.
Koenig, D. 2006. "Enhancing local development in development-induced displacement resettlement projects." In *Development-induced Displacement: Problems, Policies and People*, edited by C. de Wet, 105–140. New York: Berghahn.
Koenig, D. 2018. "Problems endure despite policies: urban livelihoods after forced displacement." In *Challenging the Prevailing Paradigm of Displacement and Resettlement: Risks, Impoverishment, Legacies, Solutions*, edited by M.M. Cernea, and J.K. Maldonado, 75–94. Abingdon: Routledge.
Lelévrier, C. 2013. "Forced relocation in France: how residential trajectories affect individual experiences." *Housing Studies* 28 (2): 253–271.
Lemanski, C., S. Charlton, and P. Meth. 2017. "Living in state housing: expectations, contradictions and consequences." *Transformation: Critical Perspectives on Southern Africa* 93: 1–12.
Meth, P., F. Masikane, S. Buthelezi, and M. Belihu. 2020. *Not Always Displacement: Conceptualising Relocation in Ethiopia and South Africa as 'Disruptive Replacement'.* Unpublished manuscript.
Meth, P., and S. Buthelezi. 2017. "New housing/new crime? Changes in safety, governance and everyday incivilities for residents relocated from informal to formal housing at Hammond's Farm, eThekwini." *Geoforum* 82: 77–86.
Mitlin, D. 2018. "Beyond contention: urban social movements and their multiple approaches to secure transformation." *Environment and Urbanization* 30 (2): 557–574.
Morange, M., F. Pilo', and A. Spire. 2018. "Experiencing regularisation in Accra, Cape Town and Rio de Janeiro: the actual right to the city, neoliberalisation and everyday life." *City* 22 (5–6): 685–702.
Navez-Bouchanine, F., and F. Dansereau. 2002. "Les stratégies résidentielles dans la ville fragmentée: Le cas de la ville marocaine." In *Gestion du Développement Urbain et Stratégies Résidentielles des Habitants*, edited by F. Dansereau and F. Navez-Bouchanine, 19–65. Paris: l'Harmattan.
Nikuze, A., R. Sliuzas, J. Flacke, and M. van Maarseveen. 2019. "Livelihood impacts of displacement and resettlement on informal households: a case study from Kigali, Rwanda." *Habitat International* 86: 38–47.
Otsuki, K. 2019. "Who is in 'the public'? Infrastructure of displacement and urban resettlement in Mozambique." *Built Environment* 44 (4): 493–508.
Pankhurst, A., and F. Piguet, eds. 2009. *Moving People in Ethiopia – Development, Displacement & the State.* Oxford: James Currey.
Parnell, S., and S. Oldfield, eds. 2014. *The Routledge Handbook on Cities of the Global South.* Abingdon: Routledge.
Parnell, S., and E. Pieterse. 2010. "The 'right to the city': institutional imperatives of a developmental state." *International Journal of Urban and Regional Research* 34 (1): 146–162.

Patel, S., R. Sliuzas, and N. Mathur. 2015. "The risk of impoverishment in urban development-induced displacement and resettlement in Ahmedabad." *Environment and Urbanization* 27 (1): 231–256.

Payne, G. 2014. "Policy and politics in urban land market management: lessons from experience." In *Affordable Housing in the Urban Global South: Seeking Sustainable Solutions*, edited by J. Bredenoord, P. van Lindert, and P. Smets, 19–39. Abingdon: Routledge.

Planel, S., and M. Bridonneau. 2017. "(Re)making politics in a new urban Ethiopia: an empirical reading of the right to the city in Addis Ababa's condominiums." *Journal of Eastern African Studies* 11 (1): 24–45.

Ramakrishnan, K. 2014. "Disrupted futures: unpacking metaphors of marginalization in eviction and resettlement narratives." *Antipode* 46 (3): 754–772.

Robinson, J. 2002. "Global and world cities: a view from off the map." *International Journal of Urban and Regional Research* 26 (3): 531–554.

Roever, S., and C. Skinner. 2016. "Street vendors and cities." *Environment and Urbanization* 28 (2): 359–374.

Rogers, S., and B. Wilmsen. 2020. "Towards a critical geography of resettlement." *Progress in Human Geography* 44 (2): 256–275.

Rolnik, R. 2019. *Urban Warfare: Housing Under the Empire of Finance*. London: Verso.

Roy, A. 2014. "Slum-free cities of the Asian century: postcolonial government and the project of inclusive growth." *Singapore Journal of Tropical Geography* 35 (1): 136–150.

Roy, A., and A. Ong, eds. 2011. *Worlding Cities: Asian Experiments and the Art of Being Global*. Chichester: Wiley-Blackwell.

Rubin, M., and S. Charlton. 2019. "State-led housing provision twenty-five years on: change, evolution, and agency on Johannesburg's edge." In *Massive Suburbanization: (Re) building the Global Periphery*, edited by K.M. Güney, R. Keil, and M. Üçoğlu, 241–266. Toronto: University of Toronto Press.

Satterthwaite, D. 2009. "Getting land for housing: what strategies work for low-income groups?" *Environment and Urbanization* 21 (2): 299–307.

Schramm, S. 2017. "People's room for manoeuvre in a fragmented city: state housing in Kibera, Nairobi." *Transformation: Critical Perspectives on Southern Africa* 93: 116–141.

Shannon, M., K. Otsuki, A. Zoomers, and M. Kaag. 2018. "Sustainable urbanization on occupied land? The politics of infrastructure development and resettlement in Beira City, Mozambique." *Sustainability* 10 (9): 3123.

Shatkin, G. 2008. "The city and the bottom line: urban megaprojects and the privatization of planning in Southeast Asia." *Environment and Planning A* 40 (2): 383–401.

Sigona, N. 2015. "Campzenship: reimagining the camp as a social and political space." *Citizenship Studies* 19 (1): 1–15.

Smith, S.J., ed. 2012. *International Encyclopedia of Housing and Home*. Oxford: Elsevier.

Spire, A., and A. Choplin. 2018. "Street vendors facing urban beautification in Accra (Ghana): eviction, relocation and formalization." *Articulo – Journal of Urban Research* 17–18 (online).

Spire, A., M. Bridonneau, and P. Philifert. 2017. "Droit à la ville et replacement dans les contextes autoritaires d'Addis-Abeba (Éthiopie) et de Lomé (Togo)." *Métropoles* 21 (online).

Steel, G., F. van Noorloos, and K. Otsuki. 2019. "Urban land grabs in Africa?" *Built Environment* 44 (4): 389–396.

Steinbrink, M. 2013. "Festifavelisation: mega-events, slums and strategic city-staging – the example of Rio de Janeiro." *Die Erde* 144 (2): 129–145.

Turok, I. 2016. "Housing and the urban premium." *Habitat International* 54 (3): 234–240.

United Nations. 1998. "*Guiding Principles on Internal Displacement.*" Accessed 22 May, 2020. https://www.refworld.org/pdfid/3b00f4234.pdf

Van Blerk, L. 2011. "'Managing' Cape Town's street children/youth: the impact of the 2010 World Cup did on street life in the city of Cape Town." *South African Geographical Journal* 93 (1): 29–37.

Van Gelder, J.L. 2010. "What tenure security? The case for a tripartite view." *Land Use Policy* 27: 449–456.

Van Noorloos, F., L.R. Cirolia, A. Friendly, S. Jukur, S. Schramm, G. Steel, and L. Valenzuela. 2020. "Incremental housing as a node for intersecting flows of city-making: rethinking the housing shortage in the Global South." *Environment and Urbanization* 32 (1): 37–54.

Van Noorloos, F., and M. Kloosterboer. 2018. "Africa's new cities: the contested future of urbanisation." *Urban Studies* 55 (6): 1223–1241.

Wang, Z. 2020. "Beyond displacement – exploring the variegated social impacts of urban redevelopment." *Urban Geography*. Advance online publication.

Watson, V. 2014. "African urban fantasies: dreams or nightmares?" *Environment and Urbanization* 26 (1): 215–231.

Watt, P. 2018. "'This pain of moving, moving, moving.' Evictions, displacement, and logics of expulsion in London." *L'Année Sociologique* 68: 67–100.

Werlin, H. 1999. "The slum upgrading myth." *Urban Studies* 36 (9): 1523–1534.

Wilmsen, B. 2018. "Damming China's rivers to expand its cities: the urban livelihoods of rural people displaced by the Three Gorges Dam." *Urban Geography* 39 (3): 345–366.

World Bank, ed. 2001. "*OP 4.12 – Involuntary Resettlement.*" Accessed 22 May, 2020. https://policies.worldbank.org/sites/ppf3/PPFDocuments/090224b0822f89db.pdf

World Bank, ed. 2004. *Involuntary Resettlement Sourcebook: Planning and Implementation in Development Projects*. Washington, DC: World Bank.

World Bank, ed. 2015. *Resettlement Fact Sheet*. Accessed 22 May, 2020. http://pubdocs.worldbank.org/en/628991425483120559/resettlement-fact-sheet.pdf

PART 1

Neoliberal Governance and Spatial Reordering

2

SLUM RE-DEVELOPMENT, DIFFERENTIATED RESETTLEMENT, AND TRANSIT CAMP

The Kathputli Colony Rehabilitation Project in Delhi[1]

Véronique Dupont and M.M. Shankare Gowda

Introduction

In the 2000s, the Delhi Development Authority (DDA), Delhi's public urban planning agency, acknowledged the "aberrations" of the strategy hitherto prevailing in addressing the challenge of squatter settlements – or illegal slums (DDA 2007, Section 4.2.3).[2] Slum dwellers were relocated in "resettlement colonies" on the city outskirts and allotted plots there that theoretically included basic civic amenities but no housing. The drawbacks of these site-and-service schemes were well documented by scholars and denounced by housing rights organisations (Dupont 2011; HLRN 2002; Menon-Sen and Bhan 2008). In particular, long distances between the new sites and the previous ones negatively affect access to employment and social networks, and overall, access to the city resources. Consequently, many plots were illegally resold by the allottees or were captured by real-estate agents.

The alternative strategy in the Master Plan for Delhi 2021 (DDA 2007) promotes in-situ rehabilitation – i.e., slum redevelopment – and the provision of housing in multi-story buildings, under public-private partnership, using squatted public land as a resource. This is in line with the national strategy (GoI 2010; 2015) and draws on the model applied in Mumbai since the 1990s (Nijman, 2008; Singh and Das, 1995).[3] Concretely, only part of the land occupied by the slum is used to rehouse its residents, and the rest is cleared for residential or commercial development for sale on the open market. This model therefore allows the private developer to generate enough profit to cover the construction cost of housing for the poor. Does this mean the end of resettlement on alternative sites for the concerned families? It does not, for slum redevelopment requires the demolition of the settlement and the relocation of its residents in transient accommodations, also called transit camps, during the construction of the rehousing complex.

DOI: 10.4324/9781003124559-3

The term transit *camp* is meaningful, and the literature on camps provides relevant concepts and heuristic tools to analyse the effects of such temporary resettlement on the displaced families' lives. Picker and Pasquetti (2015) conceptualised camps as "durable socio-spatial formations that displace and confine undesirable populations, suspending them in a distinct spatial, legal, and temporal condition" (681). "*Undesirable* populations" may apply to slum dwellers, particularly in Delhi, insofar as urban authorities and the judiciary consider them as squatters encroaching upon public land and causing public "nuisance" (Ghertner 2008). Despite the apparent oxymoron, "*durable* socio-spatial formation" also applies to *transit* camps in the slum rehabilitation context, as suggested by the Mumbai experience, where many evicted slum families still await their final resettlement after spending two to four decades in such camps (Dodhiya 2017; Tatke 2013; Times of India 2019). This invites us to question the "regime of permanent temporariness" (Picker and Pasquetti 2015, 683) that may be operating in transit camps. We will further investigate the "distinct spatial, legal, and temporal condition" of the transit camp for slum dwellers in this chapter with a resettlement case in Delhi. The transit camp can be moreover explored as a spatial *dispositif* (Foucault 1994: 299) and a tool for controlling its population.[4] In this regard, the literature on camps intersects with the critical geography of resettlement, where resettlement is understood as "a governmental program with inherent spatial effects" that "seeks to render people and space more governable" (Roger and Wilmsen 2020, 256, 268). The camp's function of containment and control, however, does not preclude its residents from exerting their agency in their everyday practices or even contestation, as captured by Sigona (2015) through his concept of "campzenship".

To contribute to the reflection on resettlement of evicted slum dwellers in transit camps, this chapter considers the case of the first in-situ slum rehabilitation project implemented in Delhi, that of Kathputli Colony (Dupont et al. 2014). This settlement's evacuation displaced around 18000 people from 2014 to 2017. While construction of the rehousing complex progresses at a slow pace, most of the families eligible for rehabilitation have been resettled in a transit camp located around three kilometres from the initial settlement, some have been relocated in flats in a remote township, Narela, and others have been excluded from the rehabilitation programme without compensation. We first provide an overview of the redevelopment project and detail the eligibility criteria that are intrinsic to the governmental programme and that generate differentiated resettlement. We focus hereafter on the transit camp, starting with the settling-down conditions and the camp *dispositif*. Next, we examine the multiple effects of resettlement in the camp on the affected families, including their living conditions, livelihoods, and socio-spatial practices. Finally, we analyse the transit camp as a space of "formation of more governable citizens" (Rogers and Wilmsen 2020, 262), while also considering the capacity of these citizens under control to exert their agency.

This case study is based on extended research conducted since 2009 in Kathputli Colony and the relocation sites (Figure 2.1), comprising in-depth interviews with the residents, their local leaders, and other stakeholders: representatives of

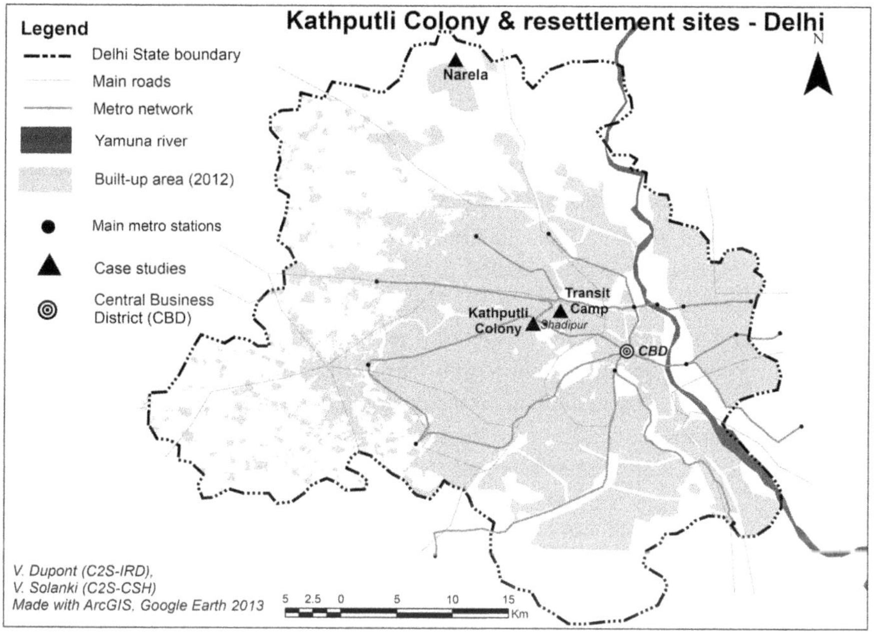

FIGURE 2.1 Kathputli Colony and resettlement sites, Delhi.

nongovernmental organisations (NGOs), activists, elected politicians, government officers, private firms executives – developer and consultant – and resident welfare associations of neighbouring localities. This was completed with regular follow-ups and field visits, numerous informal conversations, participant observations in various meetings, and attendance at hearings of related cases in the High Court of Delhi.

In this chapter, we analyse more particularly the information collected in the two relocation sites, including: a random sample survey conducted between April and June 2015 of 50 households living in the transit camp from the first group that moved from Kathputli Colony and a qualitative survey conducted from September to December 2019 of 22 households in the transit camp and 10 households in the Narela resettlement flats, following a purposive sampling strategy. The main objective of these two surveys was to assess the impact on the households of the displacement to the relocation sites, with reference to the living, working, and schooling conditions in Kathputli Colony, covering various aspects of their spatial and social practices.

The Kathputli Colony Redevelopment Project

This section outlines the rehabilitation project and its timescale. We focus on the eligibility criteria to access a flat in the rehousing complex, which explain differentiated resettlement modalities and exclusion.

A Slow-pace Project for a Five-decade Old Settlement

Kathputli Colony was a 50-year-old squatter settlement spread over 5.22 hectares of valuable DDA-owned land in a centrally located area. When its redevelopment project was announced in 2009, the Colony housed around 15,000 people, amongst them a large group of folk artists and artisans from Rajasthan who settled in this locality in the late 1960s. Kathputli Colony was named for the many puppeteers who lived there. Other groups of migrants from various regions, with diverse lines of work, had since settled down. It had become a heterogeneous settlement comprising a number of distinct communities, differentiated mainly along lines of geographical origin, but also along religious affiliation, caste, and occupation. The resulting social segmentation translated into spatial segregation, with distinct sections of the settlement corresponding to different communities, and where varying housing conditions reflected socio-economic disparities.

The Kathputli Colony redevelopment project is significant not only for the size of the affected population but also as a pilot project of in-situ rehabilitation under public-private partnership, which was promoted as "a benchmark for many such projects to follow to make Delhi a slum-free state".[5] The private company, who won the development contract in 2009, will use only 60 per cent of the land occupied by the slum to build a 14-story housing complex of 2,800 two-room flats of 25 sqm for the slum dwellers. The blocks of flats along with the mandatory amenities (community centre, school, health centre, convenient shopping, and playground) are to be delivered cost-free to the DDA. To generate profit, the Indian developer had an ambitious joint-venture plan with a Dubai-based company: to build on the rest of the land a high-end 54-story residential tower that would be the tallest building in Delhi and a commercial complex. Each beneficiary family will also need to contribute financially to obtain a flat in the slum rehousing blocks.[6]

The project involved transferring the families to a transit camp to be built by the developer before construction work could start. Finding vacant public land nearby was an important delaying factor in the project's implementation. A significant obstacle was the mobilisation of various resident and trader associations *against* the location of the camp in their respective neighbourhood. In addition to conflict in land use, the prejudicial image associated with slum dwellers also played a role in this rejection – slum dwellers were perceived as an "undesirable population". The camp was finally constructed on a site located around three kilometres from the initial settlement, on a hillock, a rocky wasteland.[7] It consists of rows of prefabricated one-room tenements of 12 sqm per household with neither kitchen nor individual water taps. Each row has shared bathing facilities, and several toilet blocks are installed along the boundary walls of the camp. Most of the 2,800 dwelling units are on one level, apart from a few two-level blocks (Figure 2.2).

The DDA launched three evacuation drives to prompt the transfer of families to the transit camp. The first one, in February 2014, entailed the resettlement of around 500 households within the next six months; the second one, in December 2016, the resettlement of around 800 households; the third one, in October 2017,

FIGURE 2.2 The unoccupied transit camp under surveillance, a couple of months before the arrival of the first batch of families.
Photo: M.M.S. Gowda, December 2013.

was followed by the total demolition of the settlement.[8] During the final evacuation, an estimated 2,600 to 2,700 households were forcibly evicted in three days by about 350 police forces. Altogether, the aggregate number of displaced households proved to be far beyond the transit camp's receiving capacity and the number of projected rehabilitation flats. This discrepancy in numbers is at the root of differentiated resettlement and exclusion; it calls for an examination of the eligibility criteria to access a flat in the rehousing project.

Eligibility Criteria and Differentiated Resettlement

The Kathputli Colony redevelopment project was planned for 2800 households, based on contested identification surveys, the first one conducted in 2008. The settlement population naturally increased over the years, new households were formed, and new migrants arrived. Meanwhile, the "cut-off date" of arrival in the settlement, used as the main eligibility criteria, was extended several times following changes in the slum policy at the state level. To be eligible for the rehousing project, each household head has to prove his/her residence before a given date, based on a list of recognised documents, including registration on the voter list and the "ration card", an official document giving access to fair-price shops, locally known as "ration shops", where the poor can purchase staple items at subsidised rates.

Two cut-off dates eventually applied for the Kathputli Colony rehabilitation project. This introduced a difference of treatment among the residents. Households with proofs of residence before 2011 were eligible for flats in the in-situ rehousing complex – and for accommodations in the transit camp. Those with proof of residence between 2011 and 1 January 2015 were eligible for direct allotment of flats in Narela in a DDA housing scheme on the northern outskirts of the city. Those who could not prove their residence before 2015, or that they formed a distinct household, were considered as ineligible for any alternative allotment. Based on these criteria, the DDA established three lists of applicants[9] that were released at the time of the final evacuation. They included, respectively, 2,800 eligible for in-situ rehabilitation, 492 eligible for resettlement in Narela, and 771 ineligible. In other words, almost 20 per cent of the applicants were excluded from the rehabilitation scheme and left to fend for themselves with no compensation. Those residents listed as ineligible could appeal to the DDA Appellate Authority to contest their exclusion. As per DDA figures, by July 2018, 475 applicants filed an appeal; by October 2018, 324 cases were examined, 260 (80 per cent) were rejected, and only 51 were found eligible.

The families relocated in Narela were allotted flats equivalent to the flats designed for the in-situ rehousing complex, namely two-room flats of about 25 sqm with kitchen, attached bathroom, and toilet. Financial conditionalities should also be similar, although to date no payment was asked from the occupants who consequently did not receive any tenure title. On the one hand, these families definitely accessed better housing conditions compared to their previous situation – and to the families resettled in the transit camp. On the other hand, they suffer from all the usual inconveniences attached to resettlement in outlying sites, Narela being about 30 kms away from Kathputli Colony. Hardships include considerably increased commuting time and cost to keep previous jobs, difficulties finding employment in the vicinity, lack of adequate school facilities, difficult access to health facilities, disruption of earlier social networks, and security issues in the surrounding area. The resettlement conditions in Narela and their impacts on livelihoods and other socio-economic issues deserve a full-fledged essay that goes beyond the scope of this chapter. We will focus here on the situation of the families resettled in the transit camp and on the specific features of this transient resettlement.

Settling Down in the Transit Camp

In what context and under what legal conditions did the evicted families arrive in the transit camp? What kind of *dispositif* did they find in this new space? These are the main questions addressed in this section. We underline another differentiated treatment of the families as well as the evolution of the *dispositif* deployed to control the population.

Three Batches of Arrivals with Differentiated Treatment

The stepwise evacuation pattern of the settlement reflects the residents' varying levels of acceptance of – or resistance to – the redevelopment project, depending on the perception of its impact on their future living conditions. It also involves the manoeuvres deployed by the DDA and the developer. The developer endeavoured to convince some local leaders to move to the transit camp and prompt their community members to follow, allegedly by paying them substantial sums. In parallel, the DDA intensified the pressure on the residents, increasingly resorting to intimidation tactics and finally to bulldozers and police violence. Changes in the transfer conditions to the camp were equally significant. The developer arranged free transportation for the first group of families who moved in 2014. Upon arrival in the camp, they were provided with free meals for a couple of weeks and were given 500 rupees – monetary help that was extended for a few days for the neediest families. Those who moved in December 2016 also got free transportation, but support during the first days in the camp was less systematic and less generous.

The resettlement process deteriorated dramatically between October to November 2017. The forced eviction of over 12,000 people in three days led to complete chaos. In the days following the demolition, many families were shelterless, staying on the debris or near the demolished site – on the roadside, along the nearby railway tracks, or under the adjacent flyover. For some, the transitory period before they were allotted a room in the camp (or a flat in Narela) lasted for several weeks under the most precarious conditions. The transit camp became overcrowded, with insufficient dwelling units, leading some households to squat in the open. The transport arrangement to transfer the families coordinated by the DDA and the developer was grossly inadequate, and the majority of the people had to arrange transport at their own cost. The last comers to the camp got neither free meals nor monetary help. Given the rush and line-ups to get a room allotted after due verification of their documents by the DDA, many people, including ineligible households, started breaking the locks of the rooms to settle in. The few guards on site, faced with this multitude in a chaotic situation, could not prevent such practices.

The households' legal occupation status in the transit camp has also varied over time, with a definite precarity for the last comers. In 2014, the first comers signed a tripartite agreement with the DDA and the developer. However, this notarial deed was very loose and lacked the accuracy expected in a proper legal document. In particular, a handwritten last point was added that "after taking over the land, *around* two years will be required to construct flats" [*emphasis added*]. This agreement concerned mainly the obligations of the "beneficiaries" in the transit camp, such as not encroaching on the camp and maintaining the place "in such a way that it can be returned in a proper condition to the developer". It did not however guarantee the allotment of a flat in the rehousing complex. The households who moved in December 2016 and in the next few months benefitted from the active negotiations that took place in 2016 between the DDA and up-and-coming leaders of a pro-project group of residents that gained importance in Kathputli Colony

(Dupont and Gowda 2020). Thus, the revised tripartite agreement was more accurate; it provided the beneficiary households with guarantees to be allotted a flat and included specification such as size, financial contribution and maintenance charges, and type of ownership. Most of the households forcibly evicted in late 2017 did not sign any formal agreement. They only got a "Demolition-cum-provisional-allotment" letter, which is not a notarial deed and are therefore maintained under an extremely insecure status.[10]

The transit camp population is indeed suspended in a distinct legal condition (Picker and Pasquetti 2015). The legal status of most households remains very precarious regarding their future. The two-year transit period mentioned in the agreement (for those who signed it) is now over, and temporariness becomes durable. This situation exacerbates the residents' feeling of uncertainty and their frustration as they have to cope with new difficulties (examined later).

A Space Under Surveillance?

Boundary walls, with three entrances, surround the transit camp. Until the final evacuation of Kathputli Colony in late 2017, the developer employed about eight security guards to patrol the camp, controlling especially its entrances (Figure 2.2). The entrance gate near the DDA and the developer's site offices was closed at night. The guards were instructed to bar entry to journalists, photo-reporters, NGOs' activists, and researchers. The developer meant to prevent adverse reports on the transit camp that could have been used to dissuade the remaining families in Kathputli Colony from resettling. In 2015, we experienced this control at our expense when, despite our being invited by a local leader,[11] the officer on duty (from the developer's firm), alerted by a guard, came to the leader's room and interfered in our discussion, eventually compelling us to pursue the interview outside the camp. For the leader who claimed the right to receive guests in his room, it was a demeaning incident, signifying that the camp authority surveillance extended to his private space.

Close-circuit television (CCTV) cameras, monitored from the developer's office, were also installed at important points in the camp but were removed after a couple of years. According to the developer, the residents had destroyed some cameras and disconnected the cables. The residents claimed instead that no camera was working. Whether an effective tool of surveillance or essentially for show, the CCTV equipment can be read as part of the *dispositif* to control the camp population.

The developer relaxed control on outsiders' visits after the complete demolition of Kathputli Colony – to wit, after the main hindrance to start construction was removed. The number of security guards was reduced to two or three, mainly to keep watch on the DDA and developer's offices. Excluding the 68-day national lockdown during the 2020 COVID-19 pandemic, the camp has become a space more open towards the outside, whereas tactics that seek to render the population inside the camp more governable were deployed – as expounded later.

Impact of Resettlement in the Transit Camp

In this section, we question the multidimensional impact of resettlement in the transit camp, with reference to the residents' situation in their previous settlement. We examine their new housing conditions and access to basic services, to workplaces, schools, and market places, as well as the disruption of socio-spatial organisation and networks.

Impact on Housing Conditions and Living Environment

The first comers to the transit camp are families who lived earlier under the most precarious conditions, in cramped shacks of makeshift materials, and a 12-sqm room in prefabricated blocks is an improvement on their previous condition. Conversely, the most prosperous families in Kathputli Colony had consolidated houses of two or more rooms, sometimes an additional floor, a roof terrace, an exclusive courtyard, or even a private bathing place on their premises. For them, living in the transit camp entails a consequent loss of space and comfort, even of status. Since the allotted floor area is the same for all, irrespective of the household size, adjustment is obviously more difficult for extended families, sometimes up to nine members. Accepting constrictive housing conditions requires believing in a short transitional period, with a view to a better future.

The massive arrival of the last batch of families in November 2017 increased the strain on basic infrastructure and services, especially on sanitation and water supply. In summer, water scarcity has become chronic, often entailing two-hour queues, at irregular times, to get a limited amount of water (two jerrycans) from shared outdoor taps. Furthermore, the quality of this supposedly potable water has deteriorated. All camp residents interviewed in 2019 complained the water was unclean; several reported skin diseases, some who can afford it buy drinking water in containers. Paradoxically, public water supply was better, in quantity, regularity, and quality, in Kathputli Colony despite it being categorised a slum. Similarly, residents complain of daily electricity cuts for a couple of hours in the camp for the last year or so, whereas power cuts were rare in the "slum". There, each house, even the most precarious shack, was equipped with an individual electricity metre and dwellers paid the bills. In the camp, electricity supply is paid by the developer and becomes another tool to control the residents. Regarding street cleanliness, maintenance, and solid waste disposal, the residents generally acknowledge that the situation in the camp is better compared to Kathputli Colony. The living conditions of those living close to the overflowing garbage containers remain, however, unhealthy.

The camp was initially built for a two-year transit period and was overall well-maintained when only the first batch of families occupied it. At that time, the developer wanted to attract other families from Kathputli Colony by providing good facilities. Since the entire evacuation of the colony, this is not the case anymore. After six years of occupation, the prefabricated structures and the physical infrastructure, especially evacuation pipes, concealed drains, cemented alleyways and platforms, have started deteriorating. Altogether, over-crowdedness, inadequate basic services, badly maintained public toilets, and fast degrading infrastructure tend to reproduce slum conditions (Figure 2.3), whereas resettlement in the transit camp was justified in the name of a slum rehabilitation project. One illegal slum was eradicated, but another one, planned, is emerging. As put by one resident, "we shifted from one *jhuggi* [shack] to the other" (Authors' interview, 26 September 2019).[12]

Impact on Spatial Practices and Major Spheres of Life

On a map the transit camp seems close to the initial settlement, around three kilometres. Nonetheless, this distance, combined with a much poorer connectivity, affected everyday spatial practices. Kathputli Colony was located on a main road where cycle- and auto-rickshaws were easily available, and its proximity to a bus depot and a metro station connected it particularly well to the rest of the city. In contrast, the camp is located on an out-of-the-way hillock, and bad transport facilities and dependence on electric rickshaws to reach the main road are general complaints. This entails increased commuting time and cost for all those who depend on public transport or rickshaws.

Adverse Impact on Livelihoods

Compared to the families resettled in Narela, those in the transit camp were certainly less impacted, as the majority of them could keep their previous work. Nevertheless, when commuting to work becomes unaffordable, it causes longer walking distance and time, and may eventually lead to leaving a job. Notably, women domestic

FIGURE 2.3 General view of the crowded Kathputli Colony transit camp.
Photo: M.M.S. Gowda, January 2019.

workers who used to walk to their workplaces in the adjoining neighbourhood had to leave their earlier placement after moving to the camp. For some this meant being unemployed for some time before finding closer workplaces. For others it meant stopping work definitively, with subsequent loss of income for the household.

The community of folk artists and artisans has been particularly impacted by resettlement in a remote place unknown to their potential clients. Because of transportation difficulties, several interviewees complained that they missed their shows, or had to refuse last moment proposals, with resulting falls in earnings. They often face similar transportation problems compounded by inflated night fares to come back after the shows. Interestingly, enterprising artists tried to overcome the camp's remoteness and poor physical connectivity by adjusting their mode of communication with their clients; they resorted to social media and circulate videos of their performances. Furthermore, due to lack of space in the dwellings and lack of customers in this new place, several artisans making puppets and other artefacts that they could sell easily in the well-known Kathputli Colony have now stopped or reduced this trade, while some try to find new market channels. Within the family, handicraft production was combined with performing activities and involved many women. They were the first ones to be impacted, entailing losses in household income. In the Colony, an artisan cooperative provided the woodcarving craftsmen with working space, advance money to buy materials, and occasional orders. All this support ceased with the settlement demolition and the disbanding of the cooperative society. Older woodcarvers stopped their activity, while others turned to repair work or focused on puppet and other shows. In Kathputli Colony like in other informal settlements, shops, workshops, and miscellaneous economic activities were commonplace. In the camp, there is no dedicated space provided for economic activities. This underlines a generic shortfall of resettlement schemes in India: they tend to address only the shelter issue and overlook the livelihood dimension (Sivaramakrishnan 2011).

Disruption of Schooling

The planners also neglected the difficulties of accessing schools post-relocation. The developer never kept his promise to provide free transportation allowing the children to stay in the same school. As a result, the poorest families, unable to afford the commuting cost, stopped sending their children to school, thereby reducing their chance to rise out of poverty. Another adverse effect of relocation to a new place involved security issues. The camp location entails crossing a major road with heavy traffic to reach the primary school where the Kathputli Colony children used to go – a worrying factor mentioned by several parents. Other parents were reluctant to send their daughters out alone in new surroundings perceived as unsafe for girls. Again, the Rajasthani artist community who used to send their children to a vocational NGO-run school in the colony itself was especially impacted. The demolition of the entire settlement entailed the demolition of the school and interrupted the children's studies. It took around a year for this NGO to reopen a vocational school in the transit camp, but not all children resumed their studies. Altogether, these various disruptive factors resulted in marked dropouts from school, negatively affecting the younger generations and limiting their future prospects.

Less Convenient Access to Marketplaces

Convenient access to fair-price shops is essential for the economically weaker sections. The camp residents, with their old address on their ration cards, remain administratively attached to the ration shop adjacent to the demolished settlement. The government has ignored their demand to relocate their ration shop closer to the camp, so they have to hire an electric rickshaw to reach the old place and bring back all their subsidised supplies. This again involves additional commuting cost and time, as well as advance planning to ensure that the shop will be open and stocks available. More generally, most residents lament the lost facilities of having well-stocked and cheap markets round the corner.

Impact on Social Networks and Socio-spatial Organisation

The resettlement to the transit camp has not only affected major spheres of life through the disruption of everyday spatial practices, it has also affected the residents' social and political networks, as well as social organisation among the relocated communities.

First, the relocation has severed some social connections, especially important for poor people. Thus, the long-term relation that the residents had built with shopkeepers in the market adjoining Kathputli Colony allowed them to buy on credit, a facility that the transit camp residents cannot benefit from in new places. Furthermore, charitable organisations were active in the well-known colony and used to supply free medicine and food to the poorest sections, but until at least the time of our survey in 2019, the camp remained out of their scope. Second, the residents lost some of their democratic prerogatives, such as resorting to their constituency elected representatives – the municipal councillor and the member of the state legislative assembly – to address problems of street maintenance, garbage removal, water supply, or other local issues. Unlike "ordinary" neighbourhoods, including slums, the transit camp is under the developer's purview for the provision of basic services. In this regard, it may be construed as a "space of exception" (Agamben 1998, 169). In the next section, we examine the nature and consequences of this control.

The relocation to the transit camp has disrupted the previous socio-spatial organisation. The pattern of community-wise quarters inside Kathputli Colony, each one with its own local leader, was not reproduced identically. Although some blocks in the camp are occupied exclusively or mainly by a single community, in many others, different communities are mixed. Women often feel less secure – or at least less comfortable – in mixed-community blocks than in their earlier homogenous and confined cluster inside Kathputli Colony, where social control by the community prevailed. This particularly concerns the third and largest batch of families, who moved in late 2017 under chaotic circumstances after the final demolition. In the socio-spatial reconfiguration of the camp, the local leaders have lost their authority as well as their traditional role of conflict resolution and control over people. The leaders are themselves watched by the DDA and the developer, and their concord for defending common interests has faded. Many residents have lost confidence in leaders, who are suspected of protecting only their own interests and of having benefitted from the developer's undue favours.

Communities, sometimes families, were also split due to differentiated allotment: either in the transit camp or in Narela flats, 30 kms away, not to mention those ineligible for allotment. Furthermore, since its announcement in 2009, the rehabilitation project itself had introduced new lines of fragmentation among the residents, including inside a same community, between those pro-project and their opponents. The three-phase evacuation of the settlement exacerbated this division, compounded by shifts in position and alliances over time.

In sum, resettlement in the transit camp has adversely impacted the residents' social capital three-dimensionally: their "bonding social capital" (the strong ties connecting people to members of their own community); their "bridging social capital" (their horizontal connections with people from different social groups, such as shopkeepers and social workers); and their "linking social capital" (their vertical connections with more powerful people, such as elected representatives).[13]

The Camp as a Space of "Formation of More Governable Citizens"[14]

In this last section, we analyse resettlement in the transit camp as a governmental programme that "seeks to render people and space more governable" (Roger and Wilmsen 2020, 256). We ask, to what extent and how are the camp residents controlled, and conversely to what extent and how can they exert their agency?

Biopolitics at Work in the Camp

Following Foucault (1997), we refer to the concept of biopolitics to examine the mechanisms at work in the transit camp to manage its population, including in the most basic functions of the human life process. The camp is under the surveillance of the DDA site manager in concert with the developer's staff. As noted above, the provision of basic services and the camp maintenance are the developer's responsibility and at his expense. This has turned into a way to control the population. For instance, daily two-hour power cuts aim at reducing the families' electricity consumption. Other incidents provide striking evidence of management through biopower. In August 2019, the women's toilets in one block were locked by order of the DDA site manager to "punish" the residents for arguing with him over drinking water shortage. The toilets remained locked for a few hours, until some leaders' intervention managed to unblock the situation. Around that time, the same officer cut off electricity connection to another block after some residents questioned the poor cleanliness of the toilets. The electricity was eventually restored after the residents protested.

Some residents do complain to the camp office about various deficiencies in the provision of basic services and maintenance. However, most of our interviewees reported poor or belated responses to their demands or lack of solutions to the problems. What also transpires from the interactions between the residents and the camp staff is the persistence of common prejudices against slum dwellers, reflected in the use of abusive language and the lack of respect, which may discourage further complaints. By way of examples:

> "Sometimes they humiliate us saying that you are *jhuggi* [shack]-people who don't know how to live properly".
>
> *(Authors' interview, 6 October 2019)*

> "They don't really consider us as human beings" – expressed a resident regarding the unattended demands for drinking water and better sanitation.
>
> *(Authors' interview, 25 October 2019)*

> "They don't treat *jhuggi*-people with respect, and they think we are beggars living on their mercy".
>
> *(Authors' interview, 13 November 2019)*

Furthermore, everybody is aware of the risk of protesting and shares the feeling of being at the DDA and developer's discretion. The fear of losing one's entitlement to rehousing impedes the residents' mobilisation for better amenities. As explained by one lady:

> DDA always threatened us with cancellation of our allotment if we ask something from them. We cannot demand anything from them but we have to take whatever they give us. That's why people don't want to question DDA, fearing their allotment can be cancelled.
>
> *(Authors' interview, 30 August 2019)*

Such fear is fuelled by the DDA and the developer's manoeuvres. To understand the effectiveness of this threat, one has to recall the conditions of the Kathputli Colony evacuation. To overcome the residents' resistance to move, the DDA – in concert with the developer – targeted some community leaders likely to influence their followers and favoured them by giving them, as part of the negotiation, additional allotments for family members who did not fulfil the eligibility criteria for a separate rehabilitation flat. A few allotments in the name of minor offspring were even reported. This was the strategy followed especially for the second evacuation drive. For the beneficiary families, this meant more rooms allotted in the transit camp – thus more comfortable housing conditions – and the promise of additional flats in the rehousing complex. However, such favours have become a way to control these erstwhile-influential denizens who know that their undue allotments might be cancelled if they challenge the DDA or the developer.

Other households are under a threat of eviction from the transit camp. At the time of the final demolition, the DDA priority was to vacate the site and allow the project to move on, hence their staff did not (or could not, given the chaotic situation) control strictly who was settling in the camp in late 2017. Consequently, many households that were deemed ineligible occupied rooms. In 2019, the DDA started evicting "illegal" residents from the camp, after the period for all appeals was over (to wit, first to the DDA Appellate Authority to contest one's ineligibility,[15] then, as the case may be, in the High Court of Delhi to challenge the rejection order of this Authority).[16] Thus, in January 2019, the DDA brought in over 100 police forces to evict around 60 families. Evictions were pursued later in the year, targeting smaller groups of families at a time.

These eviction drives did not trigger any protest from either leaders or other occupants. Undue favours had the effect of silencing the leaders. Outspoken denizens were subdued through other disreputable means, including false allegations, as described by one affected resident:

> The modus operandi is like this, if you oppose or criticise or question DDA or the developer, DDA encourages someone in the camp to file complaints against that person, and DDA initiates investigations. DDA asks the concerned person to provide this document and that document – why don't you have this and that, etc., etc. It is basically to harass and silence him.
>
> *(Authors' interview, 6 January 2019)*

This testimony reveals two important and complementary means to control the camp population. First, the DDA keeps informants to report on residents' "inappropriate" actions. Next, it issues notices to residents requiring them to submit additional proofs of eligibility, under threat of eviction. This type of harassment also affects residents who had been considered as eligible by the DDA eligibility determination committee. It hangs as a sword of Damocles over all critical and vocal residents. "Inappropriate" action as per the DDA and developer's standards also includes mobilising the residents to hold proper elections to renew the president of the Residents Welfare Association. This is mandatory for such an association, but it defies the incumbent candidate who is in league with the developer and serves as the main informant. Harassment may include more serious intimidation tactics, such as being locked in the developer's office and threats of being "taught a lesson".[17] Fear of complaints filed with the police against the residents in case of protest is also frequently expressed. Such harassment practices impede the emergence of a new leadership.

The practice of issuing notices with threat of eviction to eligible households who had already submitted all required documents reached such an extent that it prompted a delegation of leaders to meet with the DDA Vice-Chairman a few times and complain about the harassment by the camp manager. However, the harassment continued unabated. The delegation also met with the Lieutenant Governor of Delhi (who is also the DDA Chairman) to express their concern about the rehabilitation project delay and to put forward other issues. In contrast with the practice of "occupancy urbanism" analysed by Benjamin (2008), where poor urban groups try to secure their territorial claims through interactions with the *lower level* of state bureaucracy, here the camp residents seek to address the *highest* level of the state bureaucracy, in order to counteract the lower-level officer who threatens their housing entitlement. This also shows that the everyday biopolitics deployed in the camp over its population has not completely suppressed the residents' agency.

"Campzenship" … Nevertheless

Notwithstanding the mechanisms and strategies aimed at controlling them, the camp residents are not passive occupants. The situations described above show they are capable of protest against deteriorating living conditions as well as against the manager's abusive methods despite the risk of retaliation. Before the final demolition of Kathputli Colony, the first two batches of residents, who had already settled in the transit camp, also participated in several protests in 2016 and 2017, asking for the speedy implementation of the rehabilitation project.

The residents' agency further emerges in spatial practices of appropriation, evoking what Bayat (2010) coined as "the quiet encroachment of the ordinary" (43). For instance, some families have privatised public toilets by affixing their locks on the doors. Many others have closed their verandas with scrap materials to extend their private living space (Figure 2.4). Still others have extended their dwelling units into small shops or installed a makeshift shop on the roadside. The camp authorities tolerate converting part of one's room into a shop (Figure 2.5), but encroaching upon public space is prohibited, as specified in the tripartite agreement. However, people have often violated this prohibition. Despite recurrent clearing drives of commercial activities operating in public space, the DDA finds it difficult to completely stop such practices. The authorities also imposed restrictions on using extended power connections from the dwelling to the shops. Other examples of appropriation of available resources include recharging electric rickshaws from the power connection provided in the dwelling and paid for by the developer.

Thus, the camp residents exert their agency in the interstices of their confined space, in the details of their living arrangement, and in the appropriation of some

FIGURE 2.4 A row of dwellings with closed verandas in the transit camp. Photo: M.M.S. Gowda, November 2019.

resources, as well as in their interactions with other actors inside and outside the camp. In other words, they assert their "campzenship" (Sigona 2015).

Conclusion

"We feel like we are refugees here" (Authors' interview, 20 September 2019). The complaint of a resident resettled in the transit camp summarises the frequent feeling of uprootedness among those who resisted their eviction, the majority of Kathputli Colony residents. This metaphor also validates the relevance of the concepts borrowed from the literature on camps — notably refugee camps – to analyse the situation of transit camps for displaced slum dwellers. As shown by the case of the Kathputli Colony redevelopment project, the transit camp has confined and suspended its population in "a distinct spatial, legal, and temporal condition" (Picker and Pasquetti 2015, 681). Legal precariousness with regard to future rehousing, along with durable temporariness, characterise the condition of the camp residents.

Although the relative proximity between the camp and the initial settlement mitigates the disruptive effects usually observed in resettlement programmes, relocation has nevertheless affected housing conditions, livelihoods, and everyday spatial practices, as well as social organisation and networks. Variegated lived experiences emerge behind this multidimensional impact. Among the most affected

FIGURE 2.5 A small shop opened in a dwelling room of the transit camp.
Photo: M.M.S. Gowda, August 2014.

are the poorest families for whom accessibility of urban resources is contingent upon their close proximity. Furthermore, habitat conditions in the camp, in particular over-crowdedness, fast deteriorating infrastructure, and inadequate basic services, tend to reproduce slum conditions. These structural conditions are combined with a general climate of uncertainty about the future. The manoeuvres deployed by the planning authority and the developer to control the camp population foster the residents' fear of being excluded from the rehousing scheme. This impedes the residents' mobilisation, without entirely suppressing their capacity to protest. Their everyday adaptation and circumvention strategies further demonstrate their "campzenship". Yet, if transience persists, the material conditions of the camp, as well as the residents' anxiety about their future, are likely to worsen further. After enduring the hardships of demolition and uprooting, the camp residents are kept in an insecure state that restrains their ability to embrace the future and move on to a construction phase. Resettlement remains uncompleted.

This case study also highlights how the resettlement process involves exclusion and differentiated treatment of the slum dwellers, depending not only on official criteria such as the length of residence in the settlement, but also on more subjective factors. These include: the residents' local power position and influence over the members of their community; their negotiation capacities; and their degree of support for – versus resistance to – the redevelopment project. However, the leaders' preferential treatment during the relocation process has subsequently turned into a tool for controlling them. Should temporariness last, the evolving social dynamics in the camp, the possible reconfiguration of leadership, and the capacity to mobilise against delays in the rehousing project, will open new research avenues[18] to follow up on this resettlement case and enrich our understanding of the effects of such governmental programme.

Notes

1 This research is part of a collaboration programme on subaltern urbanism in India, between IRD (French National Research Institute for Sustainable Development) and the Centre for Policy Research in Delhi. It benefitted from IRD funding especially through the JEAI programme "India – Urban Rural Boundaries and Basic Services" (2015–2018).
2 The DDA terms "squatter settlements" informal settlements with no tenure rights, therefore they are considered illegal slums. The words "slum" and "squatter settlements" are often loaded with stigmatising connotations. We only use these terms for ease of reference to policy documents and other official records that use them.
3 For a critical examination of this "slum-free city" policy and the broader political economy context of urban development strategies and mode of governance, see Dupont (2018) and Dupont and Gowda (2020).
4 By *dispositif* – or apparatus – Foucault refers to the various institutional, physical (including architectural forms), regulatory, and administrative mechanisms, as well as knowledge systems, that altogether consolidate and maintain the exercise of power.
5 Source: "Raheja bags Delhi first slum redevelopment project", *Impression* – Quarterly Newsletter, IV(1), New Delhi, January 2010, p. 1.
6 This comprises a one-time payment of INR 112,000 (US$ 1,650) and another of INR 30,000 (US$ 442) covering five-year maintenance charges.
7 Part of an informal settlement was demolished to extend the camp. Hence, some "squatters" were forcibly evicted in order to relocate other "squatters".
8 The various factors behind delays in this project were expounded in Dupont and Gowda (2020).
9 Here an "applicant" is not an individual but represents a distinct household.
10 In this respect, the situation of the families resettled in Narela is identical.
11 Field-visit, 29 August 2015.
12 All residents' quotes are translated from Hindi.
13 We refer to the distinction proposed by World Bank experts (World Bank 2000, 128). Although the concept of social capital, especially "linking social capital", helps understand the slum dwellers' vulnerability, we subscribe to Harris' (2002) critical analysis regarding the promotion of social capital as the "missing link" in development whilst

obscuring power relations and class oppression – essentially whilst "depoliticizing development".
14 Rogers and Wilmsen (2020, 262).
15 As noted above, out of 771 ineligible applicants to the rehabilitation scheme, only 53 were declared eligible by the DDA Appellate Authority.
16 By January 2019, 50 such petitions were filed in the High Court of Delhi by Human Right Law Network's advocates involved in the defence of Kathputli Colony residents.
17 Authors' interview with a resident, victim of such harassment, 20 January 2019.
18 The consequences of the 2020 COVID-19 pandemic and the ensuing lockdown, what this multidimensional crisis reveals with regards to the residents' sanitary and economic vulnerabilities, the camp social organisation, the conduct of its managing authorities, etc. – all these issues open another vast field of inquiry going beyond the scope of this chapter.

References

Agamben, G. 1998. *Homo Sacer: Sovereign Power and Bare Life*. Stanford: Stanford University Press.

Bayat, A. 2010. *Life as Politics: How Ordinary People Change the Middle East*. Amsterdam: Amsterdam University Press.

Benjamin, S. 2008. "Occupancy urbanism: Radicalizing politics and economy beyond policy and programs." *International Journal of Urban and Regional Research* 32 (3): 719–729.

DDA. 2007. *Master Plan for Delhi 2021*. Delhi: Delhi Development Authority [As Notified on 7 February, 2007. Vide S.O. No 141, Gazette of India Extraordinary, Part II.3.ii].

Dodhiya, K.A. 2017. "30 years on, transit camp tenants still wait for homes". *The Asian Age*, July 21, 2017. https://www.asianage.com/metros/mumbai/210717/30-years-on-transit-camp-tenants-still-wait-for-homes.html

Dupont, V. 2011. "The challenge of slums and forced evictions." In *Urban Policies and the Right to the City in India: Rights, Responsibilities and Citizenship*, edited by M-H. Zérah, V. Dupont and S. Tawa Lama-Rewal, 76–97. New Delhi: UNESCO and Centre de Sciences Humaines.

Dupont, V. 2018. "Du squat au nettoyage urbain: processus et enjeux de catégorisation autour du *slum* dans la capitale Indienne." [From squatter settlements to urban cleansing: Processes and issues in the categorisations around the 'slum' in Delhi]. *L'Année Sociologique* 68 (1): 39–66.

Dupont, V., S. Banda, Y. Vaidya, and S. Gowda. 2014. "Unpacking participation in Kathputli Colony: Delhi's first slum redevelopment project, Act I." *Economic and Political Weekly* 49 (24): 39–47.

Dupont, V., and S. Gowda. 2020. "Slum-free city planning versus durable slums: Insights from Delhi." *International Journal of Sustainable Urban Development* 12 (1): 43–51.

Foucault, M. 1994. "Le jeu de Michel Foucault." In *Dits et Ecrits III: 1976–1979*. Paris: Gallimard.

Foucault, M. 1997. "Leçon du 17 mars 1976: 'Il faut défendre la société'." *Cours au Collège de France*, Paris: Gallimard/Seuil.

Ghertner, D.A. 2008. "Analysis of new legal discourses behind Delhi's slum demolitions." *Economic and Political Weekly* 43 (20): 57–66.

Government of India (GoI). 2010. *Rajiv Awas Yojana: Guidelines for Slum-free City Planning*. Delhi: Ministry of Housing and Urban Poverty Alleviation.

Government of India (GoI). 2015. *Pradhan Mantri Awas Yojana: Urban Housing for All (Urban): Scheme Guidelines*. Delhi: Ministry of Housing and Urban Poverty Alleviation.

Harriss, J. 2002. *Depoliticizing Development: The World Bank and Social Capital*. London: Anthem Press.

HLRN. 2002. *Fact Finding Mission Report: Restructuring New Delhi's Urban Habitat, Building an Apartheid City?* New Delhi: Habitat International Coalition – Housing and Land Rights Network.

Menon-Sen, K., and G. Bhan. 2008. *Swept off the Map: Surviving Eviction and Resettlement in Delhi*. Delhi: Yodapress.

Nijman, J. 2008. "Against the odds: Slum rehabilitation in neoliberal Mumbai." *Cities* 25 (2): 73–85.

Picker, G., and S. Pasquetti. 2015. "Durable camps: The state, the urban, the everyday: Introduction." *City* 19 (5): 681–688.

Rogers, S., and B. Wilmsen. 2020. "Towards a critical geography of resettlement." *Progress in Human Geography* 44 (2): 256–275.

Sigona, N. 2015. "Campzenship: Reimagining the camp as a social and political space." *Citizenship Studies* 19 (1): 1–15.

Singh, G., and P.K. Das. 1995. "Building castles in the air: Housing schemes for Bombay's slum-dwellers." *Economic and Political Weekly* 30 (40): 2477–2481.

Sivaramakrishnan, K.C. 2011. *Re-visioning Indian Cities: The Urban Renewal Mission*. Delhi: Sage.

Tatke, S. 2013. "Will they continue to live in transit camp forever?" *The Hindu*, September 2, 2013. https://www.thehindu.com/news/national/will-they-continue-to-live-in-transit-camps-forever/article5083143.ece

Times of India. 2019. "Mumbai: People in transit camp to get permanent homes." *Times of India*, February 5, 2019. https://timesofindia.indiatimes.com/city/mumbai/mumbai-people-in-transit-camps-to-get-permanent-homes/articleshow/67843102.cms

World Bank. 2000. *World Development Report 2000/2001: Attacking Poverty*. Washington DC: World Bank.

3

THE POLITICS OF URBAN RESETTLEMENT

Spatial Governmentality, "Soft Constraints", and Everyday Life in Lomé, Togo

Amandine Spire and Francesca Pilo'

Introduction

As is the case for many other cities in the Global South, Lomé, capital city of the West African nation of Togo, is witnessing a growth in the number of infrastructure projects that prompt urban resettlement as populations are displaced to make way for new buildings and other infrastructure. Research has shown that resettlement processes entail not only spatial ordering, but also processes of political (re)-ordering that alter the relationship between urban authorities and urban dwellers (Doshi 2013; Spire, Bridonneau, and Philifert 2017; Amedokpo 2019). Following this argument, this chapter investigates which forms of politics these resettlement operations entail for city dwellers and how power relations are altered. In line with this book's introduction, we consider urban resettlement as the combination of a destructive process (eviction) and a creative one (the construction of new houses), but we also insist on its *selective* nature in terms of urban political integration, as seen from a governmentality perspective developed by Foucault (2004).

Through a focus on urban resettlement, we here explore how the reordering of urban space reshapes how resettled inhabitants are governed, including both the perspectives of urban authorities and urban dwellers. We specifically address the following questions: how is urban reordering governed and maintained in the period following urban resettlement? How do inhabitants appropriate, contest, or reproduce the normative framework formulated by public policies? We argue that resettlement produces dispossession, as suggested by a number of scholars focusing on other geographical contexts (Navez-Bouchanine 2012; Gillespie 2016; Brickell, Fernández Arrigoitia, and Vasudevan 2017), but also a selective urban integration in cities characterised by strong segregation and inequalities, a still-incomplete democratic transition, and a weak civic space where poor people can organise collectively. We develop this idea by showing that this reordering process is led both by the urban authority and by the city dwellers

DOI: 10.4324/9781003124559-4

themselves through a form a "spatial governmentality" (Huxley 2008) that shapes the daily lives of the resettled people. We use the concept of governmentality in order to consider how the resettlement operates as a process that restructures the urban space and power relationships not only through domination, but also through self-control, discipline, and responsibility.

This research builds on several fieldworks in Lomé in 2015, 2016, and 2018, during which we combined observations and semi-structured interviews conducted with different stakeholders (representatives of ministries, international cooperation, companies, NGOs, etc.) and resettled residents. We conducted *in situ* observations at the old and the new sites, the latter called *la Cité de Djagblé* ("Djagblé City") that was first developed in 2010 as a pilot resettlement program on the outskirts of Lomé. It follows the demolition of a range of homes in Kégué, Attiègou, and Dabarakondi due to the construction of a new bypass (Figure 3.1). The resettlement represents a transformation of the political and institutional framework as will be developed further in this chapter.

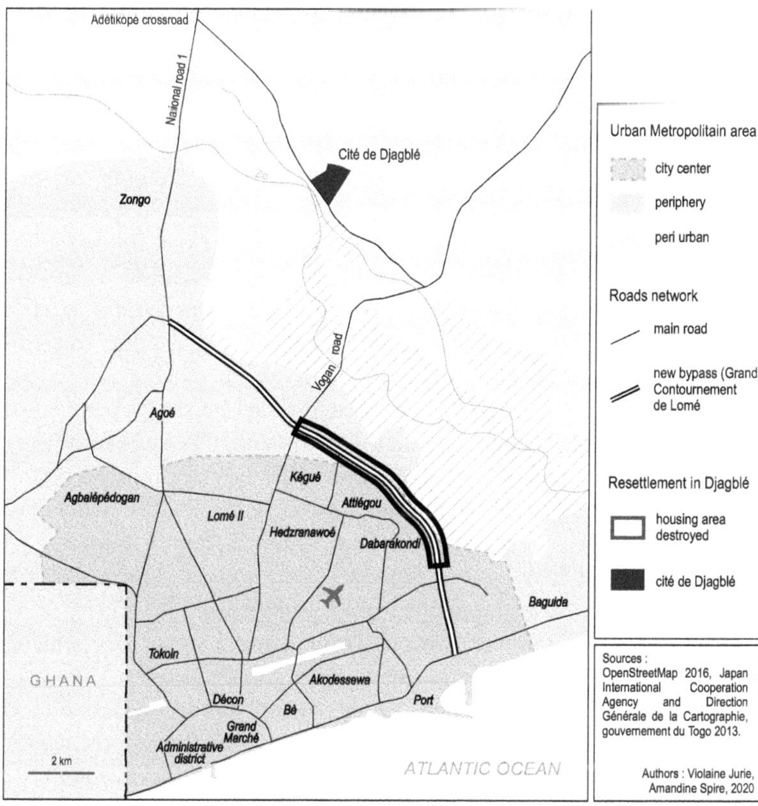

FIGURE 3.1 Djagblé : a pilot resettlement following the demolition of housing to make way for a new bypass

Source: Amandine Spire and Violaine Jurie.

After the presentation of the specific context of resettlement in Togo, we develop a critical framework to analyse the political dimension of the resettlement process, informed by the context of Lomé. We show that the state produces these new spaces through specific instruments that we define as characterised by a "soft constraint", which is used to make the resettlement acceptable. In the last section, we explore two sides of the spatial governmentality that characterise the resettlement: the daily political reordering via the *comité de quartier* ("neighbourhood committee") and the structuration of daily practices around access to urban services, namely water and electricity. These in particular reshape forms of control and responsibilities among residents and the diverse negotiations residents engage in with state agents. In conclusion, we stress the importance of focusing on resettlement in the production of new urban spaces as a possible way to reflect on techniques and logics of urban government.

Background: Governing the People Resettled in Togo

Togo is a country characterised by the dual presence of a strong authoritarian state and a proclaimed desire to open up the state to a process of democratisation (Toulabor 1999; Gervais-Lambony and Nyassogbo 2007; Biakouye 2014; Kohnert 2019). A dynastic party holds power within a highly centralised state that governs the capital city through a special delegation. Its power is highly contested by the majority of city dwellers of Lomé, who historically support the political opposition (Gervais-Lambony and Nyassogbo 2007). This paradoxical coexistence is also reflected in the urban resettlement devices that underwent transformation in 2010. On the one hand, a brutal reordering of urban space occurring in the name of "modernisation", including new infrastructure and clearance operations, showcases the strong authoritarian nature of urban governance. On the other hand, the display of a desire for democratisation opens a window for citizens to negotiate and participate in the public sphere in a way that used to be strictly controlled. The state considerably changed the technique used to resettle city dwellers at the end of the 2000s in order to make the demolition of their homes "more acceptable" in light of the growing move to democratisation in Togo and elsewhere. Thus, a paradox can be observed that we analyse in this chapter by assessing whether greater participation in resettlement processes really can sit alongside strong state control of these processes, as the pilot program suggests.

The destruction of homes and slums in Lomé is not a recent phenomenon and reflects the history of a specific district of the city, the emblematic Zongo District. In fact, it is part of the Lomé's memory in relation to the trajectory of Zongo, which has been home to Hausa and Muslim traders since the late nineteenth century (Agier 1983). As in many other West African cities in the twentieth century, the district's population was evicted several times and resettled at the city periphery in an authoritarian way, with no coordination and poor, if any, compensation to resettled persons (Blot and Spire, 2014). Except for the emblematic role of Zongo, other modernisation projects that involved the destruction of homes did not provide compensation until the 2000s. Yet, since then, the destruction of homes is no longer the sole reserve of the bulldozer that represents the brutal razing of homes through physical demolition. Some resettlements have been implemented through a new management system for evictions based on negotiation and compensation, signalling a move away from force. This change refers to the need of the municipality to respond to the demands of international donors for humane resettlement and compensation. Indeed, since the end of the 2000s, the government has encouraged an urban development where negotiating the value of a home is central, introducing with it ideas linked to "the entrepreneurial city" based on the increased role of private investments in the production of urban spaces, the multiplication of parastatal agencies, and the commodification of public spaces.[1]

In this context, the year 2010 signalled the start of a new type of urban renewal that was considered necessary in order to retain access to the financial assistance of international donors, which had been put on hold due to a lack of transparency and the absence of participatory processes in the application of development aid. To restore its reputation, central and local governments worked together to make modernisation programs more "acceptable" when the destruction of settlements is involved. This includes compensation for resettlement and the construction of a resettlement site. Hence, in 2009, the Togolese government set up a specific Inter-Ministerial Compensation Committee (CII) that is in charge of compensation procedures for populations affected by development projects and resettled.[2] The CII is under the supervision of the Ministry of Economy and Finance. According to the Directorate-General of Infrastructure and Urban Equipment, the CII managed to compensate about 200 households between 2009 and 2017 for both rural and urban resettlement.[3]

Authorities consider these processes to be a "necessary cost" of development. In order to mitigate the adverse effects of these processes in the Global South, over the past 30 years the World Bank has made a series of recommendations and guidelines (in particular the Operational Directive [OD] 4.30 created in 1990 that became the Operational Policy [OP] 4.12 in 2001) for "involuntary resettlements". These were first applied in megaprojects in rural areas and then theoretically implemented in any World Bank-funded project in urban areas (Cernea and Maldonado 2018). The main guideline stipulates that the state is to promote and distribute compensation payments for "lost assets". Consequently, World Bank guidelines have helped set standards with which states such as Togo have to comply to in order to remain a recipient of foreign aid.

In this respect, the Togolese government provides compensation for each project funded by international financial assistance on a case-by-case basis. The compensation is based on a standardised procedure used by the CII in each resettlement project: collective information sessions (an awareness phase) are accompanied by a census of those eligible for compensation. This is followed by individual negotiations with each head of household in order to avoid the build-up of collective contestations. The losses caused by the destruction of the dwelling are calculated according to criteria established by the Ministry of Public Works. In 2009, the CII introduced new rules for governing forced eviction resulting in resettlement. In Lomé, these new procedures are included in a pilot program in the Djagblé resettlement site, which we consider in this study. Before focusing on this novel urban resettlement, we would like to discuss the critical framework used for this research in order to unravel the political dimension of urban resettlement.

Critical Approaches to Urban Resettlement in Togo

A Focus on Dispossession ...

The literature on forced evictions in urban locales devotes ample attention to power relations between authorities and poor urban dwellers in the production of outcomes such as urban exclusion or dispossession (du Plessis 2005; Brickell, Fernández Arrigoitia, and Vasudevan 2017; Deboulet and Lafaye 2018; Dupont 2018). Accordingly, resettlement following eviction is read as an operation that accentuates socio-spatial inequalities (Navez-Bouchanine et al. 2012; Ninnin 2014) and the dynamics of relegation. This is well known in the context of the implementation of major international events such as the Olympic Games, where urban authorities negate the needs of marginalised city dwellers and make these "undesirables" invisible (Dupont 2013; Watt 2018; Magalhães 2016). The aim of these programs is to select, move, and replace inhabitants in order to present a competitive global metropolis. Much of this literature focuses on the asymmetry of power relationships between urban governments and city dwellers facing a build-up of dispossession processes (Harvey 2008). From this perspective, power is exercised *by* urban authorities, including public action and private actors, *over* poor, minority, or "undesirable" social groups. This is the destructive side of eviction that helps to commodify the central and most prestigious spaces of large metropolitan areas.

In a similar vein, other works have emphasised the resistance capacities of the urban poor facing forced evictions: how poor people can organise themselves and resist the neoliberal drive, even withstanding forced eviction (Bhan 2009; Crentsil and Owusu 2018). Influenced by a human rights framework, the analysis of mobilisation reveals how the poor and otherwise affected can defend their own rights to claim better compensation and even the right to remain on site (Afenah 2010; Farouk and Owusu 2012). If resistance is impossible and the balance of power too asymmetrical, then urban dwellers targeted by evictions experience a process of impoverishment and exclusion characterised by forms of dispossession in terms of jobs, education, transportation, and so on (Cernea 1997).

But Also Selective Inclusion through Governmentality

Assuming a different perspective, recent literature on forced eviction in the Global South has also highlighted the tension between resettlement processes and selective inclusion (Doshi 2013). This literature investigates resettlement from the perspective and experiences of the evicted themselves and not from a macro-economic perspective. Based on the subjectivity of those evicted who consent or contest displacement, Doshi (2013: 845) identifies a process of "accumulation by differentiated displacement", because urban development gives rise to an increase in the economic differentiation of displaced people. This differentiation helps to strengthen the social logic of land markets and the "ideologies of belonging" (Doshi 2013: 844). It embraces both the destruction and reconstruction of urban space dialectically, which enables the analysis of the political effects of such urban transformations in the mid to long term.

Similarly, the critical approach developed by Rogers and Wilmsen (2019) is useful for understanding the political dimension of resettlement beyond dispossession. They consider resettlement "a governmental program with multiple logics, one that seeks to render people and space more governable" (3). They also argue that the practice of resettlement does not only rely on the state, but engages "complex networks of agents" (10) – from international donors to local authorities. This increased governability is facilitated by specific instruments such as social evaluation and compensation. Social evaluation, including measuring, modernising, and enumerating, facilitates state intervention by making resettlement predictable and calculable. Green and Baird (2016), for example, show how compensation in Laos helped the development of capitalist social relations through new market relationships for land, goods, and even natural resources. From this critical perspective, transformation in the implementation of resettlement programs reflects techniques and logics of urban government.

Following Roy's (2009) study of civic governmentality in Beirut and Mumbai, we discuss how resettlement can mean the creation of new power relationships through techniques of government facilitated by a selective urban political integration. Roy considers that the basis of regimes of civic governmentality are how "the urban subject is simultaneously empowered and self-disciplined, civil and mobilized, displaced and compensated" (Roy 2009, 161). From Roy's dialectic perspective, resettlement becomes a tool for urban governments to reconfigure their power and reorder urban space along other lines. Using this notion of governmentality first developed in Foucault's seminal work, with some precautions we can elaborate on how people in Lomé reshape their relationship with the state *through* resettlement processes. This political dimension of resettlement is characterised by an exercise of power based on "soft constraints" instead of physical coercion, manifested through the granting of compensations as counterparts to the forced eviction.

The Production of "Soft Constraints": Secured Tenure and Integration in Land Markets in Djagblé

Resettlement in Djagblé offers a specific turn for discussing the urban transformation and the process of selective political inclusion in Togo. With the creation of counterparts, the CII's mission marks a turning point in redefining how the Togolese state intervenes in daily urban lives. In fact, through the resettlement procedures, the relationship between the state and poor city dwellers is directly redefined. Instead of using its direct force of constraint, the central government regulated counterparts in order to integrate city dwellers into the project. This process of adhesion is not the result of acceptance or the cessation of resistance. The "soft constraints" are not imposed by force, but by the promotion of new norms defined on the basis of the promise of land ownership and market value.

Before being displaced, most of the poor city dwellers did not have formal land tenure, but occupied land according to customary rules. The demolished houses were built on land with a precarious status. However, despite occupying land but not having land titles,[4] these city dwellers were eligible for compensation according to customary rules (Agetur et al. 2012). In the case of resettlement to Djagblé, the majority of the displaced city dwellers left the houses they built themselves and had turned into homes over time. These houses, called *chez* ("at") in Togolese French have strong affective and social dimensions: they evolve over time with the socio-economic trajectory of their owner (Marguerat 1989; Biakouye 2014). The demolition, however, rapidly transformed the *chez* into an economic product. In fact, the compensations for the demolition contributes to standardize the value of the *chez* according to the economic value defined by public authorities.

To integrate this exchange value, the budget allocated by the Togolese government for Djagblé's resettlement operation is exceptionally large. Under given conditions, the government was able to propose the terms of departure to the head of each household. The compensation included both a parcel of land at the resettlement site (Djagblé) equipped with water and electricity connections, and a sum of money equivalent to the estimated value of the *chez* lost through resettlement, with the amount ranging from 300,000 to 3.5 million CFA provided for the self-construction of new house (Figure 3.2). The compensation was reserved for those considered to be landowners, and tenants were *de facto* excluded from the process. According to the CII, in the case of the Djagblé resettlement, of the 312 households eligible for compensation, 258 had received it, which came to imply the monetisation of every aspect of the home. The evaluation of the value of ceded houses covered every conceivable physical and descriptive component of the

FIGURE 3.2 "Djagblé City" under construction in 2016, five years after the resettlement. Source: Photo taken by Authors, 2016.

dwelling: the land surface area, fencing, number of rooms, building materials, number of trees, and access to utility networks.

As early as 2009, the central government was using a newly developed administrative and political tool called the *certificat d'entente* ("certificate of understanding") to assess the level of compensation required for any demolition taking place as part of an urban project resulting in resettlement. This document includes a written agreement between the head of the household and the central government (Figure 3.3). For the Djagblé resettlement, the agreement stipulated that the head of the household was to vacate the original site within five months in order to receive compensation, as defined by local authorities. The compensation would cover the losses generated by the demolition of certain houses located at the site of the new bypass. The document is edited by the CII following an individual meeting with each head of household eligible for compensation. The relocated person must also pay a tax stamp of 200,000 CFA. Each person that benefits from the relocation receives a copy of the certificate of understanding, which is safely stored (see Figure 3.3). During the interviews, this document was sometimes presented to us in order to explain the origin of their installation at the resettlement site, but also to demonstrate the new sense of security of land tenure this document entails. In fact, the official nature of this document reveals the recognition of a specific and quite secured land tenure for the resettled and shows how documents serve as important mediators in the relationship between marginalised city dwellers and the state (see Pilo' 2020).

The use of the certificate in the Djagblé resettlement embodies the growing importance of individual property characterised by the increased significance of its exchange value that quickly becomes market-driven. The document thus determines the distribution of plots of land at the resettlement site and marks the transition from the status of *displaced person* to that of *resettled owner* of a plot of land whose value is thereafter determined by the market. The *certificat d'entente* is similar to a land title: it defines ownership of the plot in the resettlement area and illustrates one aspect of the transformation and the consolidation of the resettled into "landlords", the term used in the *certificat d'entente*. Transforming the resettled into landlords creates a new relationship between property and political subjectivity under neoliberal urbanism (Lund and Deslaurier 2013; Hilgers 2013). The document signifies security of tenure and boosts the market-driven value of the plot in a part of the city, Djagblé, where the logic of occupation before the resettlement was based on the collectively owned land of communities and customary authority-governed land transfers. In Djagblé, this logic has not disappeared, but instead has been refined and transformed. Different strategies confirm the growing importance of a market-driven rationality with speculative practices. Five years after resettlement, land prices had increased threefold, and strategic investments had even been made by city dwellers who were not resettled by government, but who decided to move to and invest in this new area.

Many of those resettled sold their plot of land within a few months of resettlement because of the insufficient financial capacity to build a new house or because

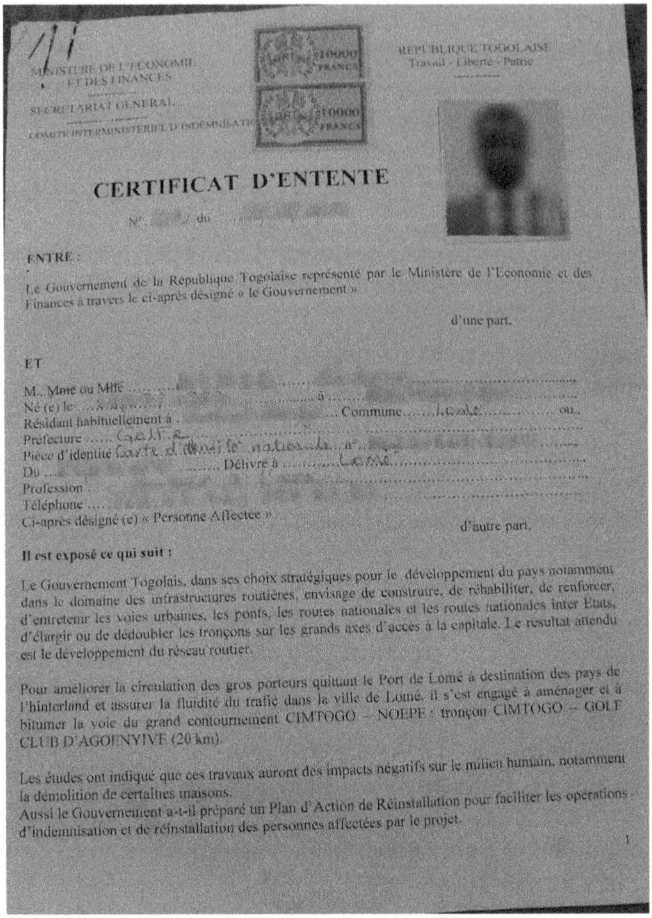

MINISTERE DE L'ECONOMIE ET DES FINANCES

SECRETARIAT GENERAL

COMITE INTERMINISTERIEL D'INDEMNISATI[illegible]

REPUBLIQUE TOGOLAISE
Travail - Liberté - Patrie

CERTIFICAT D'ENTENTE

N°: ... / du ...

ENTRE :

Le Gouvernement de la République Togolaise représenté par le Ministère de l'Economie et des Finances à travers le ci-après désigné « le Gouvernement »

d'une part,

ET

M., Mme ou Mlle ...
Né (e) le ... à ...
Résidant habituellement à ... Commune ... ou..
Préfecture ...
Pièce d'identité ... n° ...
Du ... Délivré à ...
Profession ...
Téléphone ...
Ci-après désigné (e) « Personne Affectée »

d'autre part,

Il est exposé ce qui suit :

Le Gouvernement Togolais, dans ses choix stratégiques pour le développement du pays notamment dans le domaine des infrastructures routières, envisage de construire, de réhabiliter, de renforcer, d'entretenir les voies urbaines, les ponts, les routes nationales et les routes nationales inter Etats, d'élargir ou de dédoubler les tronçons sur les grands axes d'accès à la capitale. Le résultat attendu est le développement du réseau routier.

Pour améliorer la circulation des gros porteurs quittant le Port de Lomé à destination des pays de l'hinterland et assurer la fluidité du trafic dans la ville de Lomé, il s'est engagé à aménager et à bitumer la voie du grand contournement CIMTOGO – NOEPE : tronçon CIMTOGO – GOLF CLUB D'AGOENYIVE (20 km).

Les études ont indiqué que ces travaux auront des impacts négatifs sur le milieu humain, notamment la démolition de certaines maisons.
Aussi le Gouvernement a-t-il préparé un Plan d'Action de Réinstallation pour faciliter les opérations d'indemnisation et de réinstallation des personnes affectées par le projet.

1

FIGURE 3.3 The *certificat d'entente*: an original agreement between the state and the resettled in Togo.
Source: Authors, 2014.

of the distance from or lack of transport connecting Djagblé to the city centre or workplaces. Resettlement therefore does not really meet the expectations of all displaced city dwellers and presents new difficulties for the urban poor in their daily lives to remain in the city. In fact, Djagblé is far away from central urban spaces and thereby from employment and commercial centralities. As a result, commuting becomes time-consuming, more difficult, and more expensive. The use of the personal vehicles of the few equipped households in the neighbourhood is beneficial in case of emergency. The rest of the time, reaching the city centre begins with walking up to four kilometres to reach the main road where motorcycle cabs and cabs assemble. Moreover, the purchase of a motorcycle is often the most appropriate response to these new constraints, which puts a strain on household budgets. Many households have thus changed their mobility practices following

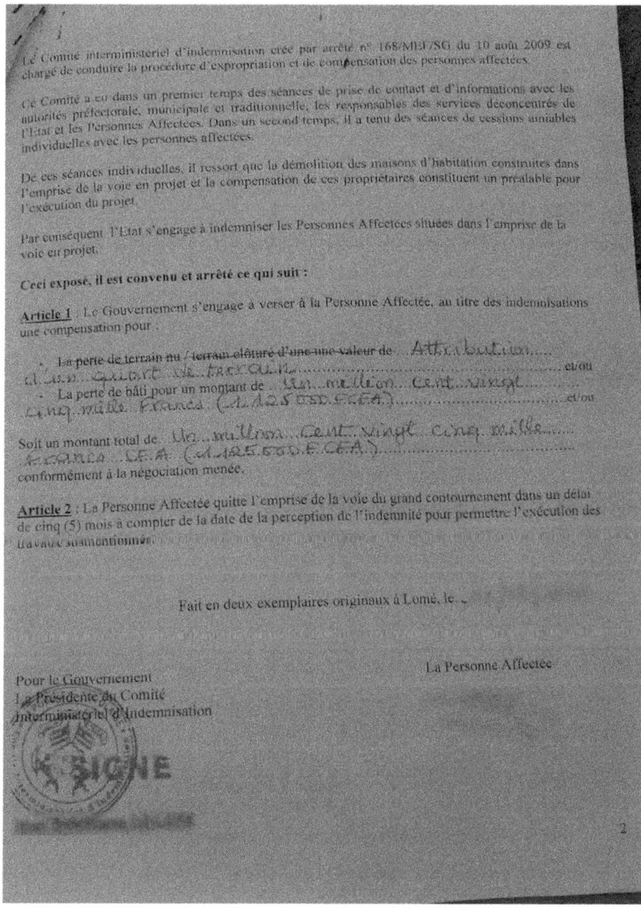

Le Comité interministériel d'indemnisation créé par arrêté n° 168/MEF/SG du 10 août 2009 est chargé de conduire la procédure d'expropriation et de compensation des personnes affectées.

Ce Comité a eu dans un premier temps des séances de prise de contact et d'informations avec les autorités préfectorale, municipale et traditionnelle, les responsables des services déconcentrés de l'Etat et les Personnes Affectées. Dans un second temps, il a tenu des séances de cessions amiables individuelles avec les personnes affectées.

De ces séances individuelles, il ressort que la démolition des maisons d'habitation construites dans l'emprise de la voie en projet et la compensation de ces propriétaires constituent un préalable pour l'exécution du projet.

Par conséquent l'Etat s'engage à indemniser les Personnes Affectées situées dans l'emprise de la voie en projet.

Ceci exposé, il est convenu et arrêté ce qui suit :

Article 1 : Le Gouvernement s'engage à verser à la Personne Affectée, au titre des indemnisations une compensation pour :

- ~~La perte de terrain nu / terrain clôturé d'une une valeur de~~ Attribution d'un quart de terrain .... et/ou
- La perte de bâti pour un montant de Un million cent vingt cinq mille Francs (1.125 000 FCFA) .... et/ou

Soit un montant total de Un million cent vingt cinq mille Francs CFA (1.125.000 F CFA) ....

conformément à la négociation menée.

Article 2 : La Personne Affectée quitte l'emprise de la voie du grand contournement dans un délai de cinq (5) mois à compter de la date de la perception de l'indemnité pour permettre l'exécution des travaux susmentionnés.

Fait en deux exemplaires originaux à Lomé, le ...

Pour le Gouvernement
La Présidente du Comité
Interministériel d'Indemnisation

SIGNE

La Personne Affectée

2

FIGURE 3.3 (Cont.)

their arrival in Djagblé: freedom of movement when the purchase of a motorcycle is possible, reduced social and family interactions outside the place of residence.

However, at the same time, other city dwellers living in the city centre have been looking for an opportunity to purchase such secure plots of land. The certificate ensures that the lot has been allocated to a single occupant, which is not always the case in Lomé, particularly on the outskirts of the city where some members of the communities subdivide property, leading to protracted and widespread family conflicts. In addition, the strong advantage of the site is not only the security of tenure, but also the connection to the electricity network and the water supply service, which opens up a way to redefine a new kind of social contract (see below). We can argue that the resettlement in Djagblé reinforces the grounds for a selective political urban inclusion based on a combination of market rationality and economic and political contractualisation. This transition to the "status" of resettled people leads city dwellers to formulate requests for state intervention. The property and the market-based value reflect the state's implementation of soft and flexible constraints for urban dwellers to adhere to new social norms and urban transformations without strong coercion. We argue that these transformations pave the way for the implementation of a spatial governmentality. The resettled are governed through logics of responsibility and control that we suggest should be explored through a focus on two aspects of daily life: political leadership and access to urban services.

Governing Everyday Life

The political dimension of the resettlement emerges from the intertwined promise made by the state (the provision of land and urban services) and the reshaping of power relations at the local level. New power relations emerge through the structure of *le comité des affectés* ("community of affected people") and the everyday official and unofficial practices of accessing urban services. Both aspects contribute to the implementation of discipline and control to rule daily interactions.

Shaping Authority and Asserting Control through the Local Committee

The arrival of displaced city dwellers at the new resettlement site rapidly transformed the local organisation of Djagblé, whose direct surroundings were already occupied by rural communities, elites, and local chiefs. The latter are witnessing the arrival of a new political and social form of organisation that may seem to compete with that which prevailed before the resettlement. In fact, CII state leaders encouraged a new kind of local social organisation in Djagblé immediately after resettlement, *le comité des affectés*. Its role is mainly to act as mediator in neighbourhood conflicts or between the different social groups living at resettled sites, and it generally ensures compliance with the rules prescribed by the state: respect for the demarcation of plots, the non-occupation of land reserves (reserved for future public facilities), and the provision and access to urban services. The daily organisation created by the leader of the special committee helps increase the acceptability of the logic of the state's actions among the resettled. A representative of the state sometimes visits the head of *le comité des affectés* in order to support their authority. Thus, daily affairs in the resettlement site are governed through negotiation, discipline, and control that transform socio-political hierarchies.

Resettled city dwellers are consequently subject to a new framework of authority set up by an intermediary who is well-anchored in the context of Djagblé daily life. The committee is chaired by a relatively young male welder (under the age of 40) who was resettled at an early stage. His relatively young age contrasts with that of traditional authorities that prevail in the district at large. This new leader directly represents the state and is in charge of ensuring respect for government rules in Djagblé. For example, the state had initially banned agricultural activities on vacant land (reserves in the initial plan) intended for the potential future development of community facilities. However, many resettled people started to cultivate the vacant land due to the lack of available land or alternative sources of livelihoods. The local representative then began a process of negotiation between the resettled people and the state to obtain a framework that would allow some of the inhabitants to cultivate this land, based on more or less clientistic relations. Thus, in general, the head of the committee is mobilised to control and find ways out of the many conflicts that arise around the use of land resources. Maintaining the initial plan or modifying it under certain conditions remains a key issue for the CII in order to keep control of the resettlement site from a distance. The role of the committee is therefore to contain tensions in a resettlement site marked by an increasing number of inhabitants and newcomers who have chosen to settle in Djagblé and are not older people affected by the past eviction. In 2017, encouraged by the CII, the committee became a neighbourhood development committee (CDQ), that is, a common intermediate level of government that mediates the relationship between the state and urban city dwellers in Togo. The CDQ is a common form of organisation at the district level in Lomé (Aholou 2008). This shift reveals the normalisation of the authority this committee wielded.

In Lomé, CDQs have developed not without difficulty and in various forms depending on the neighbourhood since the beginning of the twentieth century. In all cases, even if they constitute a participatory space, they are strongly controlled by the central authorities. The CDQs are supposed to guarantee "social peace" by formulating a series of rights and duties, providing a framework allowing for certain "citizen" actions such as the cleaning of public spaces. Thus, every Saturday morning, the Djagblé CDQ invites residents to pull up the weeds that grow along the district's unpaved roads or to clear the reserved land in the public domain (vacant spaces earmarked for the collective facilities – markets, schools – that residents are still waiting for). When the Saturday morning "gong" rings, one of the CDQ members scrupulously notes the people present at each meeting in a register. This register makes it possible to know which city dwellers are volunteers and to value responsible residents in future arbitrations. CII officials, or any other representative of the district's external authority, may consult this register. This type of operation, which is quite common in Lomé, indicates to Djagblé the implementation of control and discipline by the residents themselves in a post-resettlement context. The local political reorganisation in Djagblé contributes to consolidating the social contract that imposes respect for specific rules and responsibilities. The supply of water and electricity is another important illustration of this dynamic of responsibilisation, as we show below.

Reconfiguring Local Relations and Responsibilities through Urban Services

Urban services are recognised as enabling a specific re-ordering process that links government intervention, urban rights, and everyday practices (see Pilo' 2017). In Djagblé, the delivery of urban services definitively helps to construct a post-resettlement order characterised by new forms of responsibility among residents themselves that are facilitated in particular by heterogeneous forms of accessing these services.

Djagblé's water supply is delivered through water fountains located in different parts of the settlement, individual household connections, and wells that are increasingly being drilled in residents' yards, since this is the cheapest, albeit least safe, way to access water. A water tower is an integral and symbolic part of the resettlement site and has supplied water to the neighbourhood since 2012 (Figure 3.4). It is managed by the "water tower management committee" (*comité de gestion de l'eau*), formed by three young, resettled residents with a basic level of education and expertise in the domain in order to task some residents with the sound functioning and maintenance of the service, but also for cost recovery, since they are in charge of billing those residents who have an individual connection. This committee is consequently a mediator between the water company and water users, checking and controlling the correct technical and commercial functioning of the system.

In 2016, however, individual connections were still an exception. Only 20 households out of around 100 had a private connection, according to a member of the water committee. In fact, individual connections are still quite expensive and not everyone can afford one.[5] Consequently, most residents buy water from vendors at one of the seven water fountains in the settlement when they do not have a borehole in their yard. These are run by vendors who pay a monthly bill to the water committee and resell water at a higher price per litre. These fountains, equipped with meters, are generally installed underground and locked with a chain when the vendor is not present in order to avoid theft. In both cases, access to

FIGURE 3.4 The water tower, a symbol of the resettlement site.
source: authors, 2017

water is shaped by the market and respect for the rules enforced by the presence of a water committee and the protection of the infrastructure itself.

In contrast to the water service, the electricity is distributed through a more hybrid system formed by official and unofficial (but tolerated) practices. The grid was installed in 2012, and the residents generally have access to electricity, with the exception of traditional communities who had already lived on the outskirts of Djagblé before others were resettled there. Most of them could not afford a connection (Amedokpo 2019), which contributes broadly to the creation of inequalities between those residents who resided there before and newcomers. Beyond these more evident forms of exclusion, other types of inequality are reproduced mainly through the official and unofficial distribution system.

In the official system, households are equipped with a (prepaid or post-paid) individual meter. It is very common, however, that other meters (called sub meters) are connected to the main meter. Sub-meters "distribute" and measure electricity consumption to other neighbours who may live inside or outside the same compound where the main meter is installed. This electricity supply sub-system complies with the electricity provider's rules, and residents who have a sub-meter are customers of the electricity company (and receive separate bills). These generally offer more electricity and are cheaper than a main meter. However, a third type of meter widely used in Lomé, called an *additionneuse,* is not official. The *additionneuse* is directly connected to the main meter and is generally used to measure the consumption of tenants who live in another part of the house, within or nearby the same compound. While the resale of electricity is not officially permitted, it is generally tolerated by the *Compagnie Energie Electrique du Togo* (CEET), the country's sole electricity provider.

The installation of a main electricity meter seems to depend on three main elements: the physical possibility of installing it – the house must be within 100 meters from an electrical pole; the financial means, since it is more expensive than the other meters; and the occupancy status – owner or tenant. In general, only owners have a main meter, while tenants are considered temporary and generally do not wish to invest in one because of the price and the responsibility involved. *Responsibility* is a term that often emerges in residents' discourse associated with the main meter and is generally associated with the idea of homeownership. Thus, taking responsibility for a main meter seems to be a goal of homeowners. Although access to electricity was not new among relocated residents, resettlement has generally changed their position on the electricity supply sub-system. The formal and informal relations created by this hybrid electricity distribution system helped reshape power relations between residents along the lines of an owner-tenant structure, but also between neighbours, helping to stabilise norms governing conduct and solidarity.

Residents often describe the difference between the official system (main meters and sub-meters) and the "unofficial" system (*additionneuse*) in terms of *dependence* and *independence* among neighbours and by referring to the owner-tenant relationship. The term *independence* refers above all to having or not having an electricity supply that depends on the goodwill of a neighbour, in contrast to the *additionneuses* system, where dependence takes the form of an informal commercial relationship that ties whomever has the main meter to the person with an *additionneuse*, who is considered in the debt of the former. This hybrid electricity system seems to make the management of the commercial relationship more flexible in terms of resolving problems (technical or commercial), but it is also the product of increased control directly related to physical proximity. Thus, for example, during a daily control of an *additionneuse*, the owner of the main meter realised that one of the *additionneuses* had stopped measuring consumption. He immediately encouraged the tenant to replace the *additionneuse* as quickly as possible, which took one week. In order to calculate the amount for non-registered consumption, both parties agreed to install a new *additionneuse* and to refer to the consumption recorded for 24 hours to estimate daily consumption, and subsequently to multiply this number of kWh by seven (fieldnotes, Pilo' 2016). Actually, when it is a matter of disconnection due to non-payment, some residents explained that the reasons are generally discussed before they are disconnected or disconnect others. At the same time, there is also a strong form of control, as is visible in the modes of problem-solving in the *additionneuse* system.

The physical location of meters also helps structure forms of control, responsibility, and trust in these relations. For example, the installation of *additionneuses* in the owner's home should minimise attempts at illicit manipulation of the meter by the tenant. This is also likely to be infrequent in a system where the control of the meters is effective and carried out on a daily basis. The installation of prepaid meters is often considered as enabling the reinforcement of these forms of control in the sub-distribution system. Power relations within this system also emerge, particularly when it comes to power cuts. In fact, in a context in which electricity supply is often unstable, electricity can be a rare good. It is not uncommon for the owner of the main meter to temporarily disconnect the *additionneuses* in order to maintain his or her own supply. This situation can be interpreted as an extreme manifestation of network control.

The study of electricity and water provision in the post-resettlement period clearly indicates unequal access to urban services depending on power relations amongst neighbours and mediated by different socio-technical configurations. To conclude this article, we would like to focus on two ordinary situations demonstrating relations of dependence and control between neighbours through the electricity service.

Three Portraits for Illustrating the Resettlement-induced Transformation and the Consolidation of the Market Value

Some residents interviewed had installed a main meter for the first time in their lives after resettlement. Previously, they had accessed electricity via a sub-meter or an *additionneuse*, but they have now become "re-sellers" of electricity. For example, Kekeli installed a three-phase main meter and a sub-meter that supplies a neighbour whose home is one kilometre away. Since her resettlement in 2011, Kekeli had to leave her job because of the distance from Lomé and needed to find a new way to secure an income. In 2016, she sold juice and ice cream and was also a member of the water committee, where she worked once a week. Because of her work, she needed a freezer, which is why she installed a more powerful three-phase meter when the CEET decided to install an electricity pole next to her house. The installation of a main meter enabled her to start up a commercial activity and to have her own water supply, since she needed an electric pump to extract water from a well in her courtyard. Electricity access seems to partially offset the negative effects of having lost her job after resettlement. Similarly, Mawussi and his family had the opportunity to install a main meter in Djagblé. The short distance to an electricity pole – the last one on that side of the resettlement site – helped make his position particularly strategic. In fact, neighbours living beyond that point had to rely on him to access electricity or developed "cobwebs" – a system of informal grid extensions that is unsafe and built for limited extensions of the network (Biakouyé 2014). Thus, both these residents, Kekeli and Mawussi, upgraded their status in the electricity sub-distribution system thanks to a combination of homeownership and proximity to electricity poles. Mawussi installed two sub-meters in his house and three *additionneuses* in order to provide electricity to neighbours and tenants in his compound. Whereas the redistribution of electricity can be considered an act of solidarity ("We are in need together", Kekeli, February 2016), it also creates new relations in the form of unofficial commercial relationships.

Since payment is essentially based on a compromise established between the two parties, it can also create conflicts. Isaac, for example, decided to switch from a main post-paid meter to a prepaid meter, since several tenants receiving electricity through the *additionneuses* system stopped paying their bills. The prepaid meter was an optimal solution to avoid his growing debt, enabling him to step up the control of his neighbours' consumption and check the behaviour of his employees. Isaac had several apprentices and the prepaid meter allowed him to check whether they were using the electrical tools when he was not present. By installing the prepaid meter, Isaac sought to minimise the risk of debt, to manage the business relationship more effectively, while continuing to deliver electricity to two neighbours and to the only private school of the resettlement that could not afford to install a main meter. By deciding to provide the private school with electricity, Isaac helped with the functioning of an important social institution in the settlement, which is a form of responsibilisation.

The cases of Kekeli, Mawussi, and Isaac, together with those of other residents, illustrate how the experience of networked services in the resettlement site creates forms of dependency and responsibility among neighbours, which are reinforced by the general adherence to market logics required to access these services.

Conclusion

This chapter has discussed the process of selective political inclusion produced by urban resettlement programs in Lomé. It has analysed urban resettlement as a specific site where both the role of state and of city dwellers in defining a spatial governmentality characterised by soft (but real) constraints can be explored. Focusing on a pilot resettlement program and the Djagblé resettlement in particular, this chapter has analysed a rather emblematic experience in the Togolese political context. In fact, through this pilot, for the first time, the Togolese government compensated evicted city dwellers with the purported aim of creating a certain level of support for the ongoing urban transformations. The provision of compensation is illustrative of the increased implementation of logics of individualisation, economic rationality, and negotiation in metropolitan government practices. Urban authorities chose not to assert their traditional coercive power, rather employing "soft constraints" through different forms of compensation. These in return created new logics of self-discipline and control in regulating the everyday lives of those living at the resettlement site. This example helps shift the perspective from the dimension of exclusion and dispossession to the dimension of an uncertain and selective (reversible?) inclusion, based on the granting of individual property and formalised access to urban services.

In fact, resettlement was not only negotiated on the basis of landownership and financial means, but also on the basis of a promise of access to formal urban services such as water and electricity. Thus, different instruments, such as the creation of a specific document (*certificat d'entente*), the creation of a local organisation (*comité des affectés*), and the installation of urban services, contributed to the creation of a post-resettlement order characterised by the construction of mechanisms of control and self-responsibility among residents. The political effects of resettlement examined in this chapter highlight the recent transformation of a West African metropolis. Francophone Sub-Saharan African cities are not very visible in current international debates on resettlement. Thus, our analysis contributes to these debates, building on a relatively unexplored reality – that of West African cities. Yet, our argument, based on the emergence of a new relationship between the authorities and the "governed" through a new post-resettlement order grounded in everyday life, is not confined to Togo. In fact, we consider that resettlement – as a type of space – opens up possibilities to reflect on how city dwellers become more governable as their interactions with governments reconfigure forms of subjectivity.

Acknowledgements

The authors are grateful to the City of Paris for the support provided through its Emergence Program on the Right to the City in the Global South (2014–2019, coordinated by Amandine Spire and Marianne Morange), which made possible the collaboration and fieldwork for this chapter. The authors are very grateful for thoughtful comments of two anonymous reviewers and to Marie Huchzermeyer for her careful engagement with the work presented here.

Notes

1 Consider, for example, the historical Fréau Jardin Square, which in the 2010s was transformed into a privatised leisure space in a bid to modernise and reorder the heart of the city.

2 Created by decree n°168/MEF/SG of August 10, 2009.
3 Interview with the head office of the *Direction Générale des Infrastructures et des Équipements Urbains* [Directorate-General of Infrastructure and Urban Equipment], 13 April 2018.
4 Only a small portion of city dwellers hold an official land title in Togo. In fact, official land titles are very rare and expensive to obtain in Togo because of a lack of resources to process them. Thus, the land tenure system is characterised by a legal duality, expressed as the coexistence of customary and modern practices (an "in-between").
5 Households have to pay 1,500 CFA for the connection and 25,000 CFA to install the water meter.

References

Afenah, A. 2010. "(Re)claiming citizenship rights in Accra, Ghana." In *Cities for All: Proposals and Experiences towards the Right to the City*, edited by A. Sugranyes and C. Mathivet, 159–167. Santiago: Habitat International Coalition.

Agetur *et al.* 2012. *Stratégie de développement urbain du Grand Lomé 'Horizon 2030'*. Lomé: Agence G2 Conception.

Agier, M. 1983. *Commerce et sociabilité: les négociants soudanais du quartier zongo de Lomé (Togo)*. Paris: Office de la recherche scientifique et technique outre-mer (ORSTOM).

Aholou, C. 2008. "*Proximités spatiales, distances socio-culturelles à Cotonou (Bénin) et à Lomé (Togo). Etude comparative.*" PhD diss., Université de Paris Nanterre.

Amedokpo, Y. 2019. "Problématique des déplacements forcés de populations dans l'aménagement de l'agglomération urbaine de Lomé." Master's thesis, Université de Lomé.

Bhan, G. 2009. "'This is no longer the city I once knew': evictions, the urban poor and the right to the city in millennial Delhi." *Environment and Urbanization* 21 (1): 127–142.

Biakouyé, K. A. 2014. "*Lomé au-delà de Lomé: étalement urbain et territoires dans une capitale d'Afrique sud-saharienne.*" PhD diss., Université Paris Ouest Nanterre La Défense.

Blot, J. and Spire, A. 2014. "Déguerpissements et conflits autour des légitimités citadines dans les villes du Sud." *L'Espace Politique* 22 (1).

Brickell, K., M. Fernández Arrigoitia, and A. Vasudevan, eds. 2017. *Geographies of Forced Eviction*. London: Palgrave Macmillan.

Cernea, M. 1997. "The risks and reconstruction model for resettling displaced populations." *World Development* 25 (10): 1569–1587.

Cernea, M. M., and J. Maldonado. 2018. *Challenging the Prevailing Paradigm of Displacement and Resettlement Risks, Impoverishment, Legacies, Solutions*. New York: Routledge.

Crentsil, A., and G. Owusu. 2018. "Accra's decongestion policy: another face of urban clearance or bulldozing approach?" *International Development Policy* (10): 213–228.

Deboulet, A., and C. Lafaye. 2018. "La rénovation urbaine, entre délogement et relogement. Les effets sociaux de l'éviction." *L'Année Sociologique* 68 (1): 155–184.

Doshi, S. 2013. "The politics of the evicted: redevelopment, subjectivity, and difference in Mumbai's slum frontier." *Antipode* 45 (4): 844–865.

Du Plessis, J. 2005. "The growing problem of forced evictions and the crucial importance if community based, locally appropriate alternatives." *Environment and Urbanization* 17 (1): 123–134.

Dupont, V. 2013. "Which place for the homeless in Delhi? Scrutiny of a mobilisation campaign in the 2010 Commonwealth Games context." *South Asia Multidisciplinary Academic Journal* 8 (online).

Dupont, V. 2018. "Des camps de squatters au nettoyage urbain : processus et enjeux de catégorisation autour du slum à Delhi." *L'Année Sociologique* 68 (1): 39–66.

Farouk, B. R., and M. Owusu. 2012. "'If in doubt, count': The role of community-driven enumerations in blocking eviction in Old Fadama, Accra." *Environment and Urbanization* 24 (1): 47–57.

Foucault, M. 2004. *Sécurité, territoire, population: cours au Collège de France, 1977–1978*. Paris: Gallimard.

Gervais-Lambony, P., and G. K. Nyassogbo. 2007. *Lomé: dynamiques d'une ville africaine. Hommes et sociétés*. Paris: Karthala.

Gillespie, T. 2016. "Accumulation by urban dispossession: struggles over urban space in Accra, Ghana." *Transactions of the Institute of British Geographers* 41 (1): 66–77.

Green, W.N., and I.G. Baird. 2016. "Capitalizing on compensation: Hydropower resettlement and the commodification and decommodification of nature-society relations in southern Laos." *Annals of the American Association of Geographers* 106: 853–873.

Harvey, D. 2008. "The right to the city." *New Left Review* 2 (53): 23–40.

Hilgers, M. 2013. "À qui appartient la ville ? Urbanisme néolibéral et propriété dans trois petits centres urbains du Ghana et du Burkina Faso." *Politique africaine* 132 (4): 95–113.

Huxley, M. 2008. "Space and government: governmentality and geography." *Geography Compass* 2 (5): 1635–1658.

Kohnert, D. 2019. *Pas de changement en vue: le développement politique et socio-économique du Togo (2017–2019)*. Preprint. GIGA German Institute of Global and Area Studies.

Lund, C., and C. Deslaurier. 2013. "Propriété et citoyenneté. Dynamiques de reconnaissance dans l'Afrique des villes." *Politique africaine* 132 (4): 5–25.

Magalhães, A. 2016. "'Logique d'intervention ' et circulations: éradiquer les favelas pour gérer l'espace urbain dans le Rio olympique." *Problèmes d'Amérique latine* 103 (4): 79–93.

Marguerat, Y. 1989. "Dynamique sociale et dynamique spatiale d'une capitale africaine: Lomé." In *Tropiques, lieux et liens*, edited by F. Pinton, 341–349. Paris: Éditions de l'ORSTOM.

Navez-Bouchanine, F. 2012. "Les nouvelles voies de la négociation dans les politiques de résorption des bidonvilles au Maroc. Entre recasement et accompagnement social." In *Effets sociaux des politiques urbaines: l'entre-deux des politiques institutionnelles et des dynamiques sociales: Algérie, Maroc, Liban, Mauritanie*, edited by A. Deboulet, 167–218. Rabat: Centre Jacques Berque. Éd. Karthala; Emam-CITERES.

Navez-Bouchanine, F., and A. Deboulet. 2012. *Effets sociaux des politiques urbaines: l'entre-deux des politiques institutionnelles et des dynamiques sociales: Algérie, Maroc, Liban, Mauritanie*. Rabat: Centre Jacques Berque. Éd. Karthala; Emam-CITERES.

Ninnin, J. 2014. "Le rêve carioca: entre planification urbaine et déplacements forcés de population." *L'Espace Politique – Revue en ligne de géographie politique et de géopolitique*, 22 (online).

Pilo', F. 2017. "A socio-technical perspective to the right to the city: regularizing electricity access in Rio de Janeiro's favelas." *International Journal of Urban and Regional Research* 41 (3): 396–413.

Pilo', F. 2020. "Material politics: utility documents, claims-making and construction of the 'deserving citizen' in Rio de Janeiro." *City & Society* 32 (1): 71–92.

Rogers, S., and B. Wilmsen. 2019. "Towards a critical geography of resettlement." *Progress in Human Geography* 44 (2): 256–275.

Roy, A. 2009. "Civic governmentality: the politics of inclusion in Beirut and Mumbai." *Antipode* 41 (1): 159–179.

Spire, A. *et al.* 2014. "Localisation forcée en ville: l'injustice spatiale et les politiques de déguerpissement en Afrique." In *La justice spatiale et la ville: regards du Sud*, edited by P. Gervais-Lambony*et al.*, 127–148. Paris: Karthala.

Spire, A., M. Bridonneau, and P. Philifert. 2017. "Droit à la ville et replacement dans les contextes autoritaires d'Addis-Abeba (Éthiopie) et de Lomé (Togo)." *Métropoles* 21 (online).

Toulabor, C. M. 1999. "Violence militaire, démocratisation et ethnicité au Togo." *Autrepart* 7: 105–115. Paris: Presses de Sciences Po.

Watt, P. 2018. "'This pain of moving, moving, moving': evictions, displacement and logics of expulsion in London." *L'Année Sociologique* 68 (1): 67–100.

4

TRANSFORMING POLITICAL SUBJECTIVITIES THROUGH RESETTLEMENT IN CÓRDOBA, ARGENTINA

From Poor Citizens to Poor Consumers

Juliana Hernández Bertone, Candela de la Vega and María Alejandra Ciuffolini

Introduction

The extent of urban localisation and level of access to infrastructure, goods, and services are important metrics for assessing patterns of inequality within contemporary Latin American societies, especially considering that 80% of the population in this region is concentrated in cities (CEPAL 2012). Moreover, over the past few years, cities across Latin America have changed as a result of spatial transformations enacted through state housing policies. As Ziccardi (2008) points out, the way a city is transformed by housing policies is related not only to their impact on spatial and urban distribution of people, services, and infrastructure, but also to a diversity of economic, social, political, and cultural issues. In the same vein, a number of separate analyses of Argentinean cities, including ours (Hernández Bertone and Saccucci 2020; Ferrero 2017; de la Vega and Hernández Bertone 2011; de la Vega 2010; Ciuffolini and Scarponetti 2011; Ciuffolini and Núñez 2011), all reveal the effects of housing policies on the urban distribution of problems such as violence and environmental pollution, as well as a lack of access to land, urban infrastructure, security services, and spaces for recreation. From this perspective, an analysis of housing policies that entail the displacement and planned relocation of urban populations must understand such policies as truly consequential devices for regulating urban space, as well as social relations.

An insufficient understanding of changes in social relations effected by housing policies motivates the departure of this study from traditional approaches of states and agencies focusing on the efficiency and effectiveness of such policies. By contrast, our interest in the effects of housing policies, in general, and resettlement policies, in particular, is rooted in the understanding that such policies are underscored by a particular way of governing populations but also construct forms of political

DOI: 10.4324/9781003124559-5

subjectivities that come to replace existing citizenship imaginaries as the primary identity associated with democratic societies. As such, the production of urban space based on resettlement policies is closely connected with the production of certain subjectivities and the displacement or erasure of others.

In this line, and on the basis of a concrete analysis of an urban resettlement policy implemented in the city of Córdoba, Argentina officially called *Mi Casa, Mi Vida* ("My House, My Life" – hereafter MHMLP), the purpose of this chapter is to provide an account of how a resettlement policy configures specific types of subjectivities and influences the formation of new urban identities across urban space. This chapter shows that a hybrid "homeowner-consumer" identity comes to dominate the urban space as the new primary urban identity forced on specific urban populations. The logic of the selection of urban population groups is briefly discussed, showing that the marginalised "poor" are the target of new identity formation outcomes through influencing subjectivities by means of planned resettlement policies.

The main theoretical approaches and methods used for this study are detailed in the first section of this chapter, followed by a brief description of the MHMLP under scrutiny in this study. Then, in the third section, we address how poverty is problematised and tackled through resettlement policies and, based on this, the peculiar conceptualisation of policy beneficiaries as poor and nevertheless consumers. We argue in conclusion that far from eradicating poverty and assuring rights, resettlement policies can became devices to regulate and control the behaviour of urban residents through the creation of minimum consumption levels among the poorest inhabitants. Homeownership and related access to urban services enabled by resettlement to formal housing sites facilitates the stimulation of such minimum consumption levels.

The Neoliberalisation of Urban Space

Based on evidence from our previous studies,[1] we agree with a number of authors (such as Fraser 2017; Lorey 2016; Rancière 2016; de Lagasnerie 2015; Brown 2015; Butler 2014; Laval and Dardot 2013) that, since the 1970s, capitalism has started to become organised at a global scale through a neoliberal logic based on the generalisation of the market and competition that has completely remodelled how social relations are governed. We base this chapter on the understanding of neoliberalism as the main govern strategy of contemporary capitalism – capitalism without the burden of its old-fashioned references and fully assumed as a historical construction and general norm of life. In this light, the neoliberal order as a spectrum of narratives, practices, and devices particular to a new mode of governance is not an alternative to capitalism but one way "to make it work" (Foucault 2007, 111).

In the more than 15 years of working as members of the research team *El Llano en Llamas*,[2] we have been able to show that the expansion of the neoliberal governance has brought with it a new list of concepts and possible interpretations thereof, including those related to the market, forms of state intervention and state legitimacy, self-ownership and ownership of our bodies and others, as well as of land and nature, ways of living, producing, and reproducing, and, finally, forms of subjectivity. Hence, the growth of capitalist accumulation under a neoliberal governance not only means that a profit logic underlies economic activities, but also that these are increasingly emerging as parameters for measuring all spheres of social life, considerably affecting social and territorial relations, as well as subjective configurations.

Based on this theoretical lens, public policies can be considered prime sites for examining the neoliberal governance of urban spaces. "Governance" here refers not to the instances of public decision-making associated with the law, but to how power is exercised in the governance of specific populations that provides a possible scope of action for the behaviours of those who are governed (Foucault 2007).[3] In its goals, recipients, actions, and components, among others, public policies are key to unveiling and understanding the logics according to which the neoliberal and capitalist order is conceived and continuously produced. By focusing on the production of subjectivities through urban governance by examining a resettlement policy instead of evaluating policy impacts as mainstream policy analyses do, we highlight those ideological assumptions informing policies and the effects of their implementation on the configuration of a segregated, gentrified and socially polarized urban order. In this sense, as we have shown in previous empirical studies (de la Vega and Ciuffolini 2020; Ciuffolini and Hernández Bertone 2017; Hernández Bertone 2019; Ciuffolini and Scarponetti 2011; Ciuffolini and Núñez 2011), the characteristics of a policy design and its effects and impacts cannot be thought of in terms of "successes" or "failures" as through a rational model of policy analysis, but rather they can be interpreted as particular and historical forms in which a neoliberal governmentality strategy is able to reproduce itself in an open and non-neutral field of disputes, resistance, and social struggles.

We are thus especially interested in showing how public policies are important devices that shape subjectivities such that, in the greater scheme of things, they become the key premise of the neoliberal political order. In order to illustrate this, policies are considered part of the technologies of power used both to produce and then govern specific forms of subjects, the latter being "the goal and the instrument of government: a subject of needs, aspirations, but also an object in the hands of the government" (Foucault 2007, 132). In the most widespread modern and Western democratic imaginary, as instruments of government, public policies are legitimised ideologically by drawing on the belief that through them rights are assured to citizens.

Within this "rights discourse", as it has become known in Latin America (Pautassi 2010), citizens are the privileged political subjects of the democratic political order and beneficiaries of social policy interventions. In Argentine political culture, this citizen identity was reappropriated and featured more prominently during the "progressive cycle" (2003–2015) that re-established state intervention through social inclusion policies that were to guarantee rights (Thwaites Rey 2012). As Avalle and Brandán Zehnder (2010) show, after the social and political upheaval caused by the 2001–2002 crisis, a specific set of policies emerged in Argentina that were politically legitimised through public negotiations centring on a discourse of "universality" associated with the guarantee of rights.

Yet, the design and implementation of the studied resettlement policy in Córdoba reveal an ongoing dislocation: despite its public conceptualisation as a policy aiming to ensure citizens" rights, what we observed was the implementation of a policy aimed at serving not citizens, but poor urban dwellers. Certain populations acquire the status of subjects of public policies, but in relation to such policies are not viewed as citizens with the right of having rights, "but human beings "in need" who should receive assistance" (Dagnino 2006, 404). As will be shown, the beneficiaries of the resettlement policy recognised this shifting conceptualisation. Moreover, since it is a socially and territorially focused policy, the final result is a fragmented urban space governed according to a distinction between "the poor" and "the citizens" as inhabitants of the city. This transformation of political subjectivities and their urban distribution cannot be negated if what is of concern are the current privatising and restrictive drifts imposed on the spaces and subjects of the assertion of the exercise of neoliberal governance.

The research methodology we employed for this study flows from these theoretical underpinnings. Understanding public policies as mechanisms of governmentality means assuming that these can be analysed as material units of discourse, as they are built on a complex set of narratives used to govern populations that are also variable and arguable (de la Vega and Ciuffolini 2015). However, the effects – planned or not – of a public policy are not only inferred from the discursive frameworks present in its design and implementation, but can also be recognised more broadly from the experiences of the people and social groups reached through its implementation.

Hence, the research employs a qualitative research approach, and findings are primarily from a discourse analysis of a number of primary and secondary data sources. First, 24 publicly available policy documents related to the MHMLP were analysed; these included operative regulations, decrees, laws, official bulletins, resolutions from administrative offices, and other documents on public policies (both national and international). Documents in general contain socially produced information and allow for the reconstruction of the historical dimensions of phenomena (Valles 2000), in this case the process of resettlement sprouting from a housing policy. Second, transcriptions were analysed of a total of 56 structured interviews conducted between 2008 and 2012 with key informants – slum dwellers relocated through the housing policy to one of the three most populous new housing complexes called *Evita, Ampliación Ferreyra,* and *Ampliación Cabildo,* respectively.

Content analysis techniques were used to find instances of recurring semantic relations in the different narratives. The data processing was based on the constant coding and comparison paradigm proposed in Glaser and Strauss's grounded theory (Soneira 2006), mainly aimed at generating theory from a specific body of data in an inductive manner, in comparison to methodologies following deductive reasoning. The software program ATLAS.ti helped systematise the coding process. For this chapter, we decided to include extracts of some of the cited documents and interview transcriptions in order to provide empirical examples of some of the semantic categories that emerged during data processing. The excerpts reveal only a small number of categories, but best reflect the meanings and significant relations on which this study focuses. The English translations of these extracts are our own and have been specially adapted for this chapter. Each text fragment quoted in this chapter is accompanied by an identification code that can be used to trace the respective quotation within our database.

"Mi Casa, Mi Vida": The Resettlement Policy

Córdoba is one of the most populated cities in Argentina, home to around 1.2 million people in 2001 (INDEC 2001). At that time, it was estimated that more than 100,000 people (or 8% of the city's population) resided in one of its 158 slums ("*villas*" in Spanish) in or around the city (Buthet, Baima and Calvo 2007). In 2003, after an intense rainy season, the implementation of a resettlement policy called *Proyecto de Emergencia para la Rehabilitación Habitacional de los Grupos Vulnerables Afectados por las Inundaciones en la Ciudad de Córdoba* ("Emergency Project for Housing Rehabilitation for those Vulnerable Groups Affected by Floods in the City of Córdoba") commenced. This policy is colloquially known, and also officially referred to, as the *Mi Casa, Mi Vida* project ("My House, My Life"; MHMLP).

An "emergency rhetoric" based on the need to protect vulnerable urban residents living in slums from unpredictable weather events such as flooding drove the speedy design and implementation of the MHMLP, as we found earlier (de la Vega and Hernández Bertone 2011). The need for "agile and effective mechanisms to address a hydraulic emergency",[4] as stated in the MHMLP, is not a novel focus of resettlement policies – "emergencies" caused by meteorological phenomena have previously been invoked as the reason for diverse government interventions in Latin America related to housing policies (Rodríguez and Taborda 2009). This type of justification contributes to the consolidation of the view of resettlement of a large number of people in a short time span as necessary and urgent, despite the fact that the speed and scope of resettlement can lead to the inability of displaced persons to participate in discussions and decision-making processes related to their destination or the design of the new housing sites.

The MHMLP represents one of the last and largest investments made in housing in the city in the past two decades, financed mainly by the Inter-American Development Bank (IDB), which disbursed more than 33 million USD under loan 1287/OC-AR and some 69.5 additional USD under loan 1765/OC-AR. Between 2004 and 2008, this policy involved the resettlement of 28,000 people living in 35 slums to one of 11 different planned formal social housing complexes built especially for the purpose on government property on the urban periphery, along with related urban infrastructure (locations indicated on the city map below).[5] The new housing sites were called *Barrios Ciudades* ("Neighbourhood Cities", hereafter NCs).

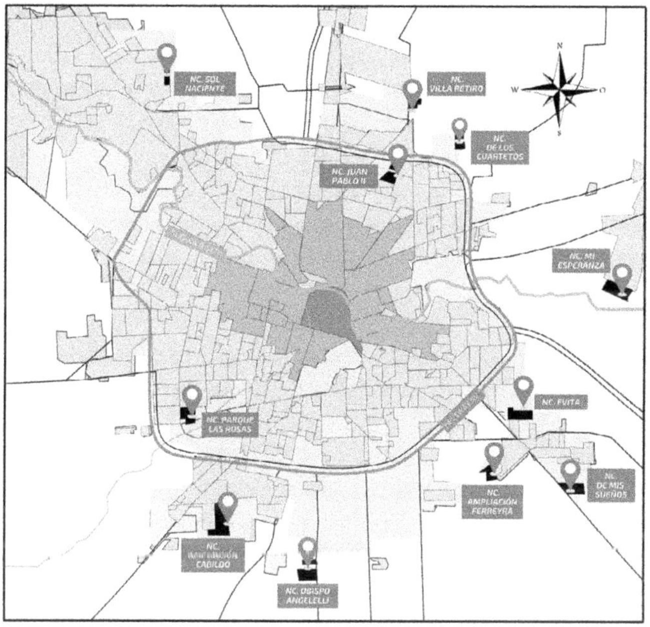

FIGURE 4.1 The location of the 11 *Barrios Ciudades* (NCs) as shown in black on a map of the city of Córdoba. The green ring indicates the ring road encircling the city.
Source: Own elaboration.

MHMLP supporting documents reveal that the resettlement of slum dwellers, considered the most vulnerable group in Córdoba, was based first and foremost on the desire to improve the quality of life of the resettled families by providing them with land and housing. This would be supported by the provision of access to services and facilities such as health centres and schools. Finally, the areas that were left uninhabited following the move to the NCs would be allowed to "heal": one of the IDB's financing requirements was the conversion of the urban areas where the slums were located into green areas to aid urban environmental recovery. These reasons were mainly what allowed the MHMLP to be framed by political classes as a rights insurance policy. A speech by former provincial governor Juan Manuel de la Sota is a case in point:[6]

> You now have what you rightfully deserve: you have adequate housing, healthcare, education, security, and recreational facilities for your children. [...] Today, you are experiencing the joy of living in neighbourhood cities such as these ones, with access to all services, so that you can say, "I, too, am a person: I have rights and I am exercising those rights by living in a neighbourhood that restores dignity".

One of the particularities that we have addressed in our analysis is that the policy was formulated based on the recommendations of the IDB's "Involuntary

Resettlement" document (IBD 1999) that stressed the improvement or restoration of the living standard of those losing their homes or their livelihoods as a result of Bank-financed projects. According to this regulation, a resettlement plan must minimise the disruption of the affected population, avoid and control risks of impoverishment, and, when feasible, ensure that those who are displaced will have access to better housing, urban services, employment opportunities, and social or labour networks at least equivalent to pre-resettlement levels.

Undeniably, housing and urban services for displaced people were truly improved by the MHMLP, as other research has also shown (Marengo and Elorza 2018; Tecco and Fernández 2009; Cisterna 2012; Martínez and Maffrand 2010; Boito, Cervio and Espoz Dalmasso 2009; Elorza 2009). Between 200 and 400 housing units were constructed in each of the NBs, depending on their respective sizes, in a neat grid formation. These "social housing" units, as they are called in MHMLP supporting documents, were 42 square metres in size, situated on a piece of land of around 300 square metres, and comprised two bedrooms, a kitchenette, and a bathroom – a frontal view of some houses can be seen in the image below. Each housing unit was connected to the formal water and electricity network, and the areas had a sewage system connected to a wastewater treatment plant and tarred roads. As required by the IDB regulation pertaining to "social facilities" and "intangible assets",[7] the MHMLP made provision for the delimitation of space for shops, an administrative centre called the *Consejo Territorial por la Identidad Barrial* ("Territorial Council for Neighbourhood Identity"), a primary healthcare centre, a police station, a primary school, and recreational areas such as football pitches or basketball courts, squares, and playgrounds.

FIGURE 4.2 Frontal view of houses located in *Ampliación Ferreyra* NC.
Source: Own picture taken in 2010.

Mi Casa, Mi Vida: "Transforming Lives through Housing"

The impact of the housing and urban improvement on the lives of former slum dwellers can be recognised in the testimonies of those relocated dwellers we interviewed. The high level of marginalisation slum dwellers historically suffered – and still suffer – in Argentina and Córdoba (Kessler 2012; Elorza 2019) influenced their memory of a "sacrificed life" in the old slums where daily life was fraught with difficulties and complications with regard to the precarious housing conditions and the lack of access to urban infrastructure and services. The desire to improve their living conditions appears in the narratives of slum dwellers when they remember their life prior to relocation:

> Living in the *villa* [slum] was a sacrifice. I'm not saying that it isn't now. But there it was like a superhuman sacrifice.
>
> *(I.23. Dweller NC Amp. Ferreyra)*

> We were forced to live in a *villa* out of necessity and a lack of resources. If the government hadn't put my husband out of work, we would have lived in a neighbourhood. My children became *villeros* [slum dwellers] and when you went to a neighbourhood school, they said, "here come the *villeros*". They were outcasts.
>
> *(I.13. Dweller NC Evita)*

However, their displacement and relocation to NCs also produced a complex range of new problems. First, the new housing units and urban infrastructure soon became a limitation in terms of social and labour relations in the NCs. Indeed, the precarious situation in which people from these sectors used to live shifted from a type of precarity based on a lack of urban infrastructure and housing conditions to a precarity related to strained and conflictive social and labour relations. For instance, inhabitants or families who had lived together in a particular slum were split up and relocated to NCs far away from each other; populations that historically had experienced conflicting relations were forced to live together in one NC. Thus, access to new housing occurred alongside the weakening or breakdown of familial and other social ties that for marginal and poor populations are essential in guaranteeing food, work, or access to education.

Additionally, relocation affected access to income sources for the vulnerable population, especially through informal jobs. Many of the displaced people formerly engaged in informal work in the slums where they used to live lost their incomes, while other residents of the NCs were forced to incur transportation expenses to travel to their former areas of work to earn a living. An increase in formal employment among residents of NCs was hardly observable; on the contrary, high unemployment levels and job precarity were observed, particularly among young people: "We suffered in the slum because we did not have a house, but now we are left without jobs" (I.13. Dweller NC Evita).

What is more, because resettlement was accompanied by the immediate demolition of old slum dwellings, the MHMLP was seen by many as forcing homeownership upon them. The perception of this "imposition" acquired such intensity because the old dwelling that each family had built or maintained was not only demolished but was demolished before their eyes as soon as they had started being evacuated for transfers. Each new house located in one of the NCs could only become an "option" to them after they "lost everything" through the demolition of their former houses:

> No, they did not give you the option to stay; they just gave you the house in the NC. [...] Either you left voluntarily or they would knock your house down. And before losing everything, we accepted the house [in the NC].
>
> *(I.05. Dweller NC Evita)*

Despite the fact that sharp social and economic divides were emerging in some NCs, an undeniable improvement of living conditions for the poor population was visible. This became an indispensable condition facilitating the creation of a new homeowner-consumer identity based on the type of dwelling, lifestyle, and type and level of consumption associated with homeownership. The next section explains how a neoliberal conceptualisation of poverty underpinning the resettlement policy in Córdoba is the core engine powering this process and how this ultimately influences social and spatial relations in the whole city.

The Neoliberal Governance of Córdoba: Poverty, Ownership, and Consumption Distribution Across Urban Space

The empirical data are supportive of our argument that the resettlement of the poorest populations in Córdoba through their relocation to peripheral urban areas was executed in a particular way and underpinned by a discourse about combating poverty. This served as an experimental platform through which certain neoliberal identities were enacted. The MHMLP prompted a process of displacement that also reformed political subjectivities in a way that could help better govern territories and populations: by identifying and classifying residents as consumers of different levels, a neoliberal market logic could be used to govern behaviour across the urban space. Two dimensions of this process of neoliberal governance through resettlement emerge from the data analysis. First, we discuss the definition of "poor" that informs resettlement beneficiary selection under the MHMLP that catalysed the forced transformation of urban residents into homeowners and consumers. Then, we propose that the resettlement policy was an exercise leading to social fragmentation as much as it led to spatial fragmentation based on consumption and the artificial borders that were created and linked to specific consumption levels. This conversion of political subjects from citizens to consumers reveals the rising assumption within the neoliberal rationale underpinning urban governance that poverty alleviation policies are likely important for ensuring some basic human needs or even some rights. What is of greater concern, however, is that they can become relevant devices to regulate and control consumption levels of urban residents through the creation of minimal consumption levels among the poorest urban inhabitants.

A Subject Conversion: From Being Poor to Becoming (Poor) Homeowners and Consumers

Echoing Laval and Dardot (2013), the neoliberal way of governing has transformed the former "fight against inequality" – a central objective in socialist projects – into a "fight against poverty". This in turn allowed for the obscuring of the unequal relations that sustain capitalism and the presentation of poverty as a given and a "positive" state instead of an unfair result of those capitalist relations. On the contrary, inequality is framed as a necessary, given that it functions as an incentive to produce goods and work. According to Hayek (2019), one of the most recognised theoretical referents of neoliberalism is the belief that in a free society the unequal distribution of wealth is not an important cause of poverty. As poverty represents a situation that manifests the inability of reaching a superior evolutionary stage for a certain group in society, it is a temporary or relative phenomenon that can be overcome through social or economic prosperity. In doing so, following Hayek's view (2019), a minimum level of economic security could be guaranteed by the state even within a competition system and without representing a threat to individual freedom.

Laval and Dardot (2013) argue that this idea serves to legitimise and reproduce a form of neoliberal governance that assumes compensations provided by the state as a necessary but temporary evil, with them having to be kept to a strict minimum. From this perspective, extreme poverty and vulnerability leave large populations outside of the consumer market due to a lack of income, education, or certain goods such as houses. However, according to this logic, policies oriented towards securing incomes, education, or houses for the poor will do so in a way that ensures that they just cross the line to stop being non-consumers and consequently acquire the ability to spend money and consume goods and services in market.[8] However, if compensation provided by such policies ensures more than this minimum level of consumption, there is a risk of generating distortions in the competition rules and the allocation of resources resulting from it. As a result, poverty is a concern because it prevents individuals from attaining a minimum level of consumption, not because it leads to suffering and a lack of dignity (Murillo 2011; Álvarez Leguizamón 2005; Czarnecki 2013).

Based on our empirical observations, we argue that also in urban governance, poverty is seen as a condition to be overcome by improving living conditions, amongst others. Doing so favours the entry of more people into the consumer market. By constantly making reference to poverty as the main objective of Argentinean resettlement policies,[9] the absolute eradication of poverty is less expected than the creation of markets and consumers where they did not exist before. Neoliberal governance through the control of urban space does not produce new consumers without improving their living conditions; on the contrary, because it can create at least minimal improvements in housing conditions, it can expect a consequent increase in general consumption.

In our analysis, we found that the MHMLP evidently improved basic housing conditions through the provision of houses and land, but by "preventing the poor from falling deeper into poverty" also gave birth to new consumers. Although the NCs included the provision of housing as well as educational, health, and social services, the documents supporting the MHMLP define the extent of the "solution" as "minimal", which NC dwellers recognised and criticised. For instance, many houses were quoted as being very small in relation to family size, while other houses presented structural or moisture-related problems. With regards to urban infrastructure, street lighting was poor and the maintenance of green spaces by the municipality practically non-existent. Educational facilities were also found wanting, as many NCs had kindergartens and primary schools, but no secondary schools, leading to an elevated school dropout level. Thereby, a number of interviewed former slum dwellers were both satisfied and dissatisfied with life in the NCs:

> Now you have a house, although I had a mansion in the slum.
>
> *(I.21. Dweller NC Evita)*

> It seems to me that obviously there are many things missing. Many people will tell you that much is missing.
>
> *(I.03. Dweller NC Amp. Cabildo)*

> Thanks go to God and the government who gave us these houses, because many people, myself included, could never have bought a house. Okay, they are small houses with only two bedrooms, but I could never have bought a house on my own.
>
> *(I.10. Dweller NC Amp. Ferreyra)*

Although access to housing was defined in the MHMLP documents as a service provisioned by the state for those who could not enter the housing market by their own means, a shift started to appear when they did enter the market after receiving houses: beneficiaries started to show and recognise new consumption practices. As many of the interviewees stated, if living conditions in new NCs were "lacking many things", the experience of being an owner is the subjective platform that triggers the consumption of services and goods related to homeownership, including purchasing building materials to expand houses, making utility payments, purchasing new appliances, furniture, or vehicles, or even the act of selling the house.

In addition, housing in the new neighbourhood represented an "insurance policy" for some interviewees that would protect them against an old fear of eviction that in most of the slums where they lived before was part and parcel of daily life. The acquired identity as homeowners helped eliminate that feeling of permanent exposure to the risk of helplessness associated with being evicted. This perception of lower risk is also essential for activating consumption:

> You have your own house – it's yours and no one will come to tear it down with a bulldozer and take you away.
>
> *(I.17. Dweller NC Amp. Cabildo)*

> I tell you, there are people who have already sold their houses. But I don't agree with that. Because after a lifetime of living in a slum, now you have a little house; you have utilities. Here, one can say: "I am going to use this – the little money I earn – to build another room or to fix the roof or something else". Sometimes people do not know to appreciate a little or a lot; they do not value things. The people who sold the house have returned to the slum just to not have to pay taxes. The tax that we are paying here, we pay every two months for the public supply of water and electricity. It is not that much money. Besides, after they sell the house, how long can that money last them? A month at the most, and then they once more have nowhere to live.
>
> *(I.13. Dweller NC Amp. Cabildo)*

> I had nothing there, only a roof that leaked all over. But now I have my bed, my room, and a room for my children. I have my washing machine, my refrigerator; I have my car – I didn't have a car before.
>
> *(I.21. Dweller NC Amp. Ferreyra)*

What is revealed from here is that the implementation of this resettlement policy has a notably powerful result: the subjective transformation necessary to keep the wheel of consumption turning – that is, the transition to becoming a homeowner-consumer. As contrasting points of view emerge from the data analysis, it is not, however, a univocal or complete transformation. The transition to a homeowner-consumer became opaque when, for instance, some new owners refused to pay taxes, even though they were very low, as the above testimony reveals. Furthermore, the strongest brake on this subjective transformation occurred when some families abandoned their new houses without selling them and decided to return to their former places – those in the slums. Although some of the areas where the old slums were located had been converted into green spaces, others had not been touched, so that some families could rebuild their houses there. The return to the former slums did not constitute a generalised movement but represents the case of some families returning to *Villa La Maternidad*, an old slum located around one kilometre from the main square of Córdoba city. This was one of the most conflictive cases at the public level.[10]

Shifting the Face of Poverty

As stated above, from a neoliberal perspective, poverty is conceived of as not only temporary, but also relative; that is, poverty is seen as a problem that affects certain groups of society and not others based on the availability of resources and individual effort. Building on this understanding, only those whose resources do not allow them to consume at minimum levels will be the object of neoliberal policies focused on stimulating consumption. A poverty reduction logic thus considers that states are supposed to identify the scope and dimensions of poverty before determining its response. The MHMLP thus classified and objectified some poverty-related societal attributes, including a low income, unemployment, or housing deficits, to determine who would be the "beneficiaries" of the housing policy.

Once in the NC, the new residents still viewed themselves as "different" from the rest of the inhabitants of the city:

> They placed us far away because we are descendants of *villeros* and because there was no space closer to the city centre to build houses. I also think the governor doesn't want slums near the city centre but far away, because he already knows "the way of life" of *villeros*: they steal; they are filthy. We are not all the same, but that is why we are also kept separate. Although there is a lot of space near the mill, for example, that is for a private gated community that generates money, while the slum doesn't.
>
> *(I.07. Dweller NC Amp. Cabildo)*

> This is not a "neighbourhood"; those from outside [the NC] also know this. You say that you live in *Barrio Ciudad Evita* and they answer you: "Those are *villeros*". There is a lot of discrimination going around.
>
> *(I.14. Dweller NC Evita)*

Despite the housing improvements enacted by the MHMLP, the stigma of being a former slum dweller ("ex-*villero*") remains. Moreover, as the first testimony shows, social differentiation is measured not so much by the metric of the type of house where people live, but in terms of who consumes more and who consumes less, thereby generating more or less money for the state. Even after being converted into homeowners and living at a new housing site, these new consumers still lacked many basic things, revealing that they have not stopped being poor. As we will show, a neoliberal logic prevents further improvements to the living standards of slum dwellers or others targeted by urban resettlement policies, as the minimum level of "affluence" needed for increased consumption has been reached through minimal resettlement policies such as the MHMLP.

Social fragmentation was also visible within NCs. Due to standardised housing solutions provided through the MHMLP across NCs despite the diversity of manifestations of poverty and inequality, formal housing and neighbourhoods could not reverse existing perceptions of distrust, fear, and insecurity that were created or compounded when strangers suddenly had to live alongside one another. The insecurity associated with the risk of eviction described in the previous section that was generated by living in an informally located slum transmuted in the NCs. The new insecurity is now linked to what has made them owners – the house:

> In the *villa*, it was very quiet, at least. But here you have to sleep with one eye open. You don't know when your house could be broken into by thieves.
> *(I.03. Dweller NC Evita)*

Through this resettlement policy, great control has been exerted over urban space through the designation of areas based on the level of consumption. The strategy of urbanising poverty through the creation of conditions of ownership and owner identities, amongst others, does nothing other than create consumers and specific spaces for these consumers to engage in consumptive behaviour. In general, as the new housing sites are on the outskirts of the city, this attempt to "address poverty" entails an inevitable polarising distribution of consumers and markets within the urban space. Moreover, a territorial distribution of different markets according to the levels and possibilities of consumption begins to be clearly displayed: certain goods and services are commercialised in low-consumption areas and not in high-consumption ones. Considering that the public transport system in the city has historically been deficient in connecting different areas, the result is geographically demarcated consumer markets.

Furthermore, this way of relocating populations to the city's periphery by ensuring access to "basic" housing stands can be interpreted as either excluding these populations by keeping them at the city margins or including them by providing them with access to housing and infrastructure in an area that, in contrast with slums, is considered to fall "within the city boundaries". The NCs in relation to the entire city can be viewed as border territories where inclusion and exclusion in both spatial and consumptive terms are barely balanced: they are consumers, but they cannot consume much; they live within the city but not so far inside; they are citizens but not empowered enough to exercise and claim all their rights.

Spatial Domination through the Distribution of Political Subjectivities

As we showed in this chapter, when poverty is taken into consideration up to the point at which a housing solution or mitigation from the state becomes a maxim – that is, when it becomes an object of housing policy – a particular form of neoliberal urban government with the aim of creating consumers and enlarging markets becomes visible. By focusing on the MHMLP, we aimed to show how this is visible in urban housing policies.

We showed that this resettlement policy not only produced major transformations by ensuring housing improvements for a spatially marginalised population, but also made a foremost contribution to a neoliberal form of urban governance based on a transformation of political subjectivity through the conversion of poor populations into a broader group of homeowner-consumers who remained poor and could consume only minimally by being provided only "basic" housing and urban services. Despite using a discourse attempting to legitimise the policy by relating it to public policies in general as providers of rights, the MHMLP was far from offering a platform for allowing the enactment of citizenship in a way that supposedly promoted equality, such as by claiming rights. Instead, through the policy, the entire city was fragmented into areas of diverse consumption. Thus, increasingly, inequality becomes the means and the "natural" form of social and territorial bonds or divisions.

If poverty is still a worrisome and structural issue in the Latin American region– which was visibly exacerbated by the ongoing COVID-19 health crisis –, it constitutes evidence of, but also represents one way of governing populations within the framework of neoliberal governance of capitalism. Therefore, carrying out a radical critique of neoliberalism requires thinking about how neoliberalism has been able to achieve certain outcomes, not only about what it has destroyed. The transformations carried out by this policy cannot only be understood according to the mandate of "fighting poverty", as the international organisations that have financed the project emphasise. Rather, the effects of this resettlement policy must be weighed in relation to a new distribution of political subjectivities deployed at an urban scale. In this sense, spatial domination could be linked to the production, destruction, and urban distribution of political subjectivities.

Notes

1 See for example de la Vega (2020), Ciuffolini (2017a; 2017b), Avalle (2017), Avalle and Hernández Bertone (2019), or Azarian, Villegas Guzmán and Whitney (2017).

2 *El Llano en Llamas* (www.llanocordoba.com.ar) is a research team at the National University of Córdoba (UNC) and the Catholic University of Córdoba (UCC) that since 2004 has been working on the analysis of contemporary conflicts and social struggles. A large part of the most significant reflections in this article are the result of current research carried out by this team.

3 For a more detailed discussion, see Bevir (2010), Enroth (2014), or Boticelli (2016).

4 As stated by the Gobierno de la Provincia de Córdoba (2001) in the *Decreto de Necesidad y Urgencia Provincial* (Provincial Decree of Necessity and Urgency) N° 2565/01.

5 Owned the government of Province of Córdoba. The Argentinean government is organised as a federal regime in which three levels of autonomous government can be distinguished: federal, provincial, and municipal.

6 A speech was made by the governor on the occasion of the inauguration of the Neighbourhood Cities in 2004 (de la Sota 2004).

7 As stated in the "OPERATIVE REGULATION IDB – 1765/OC-AR. Annex I.2 Housing Emergency" (IDB 2006).

8 In this sense, the concept of a "poverty line" reveals exactly the quantification of those goods and services provided by policies that prevent populations from being "at risk of becoming poor" or presents them with an investment that will allow them "to stay afloat".

9 For a more detailed discussion, see Boito et al. (2009) and Cervio (2015).

10 See Capdeville et al. (2013), Montoya Flórez (2006), and von Lücken (2008) for related studies.

References

Álvarez Leguizamón, S. 2005. "Los discursos minimistas sobre las necesidades básicas y los umbrales de ciudadanía como reproductores de la pobreza." In *Trabajo y producción de la pobreza en Latinoamérica y el Caribe: estructuras, discursos y actores*, edited by Sonia Álvarez, 239–274. Buenos Aires: CLACSO.

Avalle, G. 2017. "Técnicas de gubernamentalidad y degradación de derechos. Análisis de programas laborales en Argentina." *Journal Sudamérica* 1 (6): 114–136.

Avalle, G., and G. Brandán Zehnder. 2010. "*Entre la asistencia, la promoción y la inclusión. Dilemas de las políticas de empleo post-convertibilidad en Argentina.*" Paper presented at the III Jornadas de Estudios Políticos, Los Polvorines, UNGS, November 17–19.

Avalle, G., and J. Hernández Bertone. 2019. "Vidas en tránsito. El sueño de la casa propia en el programa habitacional Hogar Clase Media." *Journal Conciencia Social. Revista digital de Trabajo Social* 4: 85–100.

Azarian, F., Villegas Guzmán, S., and L. Whitney. 2017. "*Judicializar, institucionalizar, formalizar: el estado frente a las luchas por la tierra en Córdoba (Argentina).*" Paper presented at the XVIII Congreso Nacional y VIII Latinoamericano de Sociología Jurídica, Mendoza, October 11–13.

Bevir, M. 2010. "Rethinking governmentality: Towards genealogies of governance". *Journal European Journal of Social Theory*, 13: 423–441.

Boito, M.E., Cervio, A., and M.B. Espoz Dalmasso. 2009. "La gestión habitacional de la pobreza en Córdoba: antes y despúes de las 'Ciudades Barrios'." *Journal Boletín Onteaiken* 7: 50–58.

Botticelli, S. 2016. "La gubernamentalidad del estado en Foucault: un problema modern." *Journal Praxis Filosófica* 42: 83–106.

Brown, W. 2015. *El pueblo sin atributos: la secreta revolución del neoliberalismo*. Barcelona: Malpaso.

Buthet, C., M. Baima, and D. Calvo. 2007. *La evolución de las villas de emergencia de la ciudad de Córdoba, 2001–2007: localización y estimación de población*. Córdoba: Servicio Habitacional y de Acción Social.

Butler, J. 2014. "*Repensar la vulnerabilidad y la resistencia.*" Paper presented at the XV Simposio Internacional de la Asociación Internacional de Filósofas, Alcalá de Henares, November 13–15.

Capdevielle, J., D. Ceconato, and M.R. Mandrini. 2013. "Segregación urbana y mercantilización del territorio en la ciudad de Córdoba, Argentina: El caso de Villa La Maternidad." *Journal RIURB* 9: 47–71.

CEPAL (Comisión Económica para América Latina y el Caribe). 2012. *Población, territorio y desarrollo sostenible*. Santiago: United Nations.

Cervio, A.L. 2015. "*Programas habitacionales y construcción de sensibilidades en la ciudad de Córdoba.*" Paper presented at the I Congreso Latinoamericano de Teoría Social, Buenos Aires, October 7–10.

Cisterna, C. 2012. "Representaciones espaciales en la producción habitacional estatal. Programa 'Nuevos Barrios. Mi Casa, Mi Vida, Argentina." *Journal Bitácora urbano\territorial* 21 (2): 147–156.

Ciuffolini, M.A. 2017a. "La dinámica del neoliberalismo y sus desplazamientos. Para una crítica inmanente en orden a su superación." *Journal Studia Politicae* 40: 55–70.

Ciuffolini, M.A. 2017b. *Quien no se mueve no siente sus cadenas. Estudios sobre luchas político-sociales en la Córdoba Contemporánea*. Córdoba: EDUCC.

Ciuffolini, M.A., and A. Núñez. 2011. *Política y territorialidad en tres ciudades argentinas*. Buenos Aires: El Colectivo.

Ciuffolini, M.A., and J. Hernández Bertone. 2017. "Una lectura posible de las políticas públicas. Decisiones teóricas, empíricas, metodológicas y epistemológicas para su análisis." *Journal Revista Ámbitos. Revista Internacional de Comunicación*, 39.

Ciuffolini, M.A., and P. Scarponetti. 2011. *Ojos que no ven, corazón que no siente. Relocalización territorial y conflictividad social: un estudio sobre los barrios ciudades de Córdoba*. Buenos Aires: Novuko.

Czarnecki, L. 2013. "La concepción de la pobreza en el modelo neoliberal: ¿Cómo entender la lucha contra la pobreza en México?" *Journal Frontera Norte* 25 (49): 179–191.

Dagnino, E. 2006. "Concepciones de la ciudadanía en Brasil: proyectos políticos en disputa." In *Ciudadanía, sociedad civil y participación política*, edited by Isodoro Cheresky, 387–410. Buenos Aires: Miño y Dávila.

De la Sota, J.M. 2004. "Ciudad de Mis Sueños." *Prensa Oficial*, 2 November, 2004. http://www.cba.gov.ar/nota.jsp?idNota=77020

de la Vega, C. 2010. "Política habitacional y ciudadanía. El Programa 'Mi Casa, Mi Vida' en la ciudad de Córdoba, Argentina." *Journal Encrucijada Americana* 4 (1): 70–97.

de la Vega, C. 2020. "Quien aún esté vivo, que no diga 'nunca'. Resistencias contemporáneas y luchas 'sin clases'." *Journal Perfiles Latinoamericanos* 28 (56): 359–377.

de la Vega, C., and J. Hernández Bertone. 2011. "Mi casa, la emergencia; mi vida, en emergencia. El escenario del programa 'Mi Casa, Mi Vida'." In *Política y territorialidad en 3 ciudades argentinas*, edited by María Alejandra Ciuffolini, and Ana Núñez, 85–111. Buenos Aires: El Colectivo.

de la Vega, C., and M.A. Ciuffolini. 2015. "Delineando una propuesta teórica-metodológica para el análisis de políticas públicas en contextos de antagonismo." *Journal Intersticios Sociales* 9: 1–38.

de la Vega, C., and M.A. Ciuffolini. 2020. "Neoliberalismo y violencia en los conflictos ambientales de Latinoamérica." *Journal Ecología Política-Cuadernos de debate internacional* 59: 78–83.

de Lagasnerie, G. 2015. *La última lección de Michel Foucault. Sobre el neoliberalismo, la teoría y la política*. Buenos Aires: FCE.

Elorza, A.L. 2009. "Política de erradicación de Villas: impactos en la calidad de vida de las familias relocalizadas. Estudio de caso: Ciudad de los Niños." *Journal Confluencias* 67: 2–28.

Elorza, A.L. 2019. "Segregación residencial y estigmatización territorial. Representaciones y prácticas de los habitantes de territorios segregados." *Journal EURE* 45 (135): 91–110.

Enroth, H. 2014. "Governance: The art of governing after governmentality". *Journal European Journal of Social Theory* 17 (1): 60–76.

Ferrero, M.M. 2017. "*Ciudad capitalista, gobierno y resistencias. Un estudio de casos múltiples de las ciudades de Asunción, Córdoba y La Paz*." PhD diss., Universidad Nacional de Córdoba.

Foucault, M. 2007. *Nacimiento de La Biopolítica*. Buenos Aires: FCE.

Fraser, N. 2017. "¿Una Nueva Forma de Capitalismo? Respuesta a Boltanski y Esquerre." *Journal New Left Review* 106: 61–70.

Gobierno de la Provincia de Córdoba. 2001. *DNUP (Decreto de Necesidad y Urgencia Provincial) Nº 2565/01. Estado de Emergencia Hídrica y Social en el Departamento Capital de la Provincia de Córdoba*. 19 October, 2001. Gobierno de la Provincia de Córdoba, República Argentina.

Hayek, F. 2019. *Los fundamentos de la libertad*. Madrid: Unión Editorial.

Hernández Bertone, J, and E. Saccucci. 2020. "Relatos desde la precariedad: relocalizaciones territoriales, desposesiones y resistencias en Santiago del Estero, Argentina." *Journal Apuntes. Revista de ciencias sociales* 47 (87): 29–63.

Hernández Bertone, J. 2019. "El problema de la vivienda en sectores vulnerables. Lectura desde la gubernamentalidad en la política pública 'Mi Casa, Mi Vida' de la Ciudad de Córdoba, Argentina." *Journal Revista GIGAPP Estudios Working Papers* 6 (111–115): 61–82.

IBD (Inter-American Development Bank). 1999. *Reasentamiento involuntario en los proyectos del BID: principios y lineamientos*. Washington: BID.
IBD (Inter-American Development Bank). 2006. *Reglamento Operativo IBD – 1765/OC-AR. Anexo I.2 Emergencia habitacional. Desarrollo y Condiciones particulares*. Washington: BID.
INDEC (Instituto Nacional de Estadística y Censo). 2001. *Censo Nacional de Población, Hogares y Viviendas 2001*. Buenos Aires: INDEC.
Kessler, G. 2012. "Las consecuencias de la estigmatización territorial. Reflexiones a partir de un caso particular." *Journal Espacios en Blanco. Revista de Educación* 22: 165–198.
Laval, C., and P. Dardot. 2013. *La nueva razón del mundo*. Barcelona: Gedisa.
Lorey, I. 2016. *Estado de Inseguridad: Gobernar la precariedad*. Madrid: Traficantes de Sueños.
Marengo, M.C., and A.L. Elorza. 2018. "Segregación residencial socioeconómica y programas habitacionales públicos: el caso del Programa Mi Casa Mi Vida en la Ciudad de Córdoba, Argentina." *Journal Direito da Cidade* 10 (3): 1542–1568.
Montoya Flórez, O. 2006. "Enseñanzas del proceso de erradicación de asentamientos marginales en Córdoba, Argentina." *Journal Guillermo De Ockham* 4 (2).
Murillo, S. 2011. "Estado, sociedad civil y gubernamentlidad neoliberal." *Journal Entramados y perspectivas* 1: 91–108.
Pautassi, L. 2010. *Perspectivas de derechos, políticas públicas e inclusión social: debates actuales en la Argentina*. Buenos Aires: Biblos.
Rancière, J. 2016. "El Racismo, una pasión que viene de arriba." *Journal El Viejo topo* 275: 54–57.
Rodríguez, M., and M. Taborda. 2009. *Análisis de Políticas públicas. Formación, estilos de gestión y desempeño: Políticas de Vivienda. Córdoba 1991-2007*. Córdoba: Brujas.
Soneira, A.J. 2006. "La teoría fundamentada en los datos (Grounded Theory) de Glaser y Strauss." In *Estrategias de investigación cualitativa*, edited by Irene Vasilachis de Gialdino, 153–173. Barcelona: Gedisa.
Tecco, C., and S. Fernández. 2009. "Espacios urbanos estigmatizados, segregación residencial y agenda pública local." *Journal Administración Pública y Sociedad* 16: 89–114.
Thwaites Rey, M. 2012. *El Estado en América Latina: Continuidades y Rupturas*. Buenos Aires: Arcis and CLACSO.
Valles, M. 2000. *Técnicas cualitativas de investigación social*. España: Síntesis.
Von Lücken, M. 2008. "*Programas de viviendas en Córdoba: Caso Villa La Maternidad*." Paper presented at the V Jornadas de Sociología de la UNLP, La Plata, Argentina, December 10–12.
Ziccardi, A. 2008. "Pobreza y exclusión social en las ciudades del siglo XXI." In *Proceso de urbanización de la pobreza y nuevas formas de exclusión social*, edited by Alicia Ziccardi, 9–36. Bogotá: Siglo del Hombre, CLASCO-CROP.

PART 2

Experiencing Change Through Notions of Home and Shelter

5

NARRATIVES OF HOME AND NEIGHBOURHOOD

Rethinking Risk in Informal and State-delivered Settlements in Durban

Sogen Moodley and Kira Erwin

Introduction

Peoples' narratives of home and neighbourhood offer rich insights into how residents weigh up notions of risk in making a home in the city. Social and economic risks are equally important variables when assessing where and how to live in a city in which you cannot afford formal housing or when formal housing provided by the state may be far removed from economic and social opportunities. Ideas of risk, usually linked to health and safety, lie at the heart of the municipality's rationale for resettlement, where residents of informal settlements are moved into temporary or alternative state housing. As this chapter illustrates, residents in informal and state-delivered housing settlements value different risk criteria than those used by the municipality in resettlement decision-making processes. In this chapter, we explore narratives from people living in two housing settlements within the city of Durban, South Africa. The first is the long-standing informal settlement of Quarry Road West (QRW), where residents are under threat of being resettled. The second is Cornubia, a formal, state-funded housing development, where some residents from QRW have been relocated.

Drawing on narrative data we illustrate the different risk criteria and risk mitigation strategies used by residents in comparison to those used in policy regulations and frameworks. These divergent ways of assessing risk and mitigation strategies present a challenge to current South African human settlement policy objectives, particularly in relation to resettling residents from informal to formal housing. It also shows how memories and social networks of spaces left behind continue to shape experiences of making a new home for resettled residents within the city. While this chapter does not directly examine a conceptual framework of resettlement, the focus on risk and lived experiences of residents in informal and state-delivered settlements contributes to the nuanced understanding of intra-urban resettlement that is advocated for, and developed, in this book.

DOI: 10.4324/9781003124559-7

We begin the chapter by briefly positioning the two case studies within the *Narratives of Home and Neighbourhood* research project. After this, we contextualise human settlements within the broader South African policy and professional planning environments in which these two case studies are located. We then turn to how residents in the informal settlement of Quarry Road West experience and conceptualise risk in making a home and neighbourhood. QRW has been built and continues to expand on land that is deemed too risky for settlement by the local eThekwini Municipality in Durban.[1] How forms of natural disasters such as flooding and human-made disasters such as fire and health risks are planned for and mitigated against by residents are discussed. Equally important is how these mitigation strategies rely on social networks and connections with neighbours and other sympathetic partners. This makes QRW simultaneously a risky and yet socially robust and connected place to live. We contend that understanding how residents assess and mitigate risk is critically important for understanding the variegated lived experiences of resettlement.

Considering social and economic risks raises important questions for thinking through which risks are mitigated against and which are exacerbated when people are resettled from informal to formal housing by the municipality. How do people make sense of their new homes? To explore this, we examine the narrative data from participants in Cornubia, who now hold title deed units in a formal housing development. When the environmental and health and safety risks are reduced through access to formal housing, what are the impacts on the social and economic risks that make up residents' broader risk assessment criteria about feeling at home? The narratives show that the disruption of social support networks creates a fraught experience for some housing beneficiaries. Participants voice concerns around the lack of social connections between people and how this makes Cornubia feel unsafe. In addition, formal housing does not necessarily mitigate against informal practices that create risky living spaces, such as the illegal electricity connections that pose similar risks to children in Cornubia and in Quarry Road West.

Read together, the QRW and the Cornubia case studies emphasise the critical importance of residents' social networks in making homes and neighbourhoods. These social networks are built through social labour and learning that informal residents have accrued over time and that enable them to respond in robust ways to numerous forms of risk in the informal housing they live in. When residents are resettled into formal state-delivered housing developments, lessening some of the health and safety risks deemed hazardous by the municipality, their social networks and resident-led risk mitigation strategies can be disrupted, and that in turn makes residents vulnerable to new forms of social and economic risk, despite now owning a formal house. Acknowledging an expanded understanding of risk, such as that held by residents in informal settlements, requires acceptance of complexity and the contextual variables that influence these assessments. We conclude the chapter by suggesting that other forms of social infrastructure and support, beyond the provision of water, electricity, and a formal title deed, are needed to rebuild neighbourly connections after resettlement from places of informal shelter. Research that explores experiences of living informally in the city offers insights for mitigating against the current social and economic risks associated with resettlement to formal housing in South African cities.

Methodology

The narrative data discussed in this chapter is taken from a larger research project in Durban titled *Narratives of Home and Neighbourhood: Re-imagining Urban Planning.* [2] This research, carried out in seven different research sites reflecting a variety of state-delivered housing models, focused on the perspectives of housing beneficiaries in making these spaces a place called home. The project provided a much-needed qualitative micro-level focus in a field that has rich literature on macro-economic and social debates around state-delivered housing.

In each of the seven sites, research teams explored how residents attached meaning to home and neighbourliness in specific types of state housing models. Researchers paid attention to how the design of the built environment enabled or constricted social relations and peoples' sense of home, belonging, and neighbourhood, as well as how residents transformed the built environment through everyday livelihood practices and collective strategies. The aim of the broader project was to understand some of the intended and unintended consequences of living in state-delivered housing. Given the scale at which the South African government has rolled out housing since democracy, it is critical to get a sense of how housing infrastructure not only provides units for people to live in, but starts to reshape the social landscape in South African cities. Such an agenda is pertinent, particularly for the policy ideals of integration and socially mixed neighbourhoods that the latest human settlement policy aspires to.

This chapter draws from two of the seven case studies, the QRW informal settlement, and the more recent human settlement development, Cornubia. Given the nature of the research questions, research teams designed participatory methods shaped by the context of the specific housing model they were based in. The QRW team, made up of Cathy Sutherland, Vicky Sim, Ashling McCarthy, Sibongile Buthelezi, and Duduzile Khumalo, used a mixed method approach of photovoice, focus groups and community mapping. Photovoice and community mapping are both participatory research methods (see Sim et al. 2019). Participants took pictures of, or drew and mapped out, important people and places in their settlement in order to answer the research questions in ways that made sense to them. These images and maps were then used to create focus group discussions where participants analysed how the images and their captions represented possible answers to the research questions. The Cornubia research team, consisting of Doung Jahangeer, Miranda Young-Jahangeer, Ongezwa Mbele, Princess Sibanda, and Gcina Shange, used a performance-based research methodology that drew from journals, participatory workshops, and a public dance performance in Cornubia by a group of residents who had already created their own dance group. The public dance performed themes that had emerged from the project workshops and journals. Directly afterwards a public dialogue was held between researchers, audience, and performers on the themes that the dancers had highlighted.

We are grateful to both research teams; without their research within this broader project this chapter would not be possible.[3]

The Human Settlements Policy and Professional Environment in South Africa

Both research sites should be contextualised within a South African policy environment that has undergone conceptual shifts in relation to informal settlements, and the delivery of formal housing. South Africa's racist history of forced removals under Apartheid has been well-documented (see Platzky and Walker [1985]; Murray and O'Regan [1990]). Post-Apartheid, the South African state, with and without relocation plans, continues to remove people from the places they have chosen to settle in the city (Zondo and Royston 2016), albeit with different rationales and intentions to those under Apartheid. Emerging from Apartheid with a strong rights-based constitution and commitment to building a developmental state, the new democratic government focused on, amongst other things, the challenge of informal settlements that housed many of the poor in South African cities (Cirolia, Görgens et al. 2017). The first wave of post-Apartheid housing policy interpreted the presence of informal settlements as undermining the broader national transformation agenda. As Huchzermeyer (2011) argues, the mobility of international policy discourse, such as the Cities Alliance's narrative around developing slum-free cities, greatly influenced the newly elected South African government. At the time, the removal of informal settlements was legitimised not only as a means to address the goal of poverty reduction, but as a mechanism to trim down the housing backlog (Huchzermeyer 2011).

Viewing informal settlements as merely a temporary phenomenon of South African cities, this first phase of national housing policy involved the large-scale delivery of title deed formal housing under the government's Reconstruction and Development programme (RDP). RDP houses were seen as an official pass to permanence in the cities. Providing an asset base for people who had been oppressed and excluded under Apartheid was viewed as a leg up onto the property ladder (see Lemanski [2011] on why this asset-based ideology has failed to materialise). These state-provided units were allocated based on a set of criteria that determined eligibility, and for many residents from informal settlements, this sent a message of inevitable relocation to state-identified housing developments. Whilst the scale of the delivery of South Africa's RDP housing programme, compared to the rest of the continent and even internationally, has been "incredibly impressive" (Cirolia, Görgens et al. 2017, 10), the 1994 Housing Policy focussed exclusively on the delivery of units at the expense of settlement quality. Housing targets built into the municipal performance management system exacerbated an over emphasis on quantity, resulting in units frequently being built on easily available land at the urban periphery (Newton and Schuermans 2013). Not only has this housing roll-out contributed to urban sprawl (Moodley 2018), but GIS-based research has now shown that such mass delivery has done little to improve the quality of life of some residents or transform the Apartheid spatial form (Musvoto, Lincoln and Hansmann 2016).

Recognising that statistics on informal settlements are not consistent across datasets (Housing Development Agency 2013), what is clear is that, despite the large government roll-out of title deed houses, the percentage of households living in informal dwellings in South Africa has remained around the 13% mark (Housing Development Agency 2013; Statistics South Africa 2019). In Statistics South Africa's General Household Survey report of 2018, eThekwini mirrored the 13% figure of households living in informal dwellings (Statistics South Africa 2019, 33). Increased urbanisation and job-seeking meant that even with the high number of units delivered, the number of people living in informal settlements in real terms has increased, and the backlog in terms of number of people requiring homes and services has not been reduced.

In recognition of this slow progress, gradual policy shifts occurred in South Africa's housing programme (Huchzermeyer 2001). In 2004, a second wave of housing policy entitled Breaking New Ground (BNG) arrived, formulated in response to the shortcomings of the 1994 policy. There was a realisation that the state could not continue to deliver formal houses at the scale and pace required to effectively tackle the housing backlog (National Planning Commission 2011). The BNG policy recognised in-situ upgrading of informal settlements as the preferred approach to "slum improvement" (Department of Human Settlements 2004). As Huchzermeyer (2006) notes, this shift involved a more holistic approach to housing, including in-situ upgrading, flexible planning approaches, and increased community participation. The new National Housing Code also clearly identified local government as instrumental in the delivery process, performing the role of the "developer", with the municipality undertaking "all planning and project activities" in relation to housing (Department of Human Settlements 2009, 15). This was enabled through the mechanism of accreditation, which involved the delegated authority exercising functions relating to the administration of National Housing Programmes at the municipal sphere. Municipal Housing Units were responsible for "commissioning various impact assessment studies, land acquisition studies, architectural plans, and engineering surveys … to determine whether an upgrade is feasible" (Patel 2013, 212). The National Upgrading Support Programme (NUSP) set up by the National Department of Human Settlements created a toolkit for upgrading work. Informal settlements required assessment and categorisation into one of four categories. Category A settlements would receive formal upgrading, Category B1 settlements would receive incremental upgrading, and Category B2 settlements were earmarked for relocation, albeit not in the immediate future. Lastly, Category C settlements were those earmarked for immediate relocation due to being located "on land that is unsuitable for human settlement" (National Upgrading Support Programme 2017, 10).

It is important to note that in Durban, the local state adopted a proactive stance, mirroring and at times shaping national government responses to providing services to informal settlements (see the eThekwini case study in the NUSP document [2017, 11–12]). After detailed technical assessments were conducted, substantial upgrading was undertaken on sites deemed suitable for low-income housing (Sim et al. 2018). Where informal housing was demolished, informal dwellers were moved to transit camps by the municipality and subsequently resettled upon formal housing completion. The eThekwini Municipality's Housing programme has been regarded as good practice, winning numerous housing awards including the National Govan Mbeki Awards proclaiming eThekwini as the "best Metropolitan Municipality in housing delivery among the country's metropolitan Councils" (eThekwini Municipality 2015).

Despite the supportive policy environment for in-situ upgrading nationally and in the city of Durban, these principles have gained slow traction as a mechanism to address the housing challenge, and implementation remains inconsistent (Sim et al. 2019). In 2009, Huchzermeyer noted that even after the policy shift into BNG, requests for upgrading by informal settlement residents were met with reluctance by local government. She argued that local authorities favoured resettlement over upgrading because of a dominant technocratic understanding and interpretation of informal settlements. Central to this understanding was an insistence on assessing occupied land only on physical characteristics. As Huchzermeyer (2009) states, "all of these indicate the planners' and officials' treatment of informal settlement communities as figures on a chessboard, to be moved around in order to solve problems (caused by poorly conceived orderly planning) elsewhere" (69).

Related to the political and technical rationale to transform the informal into the formal, we contend, is the disjuncture between municipalities' technical assessment of risk in land occupied by informal settlements and how people living in these settlements use expanded notions of risk assessment in creating a life in the city. Residents of informal settlements risk assessment and mitigation strategies do not easily align with notions of Western modernity or planners' fixation with orderly development. Municipal planning assumptions usually follow a trajectory from informal to formal where risks are apparently reduced as residents move along this linear construction. In reflecting on urban planning practice in eThekwini, Moonsammy (2017) goes to the extent of recommending continuous professional development interventions. This, she argues, would ensure planning practitioners recognise informality, and prompt them to respond in ways that relate to, and address, the issues residents are working with in the spaces they have selected to live. Bemoaning the role of planners in their refusal to recognise and acknowledge African urbanism, she raises the concern that

> planning practitioners continue to ignore the call to accept particular characteristics of African urbanism, "grey" areas, informality, survival, and opportunity-making as part of planning knowledge that gives recognition to innovation, efficiencies, and varying material conditions. Instead, the planning practitioners adhered to what they know, continuing with a planning approach and planning knowledge that has failed.
>
> *(Moonsammy 2017, 402)*

Moonsammy's statement raises an important critique, but we are cautious of blaming planners in their individual capacity. Given the progressive shifts in the human settlement policy, it is useful to try and understand the structural and professional constraints that make a return to the technocratic bias so easy. Moonsammy (2017) also notes that urban planners empathetic to arguments to recognise and support informality work in a professional structure and governance framework that can constrain their practice. Indeed, many planners have themselves grown up with informality through living in South African cities and may well be both familiar and comfortable with its workings. Assumptions about risk and the linear trajectory from informality to formality within the planning profession, coupled with bureaucratic structures and party politics, create messy dilemmas for how planners practice once inside a local government structure. For example, many municipalities have been slow to commission and initiate the rapid assessment and categorisation process for informal settlements despite this policy objective (Housing Development Agency 2014, 3).

Risks related to health and safety are explicit drivers in urban planning assumptions about what traditionally constitutes good urban settlements. In planning education and professional practice, two of the basic non-negotiables in settlement planning and design have always been the clear demarcation of the 1:100-year flood line, and the delineation of major road reserves. It is a technically valid assumption that any land on the floodplain or within the road reserve should not be considered for human habitation due to the threat of flood risks and future road expansion, respectively. As a logical extension of this argument, any settlement already within these areas is generally regarded as "risk-prone" and earmarked for urgent relocation to safer locales. Yet many people live in these demarcated areas, and have done so in some cases for around 35 years or more. How do the people living in these areas assess risk? What risk criteria are they using to weigh up and make trade-offs about their place of residence?

Divergent Ways of Assessing Risk: Official Versus Unofficial Assessments in Quarry Road West

Quarry Road West is located next to the middle-income suburb of Palmiet/Clare Estate (under Apartheid a previously designated Indian area), with the first informal houses being built around 35 years ago (Williams et al., 2019). Since then, it has grown significantly, although households and population figures differ slightly depending on the study, a recent publication reports that the settlement consists of approximately 3000 residents living in 1030 households (Mazeka et al. 2019). Whilst the settlement has expanded consistently since the first residents from the Eastern Cape arrived in 1984, there has been a rapid population increase over the last five years. QRW is an interesting settlement in that it has received fairly extensive attention from urban and development scholars (see Mazeka et al. [2019] on community mapping and climate change, and Williams et al. [2019] on resilience to flooding in QRW as two examples), as well as media reports on waste management, service delivery protests, and flooding.

Sim et al. (2019) in their report of QRW note that most of the settlement is located either in the road reserve or within the 1:100-year flood line. QRW is of interest here precisely because it is an informal settlement that is not deemed acceptable for in-situ upgrading to formal housing as "the land is prone to flooding" (National Upgrading Support Programme 2017, 10). Identified by the municipality as one of the most risk-prone in Durban, this settlement has been subject to frequent flooding, and fires from illegal electricity connections have led to extensive loss of property. This latter risk is consistent across many informal settlements in South Africa regardless of spatial location. Moreover, Sim et al. (2019) report a range of health and safety risks associated with a lack of basic services, including refuse collection and pollution in both the river and settlement. All of these impact negatively on residents' quality of life. As Sutherland (2015) further notes, uncollected rubbish has in the past resulted in a large rodent population and an increase in snakes, including the dangerous black mamba. In this sense, it is clear that residents live with a multitude of risks that roughly align to the criteria used to classify a Category C settlement that requires resettlement.

It is worth noting, however, that many of the risks experienced in QRW, such as the health risks of using polluted water and living without refuse removal or safe electricity connections, emanate directly from a lack of infrastructure and municipal service delivery to the settlement. In the field of disaster risk reduction, disasters "are increasingly viewed as a consequence of human action and as phenomena that can be prepared for and mitigated" (van Riet 2009, 194). Arguably the fires that occur from illegal electricity connections fall into this human-created risk category and could be mitigated against through service delivery. Over the last few years, the municipality has shifted their response to some informal settlements built on risky land. Despite QRW being categorised as Category C, ablution blocks, formal electricity, and water connections have now been provided to a portion of the settlement (Sim et al. 2019, 7).

Flooding remains an annual risk faced by residents. As one participants explains, "I build the house and I keep changing it because of the river" (Focus group P7, 12/04/2018). Certainly, residents are well aware of, and concerned about, the risks of living in QRW. In a focus group discussion with participants, one resident explains the dangers of living there:

> We were not expecting that our children, who are visiting us in the settlement, to be injured because of the illegal electricity. We are also worried about that river, maybe one day [it] will wash us away. The risk also [is] of the fire in this area.
>
> *(Focus group P29, 12/04/2018)*

The critical point to be noted here is that despite residents' exposure to living in a precarious settlement with high environmental risks, many continue to remain averse to moving to formal housing projects elsewhere in the city. In 2009, nearly ten years prior to the current research, more than half of all dwellers mobilised

FIGURE 5.1 Quarry Road West informal settlement.
Source: Photo credit, Photovoice Participant 14.

against resettlement by the municipality to formal houses in Parkgate, a housing development in Verulam 30 kilometres further north of the city (Sutherland 2016). Therefore, local state planners' assumptions around location, safety, and vulnerability are different to those held by residents in QRW. How residents balance a multitude of risks to make choices about locations and their perceptions of home are therefore important considerations, especially if we are to make sense of why people not only build settlements in spaces that are professionally perceived as unsafe, but fight to remain there when offered title deeds to formal housing.

QRW residents take a much broader view of risk than the technocratic assumptions around risk in municipal assessments. For many residents, one of the benefits of living in QRW is the close proximity to jobs. This common theme is articulated succinctly by one participant who states:

> I am living there because everything is convenient for me to carry on with my life. It is easy to get jobs around … We are near the road; taxis wake me in the morning. There are jobs across the road.
>
> *(Photovoice P15, 28/02/2018)*

Having easy access to jobs is a key determinant in deciding where to live for informal settlement residents. These economic logics around employment resonate with the majority of scholarly work on informal housing in both South Africa (see

Hunter and Posel's 2012 article on how the shifts in the nature of work also shape these logics), as well as elsewhere (Bhan 2014). Besides jobs, however, access to other social infrastructure and services are equally important variables in making a home in the city:

> What I like about this home in Quarry Road is that we have services and facilities which are near to the people, such as the shops, schools, clinic, and hardware across the road. In rural areas, the children are walking long distances to go to school.
>
> *(Photovoice P23, 28/02/2018)*

In QRW, easily accessing social and retail resources, as well as work – no matter how temporary – are equally if not more important than the risk of flooding and fires. Beyond the obvious benefits of these resources for all urban residents, locations of this kind are highly valued precisely because residents have lived experiences of disconnected and excluded spaces where these resources are scarce. Actual experiences or intergenerational memories of living in townships under Apartheid or coming from the rural Eastern Cape, or more contemporary stories of being relocated to housing developments that are poorly connected into the urban fabric, undoubtedly shape these decisions. Locations that are well integrated into the social and economic life of the city are especially prized as good spaces to "make a go" of urban life.

Residents of informal settlements are already economically and socially marginalised. In their immediate context however, the location of the informal settlement mitigates against further risks of social and economic exclusion in the city. This explains why, in QRW, there are also narratives such as the below:

> To stay in Quarry Road means many things to me. It is like my home. I am now used to everything. Life in this place is good. We have everything we need. The community is united.
>
> *(Photovoice P23, 28/02/2018)*

The *Narratives of Home and Neighbourhood* data highlights the extent to which residents feel invested in Quarry Road West. Making a home and neighbourhood takes extensive social labour (Dossa and Golubovic 2019, 172). Residents have developed a self-made settlement into a vibrant mixed-use environment, creating income-generating opportunities through providing a range of services to their neighbours. Residents run small shops from their houses (*spazas*), grow food in unused land, and run childcare facilities.

Beyond the functional attachment to the location of QRW, for many participants there was also a strong sense of belonging to the people who live there. Neighbours feature often in these descriptions, for example when a participant says

> My home is everything to me. If I am here, I feel at home. My neighbour is my key of my life. When I came here, it was a forest and I cut it down and

made the land a level. I put some planks together and I made a door and a wardrobe, a cupboard. I painted and I also made a washing line.

(Photovoice P22, 28/02/2018)

Using community maps and photographs, participants identified important landmarks that were special to them both personally and as a collective. In the following quote, a participant reflects on how the mango tree they once climbed is now a tree stump used as a meeting place:

There was an open space when we were young. All the children made it into a park using sticks to mark it off. Our own special park. There was a big tree … we used to climb the mango tree and harvest the mangoes. Now it is just a tree stump. We have many memories because we played there and ate mangoes. The municipality cut the tree. Now it is used as a meeting place – people sit on the stump.

(Photovoice P17, 28/02/2018)

Rather than perceiving the space as a precarious living environment, the case study showed how residents actively sought collective strategies to make the settlement more liveable. Social connections and communications are identified by the majority of participants in QRW as critical networks for survival. Being cognisant of those living in the same space illustrates the sense of rootedness needed to build social networks (Lewicka 2011) through familial, interpersonal, and communal interaction (Galster 2001). As in any neighbourhood, there are of course conflicts and tensions in the settlements. Stories about noisy neighbours and more serious violent conflicts between drunk people at the *shebeen* (informal bar or tavern) are also present in the narratives of residents (Sim et al. 2019, 80). But these tensions exist within a rather robust and committed social network of residents who come together to take collective action. As one participant explains, "as I have mentioned earlier, we are respecting each other a lot. Even if people are fighting, we have something called committees, those people are brought to the committee get disciplined" (Community mapping P15, 17/04/2018).

These resident structures and neighbourly connections are critical livelihood strategies to mitigate against risks in the settlement. They function as preparation for, and response to, flooding and fire disasters, as well as mitigation against the human-made risk of illegal electricity connections. The wires and insecure connections are often responsible for electrocution and fires that result in loss of life and property. Disconnection of what is commonly known as *izinyokanyoka* (wires that look like and bite like a snake) by municipal officials rarely last long, as one participant explains:

We choose to live like this although it is not safe. This tree we are using for electricity. In some areas they buy it, but we get it for free. If the municipality comes and cuts off the wires, we wait until they go away and reconnect again.

(Photovoice P23, 28/02/2018)

Given the prevalence of this practice and the necessity of electricity for a more dignified life, residents in QRW have created strategies to lessen this danger:

> I can clearly remember before when the electricity were on the ground – children were dying. So, we decided they must go up. It is not nice to see our children dead because of the carelessness of the community. The community worked together to put all the wires up to protect the children of the community.
>
> *(Photovoice P23, 28/02/2018)*

This kind of preventative measure is only possible when sufficient social connections and networks have been established in a neighbourhood. Establishing such risk mitigation strategies takes substantial labour to build trust and cooperation in order to create collective solutions (Dossa and Golubovic 2019, 172).

Communal responses to risks have also created an informal early warning system for the fires that break out in the settlement. This is often through natural surveillance by neighbours. Many participants spoke about how since "we are using *izinyokanyoka*, it is easy for my neighbour to see before the fire causes a lot of damage and cut off those electricity wire" (Focus group 2 P32, 23/04/2018). Another resident explained:

> Neighbourliness can be practiced anytime. For example, if I go to the tuck shop and notice that the house has smoke coming from inside, then I can do something to help by calling other people. We can break the door and take out the clothes and stop that fire.
>
> *(Focus Group 1 P6, 12/04/2018)*

Interestingly, residents in QRW find another support network in their middle-class neighbours who live in the formal houses across the road. Participants explained how these more well-off neighbours "are always on the road driving cars. If we are sleeping at night and not noticing the fire, they help us by phoning the fire engine to help us" (Focus group 1 P28, 12/04/2018), and that "in the neighbourhood, if we experienced fire, the Indians from the neighbourhood provide the community with food and clothes" (Focus group 1 P26, 12/04/2018).

These social connections and support structures include sharing knowledge about building materials and fire. For example:

> We discussed as the community what we have to do to protect ourselves from fire. The house burnt down and the neighbours used the free sand from the river to build bricks to rebuild the house. We are not using wood anymore. This is my neighbour's house; he made the bricks himself for his house.
>
> *(Photovoice P1, 28/02/2018)*

The QRW case study indicates how social networks and connections between neighbours create a formalised response to risk in this settlement. In this sense, as other studies in disaster management have shown, QRW residents illustrate how "socially mediated access and mutual aid play an important part in coping strategies and, in turn, the resilience of livelihood systems" in preparing for and mitigating against forms of hazardous risk (Wisner 2003, 183). This suggests a disjuncture between municipal understandings of risk (flooding, fires, and road reserve) and mitigation strategies (removals and resettlement) and residents' understanding of risk (flooding, fires, lack of services, and being disconnected from economic and social resources) and their mitigation strategies (communal meetings, changing to fire proof building materials, setting up warning systems, and providing support for affected neighbours). QRW residents are not the only people to make use of this expanded concept of risk to reject state housing relocation. In a study on why people actively choose to remain living within radiation zones after the Chernobyl disaster in the Ukraine, Davies and Polese (2015, 41) explain that "people also rejected [the state's] relocation welfare because of a reliance on informality that connects people to place", where the "social networks that informality relies upon and reproduces, [are] key factors that dissuade people from leaving the spaces they inhabit".

Unfortunately, "the differences between disaster 'experts' [ideas of risk] and lay people often lead to a dismissal of lay people's perceptions" (Quarantelli 2003, 211). If we are to take lay perceptions of risk more seriously then, as the QRW case study shows, informal settlement residents assess risk more broadly than the local municipality. What then are the risk impacts for people who are resettled to formal housing developments? We do recognise that there are situations where the risks and associated costs of letting people stay on land deemed unsafe may well require people to be resettled to other parts of the city. In South Africa this is usually to formal title deed housing units, although there are instances where residents have ended up staying in temporary housing for extended periods of time (Levenson 2017).

Resettlement and the Mitigation and Increase of Risk in Formal Housing in Cornubia

The second case study site discussed in this chapter is located in Cornubia, a national priority project in eThekwini. Strategically situated in the northern corridor of the metropolitan area, Cornubia was designed as an integrated human settlement development within the parameters of the Breaking New Ground (BNG) programme (Tongaat Hulett 2014, 1). The Cornubia development aimed to provide bulk stock of well-located, lower-income housing and employment opportunities through economic developments (McCarthy 2010). Developed as a private-public partnership, it was marketed as the province's largest integrated human settlement, with the developer Tongaat Hulett Developments agreeing to sell 659 hectares of its land to the municipality for the construction of subsidised housing. The multi-million-rand development was designed as a mixed-income, mixed-use development incorporating residential, commercial, industrial, and open space uses in the form of gardens, landscaped parks, and rehabilitated wetlands (Tongaat Hulett, 2014). The beneficiaries of this flagship project were mainly comprised of residents resettled from informal settlements within the eThekwini Municipality, including Kennedy Road Informal Settlement, Blackburn Village (Kemper and McManus 2019, 4), Quarry Road West (Sim et al. 2019, 6), Constantia and Stonebridge (Sibanda, Young-Jahangeer and Jahangeer 2019). The first phase of the Cornubia housing development consisted of 482 housing units allocated to low-income households from different informal settlements in April 2014. Beneficiaries occupied double-storey, semi-detached units and were given freehold tenure (Tongaat Hulett 2014, 1–2). Whilst the Cornubia development aimed to create an integrated economic and social hub, the first low-cost houses built preceded many other infrastructure developments. This resulted in housing with limited transport routes in and out of the development, disconnecting the development from the closest economic node of Umhlanga.

More recently economic developments offering commercial and retail resources are geographically accessible for residents of Cornubia. However, most of these residents are low-income families that have precarious employment opportunities, and are unlikely to afford the upmarket retail shopping offered at the Cornubia shopping mall. The social infrastructure of schools and clinics promised to the Cornubia housing residents have also been slow to materialise. Over the years, participants' limited access to social facilities makes it difficult for residents to "connect and identify with Cornubia as home and easier to disconnect to the idea of Cornubia as a community" (Sibanda et al. 2019, 25). The participants in the Cornubia study, mostly young adults, expressed dismay over the poor quality of the temporary prefabricated primary school classroom that services Cornubia

FIGURE 5.2 Cornubia houses.
Source: Photo credit, Doung Jahangeer.

(Sibanda et al. 2019, 25). A more formalised, well-equipped school is estimated to be built in the next three years. At present most children travel to neighbouring areas of Blackburn or Verulam to attend high school, which invariably places economic strain on these already economically vulnerable families (ibid).

Despite living there for four years, this sense of disconnectedness is evident when one participant, Pablo, introduces himself, "my name is Pablo. I am from Kwa-Mashu. I came to Cornubia in 2014" (Workshop discussion, September 2018), or when Lindo, another participant, says "I miss Clermont where I was born. Cornubia is very far from the beach. *Akuna namaswimming pools lana* [we do not even have public swimming pools]" (Workshop discussion, September 2018). Participants in this research process tended to connect to the spatial identity of their previous homes, such as KwaMashu and Clermont. Much has been written on circular migration in African cities and how many informal settlement residents retain membership of two households, one rural and one urban.[4] What is interesting to note here is how the rapid rate of urbanisation in South Africa is creating a nostalgia, at least for these young participants, not of a rural home, but of their childhood urban home in the Aparthcid-created townships.[5] This previous home, as with many residences in the development, was an informally constructed dwelling, the criterion that enabled their families to be approved for resettlement to Cornubia. In interpreting this finding, Sibanda et al. (2019) suggest that Cornubia does not yet have its own identity and that for many residents it does not yet mean anything to come from Cornubia.

Unlike in the QRW case study, participants in the Cornubia study showed limited attachment to the place they live in. The initial geographical isolation and the slow pace of amenities and recreational areas may well contribute towards feelings of alienation (Sibanda et al. 2019). The Cornubia development appeared to be well-intentioned in that the urban designers and planners made provision for social facilities. However, as many of these facilities have not been constructed, the vision of creating high-quality integrated living environments for low-income residents, as promoted in the BNG policy, has not yet been realised. Participants link the lack of social resources to forms of risk in Cornubia, such as when Lindo says, "I love playing soccer but *amagrounds aweko* [we do not have playing grounds]. Most of the time *sidlalela emgwaqweni* [we play in the middle of the road] and that's dangerous" (Lindo journal 2018).

Another reoccurring theme for participants was the illegal electricity connections that leave exposed live wires on the ground and the dangers this posed to children playing (Sibanda et al. 2019, 25). Illegal connections, similar to those made in informal settlements are fairly common in Cornubia, and a familiar solution when residents cannot afford electricity or choose to reallocate constrained incomes towards other necessities. Here practices associated with informality are woven into formal housing developments. The illusion of a linear move from informality to formality, and a decrease in risks as one moves along this trajectory, are dispelled. The risks in Cornubia are not only cars and *izinyokanyoka*, but also feeling socially disconnected from other residents. Many residents remain unfamiliar people who, even after four years of living in the same space, are seen as coming from different informal settlements and not sharing a collective past. Lindo lamented the absence of a sense of community as one of the reasons why he does not feel at home in Cornubia. This he expressed in his journal during the poetry and writing exercise: "Cornubia would be homely if we could all work together, respect and love each other as brothers and sisters" (Lindo journal, 26 October 2018).

As Sibanda et al. (2019) note, all the participants' dance skits, including the final public performance for residents in Cornubia, depicted domestic, gender-based, and gang violence. This performance was watched and applauded by a sizable crowd of residents in Cornubia. In discussions about this, the participants said that Cornubia *okwamanje aiko* [does not feel safe at the moment], that walking in the streets is not safe for women and children who need more protection in the housing development (Sibanda et al. 2019, 24).

Whilst some of the environmental and health and safety risks associated with living in informal settlements have undoubtedly been mitigated against by moving people to Cornubia, some of these risks, such as those associated with illegal connections, remain. In addition, social and economic risks, in the form of fragmented social networks and disconnection from economic and social opportunities, have increased after resettlement. With little existing social infrastructure or support for rebuilding neighbourhood connections after resettlement, Cornubia residents face a different trade-off to that of the residents of QRW. While Quarry Road West residents who have decided to stay in the informal settlement at the expense of formal housing infrastructure have social networks that provide risk mitigation strategies, the Cornubia residents gain formal infrastructure but at the expense of established social networks and communal structures that address residents' concerns and issues.

What an Expanded and Contextualised Understanding of Risk Means for Housing Policy and Practice

Social infrastructure that affords residents spaces and frameworks to knit together new social connections and networks is critical to building a sense of home and belonging for resettled residents. As in the QRW case study, this is critical for building resilience and risk mitigation strategies for residents, including mitigating against social and economic risks. Comparing these two case studies raises questions for the role of policy and professionals involved in the planning and development of human settlements. As noted earlier, the South African government, at a national level, has recognised the value of social networks and connections created by people living in informal settlements.[6] The National Upgrading Support Programme toolkit on *Interim Arrangement and Relocations* correctly notes that for residents in informal settlements "a primary coping mechanism is the development of mutual support that takes a number of different forms… [and] requires trust which develops slowly over time and is easily disturbed" (National Upgrading Support Programme 2017, 3). The toolkit urges municipalities to recognise that "the relocation of a household to a new setting destroys such support, making poverty much harder", and makes clear that costs of resettlement include the costs "to maintain social networks" (National Upgrading Support Programme 2017, 3–4). The document further suggests that a resettlement strategy should be co-developed with the people targeted for resettlement. This does create the necessary framework for thinking about an expanded view of risk assessment for informal settlements. But how to make sense of social connections and networks, and the types of support and risk mitigation they provide, is less clear in the official documentation. Neither is there much guidance for how municipalities could begin to implement support structures that protect and/or enable new social networks to be built. Without a more clearly defined framework that offers methods for expanding risk criteria, resettlements as seen in the case of Cornubia, may rupture the social fabric of beneficiaries in ways that create new social and economic risk for already vulnerable people.

At present, and perhaps for understandable reasons given the intersections in the political nature of housing, the quantitative targets imposed on the municipality for housing units, and the lack of clarity on what it means to assist and support social connections that residents have built over time, there is frequently a return to the technocratic evaluation of risk. This is a return to the familiar ideologies where informal settlements need to be resettled into formal housing and where the state's responsibility stops at the handover of a title deed. As van Riet (2009) cautions "overly technical quantitative risk assessments should be approached with caution", as they often overlook more contextual community-based approaches to risk (205).

Perhaps with time these social disconnections will improve for resettled residents, as some municipal officials hope. We do acknowledge, too, that it is plausible that a follow up study in another 10 years, once the Cornubia housing development has been surrounded by the urban development already growing on its doorstep, could result in very different feelings about home and neighbourliness. Increased urban developments in the area may well reduce some of the economic risks and feelings of being disconnected from the urban fabric.

Currently official state planning responsibilities and fiscus associated with resettlement responsibilities stops at title-deed handover. There is substantially less focus, if any, on how to support people in rebuilding social networks and connections after resettlement. But what may the unintended consequences of this be for the policy goals of integrated housing and the protection of vulnerable groups in the city? Given how context shapes the formation of strong social networks, how social connections re-form to produce risk mitigation strategies for resettled residents is less predictable. For example, not all informal settlements, nor formal settlements for that matter, have social networks that function in ways such as those found in Quarry Road West. Yet, if these social networks do not knit together even a loose sense of a collective for residents, then the residents face social, economic and health and safety risks with very limited first line mitigation strategies within their immediate neighbourhood. These risks will over time become the state's problem once again. Perhaps, then, it is time to explore the expanded view of risk such as that held by Quarry Road West residents, where social connections and networks are equally important criteria for assessing risk and decision-making around informal housing and resettlement. Including these intangible criteria is critically important for learning how context-specific and resident-led risk and mitigation strategies may be supported and developed in the city, as well as for thinking through how resettlement decisions by the municipality may enhance or dismantle these mitigation strategies for thousands of people living in the city.

Notes

1 eThekwini is the name of the metropolitan municipality in Durban, South Africa that was established in 2000.
2 This project was funded by the South African National Research Foundation.
3 For more details of the research project and individual reports, please see http://narrativesofhome.org.za.
4 See Leslie Bank's (2015) article on how living in urban informal settlements is reshaping the rural-urban meanings of investing in dual homesteads.
5 For a related finding see the study by Posel and Marx (2013) on how half the participants in their research indicated no desire to return to the rural homestead.
6 It should be noted that this more progressive approach has been actively pushed for by civil society organisations, particularly the Project Preparation Trust, which has put in many hours of their own intellectual capital, fieldwork, and upgrading preparation in order to contribute substantially to this NUSP upgrading toolkit.

References

Bank, L. 2015. "City Slums, Rural Homesteads: Migrant Culture Displaced Urbanism and the Citizenship of the Serviced House." *Journal of Southern African Studies* 41 (5): 1067–1081.

Bhan, G. 2014. "The Impoverishment of Poverty: Reflections on Urban Citizenship and Inequality in Contemporary Delhi." *Environment and Urbanization* 26 (2): 547–560.

Cirolia, L. R., T. Görgens, M. van Donk, W. Smit, and S. Drimie, eds. 2017. *Upgrading Informal Settlements in South Africa: Pursuing a Partnership-Based Approach*. Cape Town: Juta and Company (Pty) Ltd.

Davies, T., and A. Polese. 2015. "Informality and Survival in Ukraine's Nuclear Landscape: Living with the Risks of Chernobyl." *Journal of Eurasian Studies* 6 (1): 34–45.

Department of Human Settlements. 2004. "Breaking New Ground: A Comprehensive Plan for the Development of Integrated Sustainable Human Settlements." Accessed 15 December, 2019. http://www.dhs.gov.za/sites/default/files/documents/26082014_BNG2004.pdf

Department of Human Settlements. 2009. "National Housing Code: Part 1 A Simplified Guide to the National Housing Code." Accessed 15 December, 2019. http://www.dhs.gov.za/sites/default/files/documents/national_housing_2009/1_Simplified_Guide_Policy_Context/1%20Vol%201%20Part%201%20Simplified%20Guide%20to%20the%20National%20Housing%20Code.pdf

Dossa, P., and J. Golubovic. 2019. "Reimagining Home in the Wake of Displacement." *Studies in Social Justice* 13 (1): 171–186.

eThekwini Municipality. 2015. "Newsflash: eThekwini is the best Metropolitan in Housing Delivery." Accessed 15 December, 2019. http://www.durban.gov.za/Resource_Centre/Press_Releases/Pages/EThekwini-IS-The-Best-Metroplitan-In-Housing-Delivery.aspx

Galster, G. 2001. "On the Nature of Neighbourhood." *Urban Studies* 38 (12): 2111–2124.

Housing Development Agency. 2013. "South Africa: Informal Settlements Status (2013)." Accessed 15 December, 2019. http://www.thehda.co.za/uploads/files/HDA_South_Africa_Report_lr.pdf

Housing Development Agency. 2014. "Informal Settlement Upgrading Guidelines: Rapid Assessment and Categorisation." Accessed 15 December, 2019. http://thehda.co.za/pdf/uploads/multimedia/HDA_Rapid_assessment_and_categorisation.pdf

Huchzermeyer, M. 2001. "Housing for the Poor? Negotiated Housing Policy in South Africa." *Habitat International* 25 (3): 303–331.

Huchzermeyer, M. 2006. "The New Instrument for Upgrading Informal Settlements in South Africa: Contributions and Constraints." In *Informal Settlements: A Perpetual Challenge?*, edited by Huchzermeyer, M., and A. Karam, 41–61. Cape Town: UCT Press.

Huchzermeyer, M. 2009. "The Struggle for In Situ Upgrading of Informal Settlements: A Reflection on Cases in Gauteng." *Development Southern Africa* 26 (1): 59–73.

Huchzermeyer, M. 2011. *Cities with "Slums": From Informal Settlement Eradication to a Right to the City in Africa*. Cape Town: UCT Press.

Hunter, M., and D. Posel. 2012. "Here to Work: The Socioeconomic Characteristics of Informal Dwellers in Post-Apartheid South Africa." *Environment and Urbanization* 24 (1): 285–304.

Kemper, A., and S. McManus. 2019. "Narratives of Home and Neighbourhood from Blackburn Village." *Research Report Produced for the Urban Futures Centre NRF Blue Skies Project*. Accessed 15 December, 2019. http://narrativesofhome.org.za/wp-content/uploads/2019/08/Narratives-of-Home-Blackburn-Village.pdf

Lemanski, C. 2011. "Moving Up the Ladder or Stuck on the Bottom Rung? Homeownership as a Solution to Poverty in Urban South Africa." *International Journal of Urban and Regional Research* 35 (1): 57–77.

Levenson, Z. 2017. "Precarious Welfare States: Urban Struggles over Housing Delivery in Post-Apartheid South Africa." *International Sociology* 32 (4), 474–492.

Lewicka, M. 2011. "Place Attachment: How Far Have We Come in the Last 40 Years?" *Journal of Environmental Psychology* 31 (3): 207–230.

Mazeka, B., C. Sutherland, S. Buthelezi, and D. Khumalo. 2019. "Community-based Mapping Methodology for Climate Change Adaptation: A Case Study of Quarry Road West Informal Settlement, Durban, South Africa." In *The Geography of Climate Change Adaptation in Urban Africa*, edited by Cobbinah, P. B., and M. Addaney, 57–88. Cham: Palgrave Macmillan.

McCarthy, J. 2010. "Socio-Economic Impacts of the Cornubia Development." *Annexure of the Amended Environmental Impact Report for the Proposed Cornubia Mixed Use Phased Development – Phase 1 Mount Edgecombe, A Public-Private Partnership Project*. Durban: Tongaat Hulett Developments and eThekwini Municipality.

Moodley, S. 2018. "Why Do Planners Think That Planning Has Failed Post-Apartheid? The Case of eThekwini Municipality, Durban, South Africa." *Urban Forum* 30 (3): 307–323.

Moonsammy, S. T. 2017. "An Insider-outsider's Exploration of Planning Knowledges Roles Uses and Construction in a Post-1994 Metropolitan Setting: eThekwini Municipality." PhD diss., University of Pretoria.

Murray, C., and C. O'Regan (eds). 1990. *No Place to Rest: Forced Removals and the Law in South Africa*. Cape Town: Oxford University Press.

Musvoto, G., G. Lincoln, and R. Hansmann. 2016. "The Role of Spatial Development Frameworks in Transformation of the eThekwini Municipality, KwaZulu-Natal, South Africa: Reflecting on 20 years of planning." *Urban Forum* 27 (2): 187–210.

National Planning Commission. 2011. "Diagnostic Overview". Accessed 15 December, 2019. https://www.gov.za/sites/default/files/gcis_document/201409/npcdiagnosticoverview1.pdf

National Upgrading Support Programme. 2017. "Participants: Section 6 Interim Arrangements and Relocations." Accessed 15 December, 2019. http://upgradingsupport.org/uploads/resource_documents/participants-combined/Chapter-6-Interim-Arrangements-and-Relocations-May-2016.pdf

Newton, C., and N. Schuermans. 2013. "More than Twenty Years after the Repeal of the Group Areas Act: Housing, Spatial Planning and Urban Development in Post-Apartheid South Africa." *Journal of Housing and the Built Environment* 28: 579–587.

Patel, K. 2013. "A Successful Slum Upgrade in Durban: A Case of Formal Change and Informal Continuity." *Habitat International* 40: 211–217.

Platzky, L., and C. Walker. 1985. *The Surplus People: Forced Removals in South Africa.* Johannesburg: Ravan Press of South Africa.

Posel, D., and C. Marx. 2013. "Circular Migration: A View from Destination Households in Two Urban Informal Settlements in South Africa." *The Journal of Development Studies* 49 (6): 819–831.

Quarantelli, E. L. 2003. "Urban Vulnerability to Disasters in Developing Countries: Managing Risks." In *Building Safer Cities: The Future of Disaster Risk*, edited by Kreimer, A., M. Arnold, and A. Carlin, 211–231. Washington, DC: The World Bank.

Sibanda, P., M. Young-Jahangeer, and D. Jahangeer. 2019. "Narratives of Home: Cornubia." *Research Report Produced for the Urban Futures Centre NRF Blue Skies Project.* Accessed 15 December, 2019. http://narrativesofhome.org.za/wp-content/uploads/2019/08/Narratives-of-Home-Cornubia.pdf

Sim, V., A. McCarthy, C. Sutherland, S. Buthelezi, and D. Khumalo. 2019. "Exploring an In-Situ Upgrade: Quarry Road West Informal Settlement." *Research Report Produced for the Urban Futures Centre NRF Blue Skies Project.* Accessed 15 December, 2019. http://narrativesofhome.org.za/wp-content/uploads/2019/08/Narratives-of-Home-Quarry-Road-West.pdf

Statistics South Africa. 2019. "*General Household Survey. Statistical Release P0318.*" Accessed 15 December, 2019. http://www.statssa.gov.za/publications/P0318/P03182018.pdf

Sutherland, C. 2015. "Settlement Story." In *The Politics of Slums in the Global South: Urban Informality in Brazil, India, South Africa and Peru*, edited by Dupont, V., D. Jordhus-Lier, C. Sutherland, and E. Braathen, 79–114. London: Routledge.

Tongaat Hulett. 2014. *Cornubia: Celebrating 20 Years of Building Dreams*. Information booklet. Durban: Tongaat Hulett.

Van Riet, G. 2009. "Disaster Risk Assessment in South Africa: Some Current Challenges." *South African Review of Sociology* 40 (2): 194–208.

Williams, D. S., M. Máñez Costa, C. Sutherland, L. Celliers, and J. Scheffran. 2019. "Vulnerability of Informal Settlements in the context of Rapid Urbanization and Climate Change." *Environment and Urbanization* 31 (1): 157–176.

Wisner, B. 2003. "Disaster Risk Reduction in Megacities: Making the Most of Human and Social Capital." In *Building Safer Cities: The Future of Disaster Risk*, edited by Kreimer, A., M. Arnold, and A. Carlin, 181–196. Washington, DC: The World Bank.

Zondo, N., and L. Royston. 2016. "Upgrading Informal Settlements: The importance of the Slovo Park Judgment." *Daily Maverick*, 11 April, 2016.

6

"THE HOUSE IS NICE, BUT …"

Looking Beyond "Shelter" in Shantytown Resettlement in Casablanca, Morocco

Raffael Beier

> "The houses are better than the shacks, but transport is a problem!"
>
> *(58-year-old female hawker)*

> "The house is nice and spacious. It's the neighbourhood that I don't like!"
>
> *(27-year-old waiter)*

> "It's good that they are eradicating the shantytowns, but they put us here …"
>
> *(21-year-old female student)*

Introduction

These few brief but exemplary statements by resettled former shantytown dwellers indicate that the provision of adequate housing requires city planners to move beyond the limited technical conceptualisation of housing as a shelter of four walls and a roof. As this chapter shows, housing is far more than this to resettled individuals. Six years after the first dwellers had moved from the shantytown Karyan Central in central Casablanca to the new neighbourhood Nouvelle Lahraouiyine at the city's margins under the national housing programme *Villes Sans Bidonvilles* (VSB, "Cities Without Shantytowns")[1] (see Figure 6.1), many residents were still undecided about whether or to what extent their new living environment embodied their aspirations. While the majority appreciated improved quality of shelter in comparison to where they lived before, many were also concerned with other aspects of adequate housing such as difficulties in accessing jobs and education, the need to rebuild a social life, and a lack of activities in the new town. Hence, the three statements above exemplify the consequences of the VSB's narrow and technical approach to housing that disregards other vital functions of housing

DOI: 10.4324/9781003124559-8

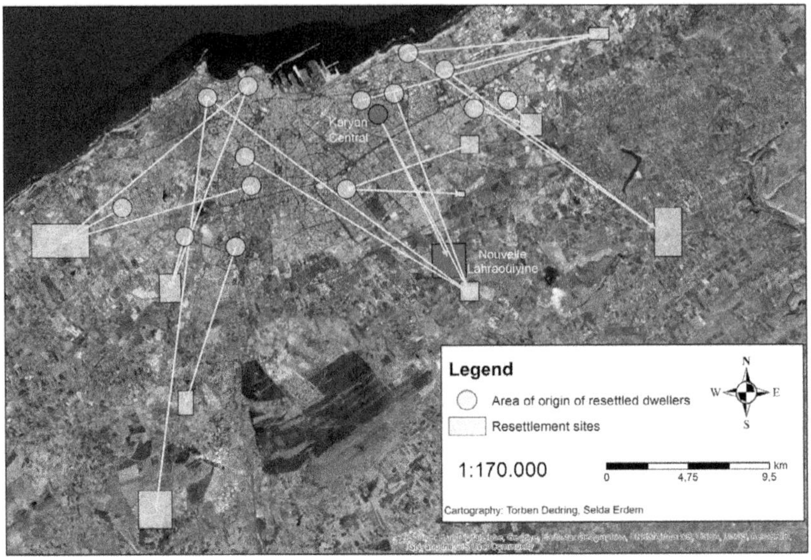

FIGURE 6.1 The VSB programme displaced *bidonville* (shantytown) dwellers to the peripheries of Casablanca.
Source: Cartography by Selda Erdem and Torben Dedring.

beyond shelter. The main objective of the VSB programme is to eradicate – in the quantitative sense of the word – all shantytowns in Morocco. To reach this target swiftly and in a way that would not lead to widespread resistance, government authorities prioritised resettlement and the cost-efficient production of standardised housing. As such, the VSB programme is a typical example of how new large-scale housing programmes in many emerging countries in the Global South are envisioned, planned, and implemented (Coelho 2016; Croese, Cirolia, and Graham 2016; Turok 2016).

The summarising statements above may remind some readers of the early ideas of Turner (1968, 1972), who urged urban planners not to view housing quality as a mere question of material quality and to analyse the quality of housing by considering the perspectives of inhabitants, from which *housing* can be considered an action (a verb). This calls for relational perspectives to housing (as Easthope et al. 2020 discuss) that require an analytical focus on people's various forms of agency in building and dwelling in a place (Caldeira 2017; Heslop, McFarlane, and Ormerod 2020), as well as their residential strategies through which they shape and navigate through different built environments (Navez-Bouchanine and Dansereau 2002; Florin and Semmoud 2010). Whereas relational approaches should acknowledge structural forces including global housing markets, finance, and politics, they emphasise the significance of contextually embedded, subjective decision-making that reveals how housing is enacted on the ground. Following this, housing emerges as a complex concept that connects people with places and that ties notions of physical shelter to subjective feelings of home (Jacobs and Smith 2008). Likewise, housing is the dynamic product of people's choices and ongoing informed comparisons of different options – even in contexts where such choices are severely constrained (Navez-Bouchanine and Dansereau 2002). As argued in the book's introduction, this requires thinking about how the material, economic, social, and emotional aspects of housing function together.

However, reflecting on a recent resurgence of large-scale standardised housing projects in many emerging countries (Buckley, Kallergis, and Wainer 2016; Coelho 2016; Croese, Cirolia, and Graham 2016; Turok 2016), I argue that the political mainstream continues to treat housing as a merely technical question. Notwithstanding the UN's acknowledgement that "adequate housing must provide more than four walls and a roof" (OHCHR and UN-Habitat 2009, 3), there is little optimism that new housing programmes will diverge from a unilateral focus on the function of housing as a physical shelter (Coelho 2016). Critical political engagement with the meaning(s) of "adequate housing" has hardly let to sustainable change (Navez-Bouchanine 2003; Huchzermeyer 2009) – Turok (2016) notes, "[v]ital aspects of functional urban settlements, such as density and connectivity, tend to get sacrificed when the short-term economics and politics of construction dominate" (234). Thus, some scholars have raised concerns that recent large-scale housing projects in many emerging countries would simply repeat past mistakes of spatially disintegrated and monotonous social housing blocks that themselves later became the targets of urban regeneration projects (Buckley, Kallergis, and Wainer 2016; Croese, Cirolia, and Graham 2016).

In addition, many large-scale housing programmes like the VSB programme do not acknowledge the potential adverse effects of resettlement. Rather, state authorities promote housing programmes as social policies that would foster the integration of socially disadvantaged population groups while reducing the vulnerability of the urban poor through the provision of "adequate" housing. Thus, they pretend to "save" residents from having to live in "slums" and other forms of "inadequate" housing. For example, Morocco's *Ministère de l'Habitat, de l'Urbanisme et de la Politique de la Ville* (MHUPV 2012) calls the shantytown "a locus of poverty and social exclusion, par excellence, within the urban fabric" (33). Therefore, the VSB is considered to be a "priorit[y] of the Moroccan Government in the areas of social development, the fight against poverty, and the reduction of exclusion in urban areas" (MHUPV 2012, 14). While housing programmes tend to have such ostensibly positive, pro-social connotations, the notion of "resettlement" as more than simply relocation (see Chapter 1) is absent. Koenig (2006, 2018) duly revealed that unlike rural "development-caused displacement and resettlement" (DCDR), urban housing programmes hardly consider the potential risks of impoverishment associated with resettlement, such as a loss of social networks and reduced access to employment, amongst others: "Most [urban resettlement] projects continue to be conceived of as housing projects and consider the reconstitution of jobs as unproblematic" (Koenig 2006, 116). This lack of consciousness persists despite a growing number of scholars having shown that urban resettlement linked to housing carries similar risks of impoverishment when compared to rural DCDR projects (Patel, Sliuzas, and Mathur 2015; Coelho 2016; Beier 2019; Nikuze et al. 2019).

Following these critical voices, the chapter challenges uniform, top-down, and shelter-centric understandings of housing. Following the book's conceptual introduction, this chapter adds a more empirical perspective highlighting the material, economic, social (incl. political), and emotional functions of housing as part of a holistic and subjective understanding of adequate housing. It asks to whom and to what extent certain aspects of dwelling matter in terms of "housing satisfaction", an evaluation metric used in quantitative housing studies (Galster 1987). Based on a people-centred analysis of the resettlement of Karyan Central in Casablanca, Morocco, the chapter further maintains that policies aimed at ensuring adequate housing must consider the adverse effects of resettlement even if people move voluntarily. Empirical and especially quantitative evidence underlying these basic characteristics of adequate housing in an urban resettlement context is still thin (Patel, Sliuzas, and Mathur 2015; Nikuze et al. 2019). The chapter therefore also seeks to reconceptualise resettlement in a way that would help to bridge between important qualitative critiques of resettlement schemes that cast them as undesired (Iraki 2006, Zaki 2006, 2007; Bogaert 2011; Harroud 2019) and the lived experiences of resettlement on the ground, and the willingness of many *bidonville* dwellers to accept resettlement even to remote places despite all known shortcomings (Arrif 1999, 302; Navez-Bouchanine and Dansereau 2002, 45–46). The chapter therefore seeks to answer the following question: Is the possibility to access one's own property and to escape the stigma of the *bidonville* more important for people than, for example, strong social bonds and better access to jobs? In other words, to what extent do certain dwelling functions affect housing satisfaction, and for whom?

This chapter builds on a larger study using a mixed-methods approach and own fieldwork in Casablanca between December 2016 and April 2017 (Beier 2019). The reasoning in this chapter follows more quantitative logics based on data from 400 survey questionnaires with former residents of Karyan Central collected, on average, six years after they moved to the new neighbourhood, Nouvelle Lahraouiyine. The survey included questions about the perceptions of housing quality, infrastructure, and social life that were answered by using Likert scales. It also included closed questions on income, transport, occupation, and household size, as well as more qualitative, open-ended questions on life in the neighbourhood. A slightly adapted survey was conducted with a similar number of households in Er-Rhamna, a shantytown of comparable size and function to Karyan Central. However, this chapter relies more on the data from Nouvelle Lahraouiyine. Both household surveys were representative, having been based on probability sampling. In Nouvelle Lahraouiyine, weighted cluster sampling determined the number of households to be questioned for each of the 158 housing blocks. In Er-Rhamna, house numbers helped to apply systematic sampling throughout the entire neighbourhood (Beier 2019, 82–86). Whenever possible, the research team, composed of the author and two local research assistants of different genders, encouraged the respondents to go beyond the survey to provide more open, qualitative views of life in the two neighbourhoods. Own observations and further qualitative interviews with key stakeholder groups, such as private developers and families that were not able to move, complemented these data.

The Resettlement of Karyan Central

Karyan Central was one of the oldest auto-constructed neighbourhoods of Morocco, known for its role in driving the country's independence movement. Similar to many other countries, Morocco's first shantytowns were the result of unjust and insufficient colonial housing policies. In the 1920s, many Moroccan labourers who arrived in Casablanca in search of jobs could not find accommodation and started to build their own makeshift shelters on vacant land close to the harbour and its attached industrial zones. In the 1930s, French colonial authorities felt urged to intervene to ensure hygiene and enforce territorial control. In the working-class district Hay Mohammadi, they resettled residents of several scattered shantytowns to a rectangular block structure, which was named Karyan Central (Rachik 2002, 45–53; Zaki 2010, 46).[2] Since then, residents themselves developed Karyan Central (and Hay Mohammadi) in an incremental way and according to their own needs, often with the assistance or authorisation of elected and non-elected state authorities. It became an important market centre and counted about 35,000 inhabitants in the mid 2000s (Figure 6.2). Several of its houses were home to large, intergenerational households and had more than one floor. Almost all houses had walls built out of solid materials, indoor bathrooms, formal access to the power grid, and an indoor water supply. Residents organised sewage collection collectively, but occasional fires, leaking roofs, dirt, and vermin largely affected shelter quality (Beier 2019). In addition to the prevailing stigmatisation of *bidonville* dwellers, this may explain why many residents were looking forward to new housing offered by the government and even took the streets to demand "decent" housing. To some

FIGURE 6.2 The market of Karyan Central prior to the eviction of its last inhabitants. Source: Author's picture, March 2015.

bidonville households, the resettlement to new, "formal-looking" houses (Beier 2021) may represent the next step in the residential journey to meeting their long-term life aspirations, offering them the chance to escape stigmatisation and to own property (Arrif 1999; Navez-Bouchanine and Dansereau 2002). For others, however, it may feel like a loss of home (Zaki 2007; Beier and Strava 2020).

In 2009, the resettlement project of Karyan Central as part of the VSB programme commenced. King Mohammed VI introduced the VSB programme in 2004 and stated its primary objective to eradicate all shantytowns in Morocco. While being mainly promoted as a social housing policy, the VSB programme should be understood in relation to security concerns and the long-term stigmatisation of informal settlements that intensified in the immediate aftermath of the 2003 suicide bombings of a few shantytown dwellers in the city centre of Casablanca (Zaki 2007; Navez-Bouchanine 2012, 171). Linked to this, the demolition of *bidonvilles* follows developmentalist and modernist logics that underlie the ambition to boost international urban competitiveness. Furthermore, the VSB programme can be considered a tool to integrate marginalised households into neoliberal governance schemes as well as formal housing markets (Bogaert 2018).

Whereas the central state mobilised public land, the implementation was led mainly by local state authorities as well as by the semi-public company Al Omrane. The former's main objective was to quickly clear the *bidonvilles* without producing much conflict. Local authorities applied a "carrot and stick" tactic combined with opaque practices of information sharing in order to avoid open resistance and make residents accept resettlement conditions "voluntarily" (le Tellier 2009; Navez-Bouchanine 2012). The latter was charged with the basic development of the new neighbourhood and derived profit from selling some plots at market prices (see also Beier 2021). In the case of Karyan Central, authorities used the relatively popular *recasement* approach, which bears similarities to a sites-and-services approach: authorities sell one subsidised plot of land (of 80 square metres) to two households and ask them to build a four-storey house according to pre-defined building standards. To improve affordability compared to previous sites-and-services projects, authorities allowed residents to ask a third party (*tiers associé*) to build the house for them (Toutain 2013; Zaki 2013). The third party is the main financer of the resettlement and not only finances the construction of the house, but also pays for the plot and the temporary accommodation of the two resettled households. In return, the third party is allocated the two lower floors of the four-storey building, while each of the two resettled households own one of the two upper-floor apartments. While many residents were happy to access property at almost no personal cost, authorities saw the third-party approach as an effective means to clear *bidonvilles* in a short time.

In late 2010, the first of the 6,000 to 7,000 households to be resettled from Karyan Central moved to the new houses in the *Zone d'Urbanisation Nouvelle* (ZUN) *de Lahraouiyine* (commonly referred to as Nouvelle Lahraouiyine) (Zaki 2013). Nouvelle Lahraouiyine is located outside Casablanca's jurisdiction, ten kilometres away from former Karyan Central, and belongs to the municipality of

Médiouna (Figure 6.1). While the majority of residents of Karyan Central deliberately accepted the conditions of resettlement, several households resisted and stayed until May 2016, when local authorities cleared the site with bulldozers and forcibly evicted the remaining 500 households (Figure 6.2). During the field research in 2016, we observed that about 90% of the houses in Nouvelle Lahraouiyine had been completed. However, some were stuck in temporary accommodation, awaiting the completion of the construction. Other residents occupied their unfinished housing units, having no formal access to electricity or water. At the same time, the first signs of deterioration had become visible in Nouvelle Lahraouiyine. Besides complaints about the sub-standard construction of houses, leading to problems such as indoor mould and crumbling bricks, insufficient public services, including a lack of waste and wastewater management, public transport, security at night, and street lighting, as well as infrastructure deficiencies such as unpaved and potholed streets, were mentioned (see Figure 6.3).

Residents' Mixed Views of the New Housing Situation

The majority of the resettled residents in Nouvelle Lahraouiyine, surveyed on average five to six years after they moved, reported being satisfied with their new overall housing situation in the new town (44%), but about a quarter were undecided, and almost 30% were not satisfied.[3] Satisfaction with material quality, particularly related to the shelter function of the house, was significantly higher: almost three-quarters were satisfied and only fewer than 10% were not satisfied. The differences in these very basic data highlight the chapter's main argument, namely that housing cannot be judged by regarding the material quality of the house alone. But is it possible to say to what extent certain housing functions are preferred over

FIGURE 6.3 Uncompleted streets and houses in Nouvelle Lahraouiyine.
Source: Author's picture, January 2017.

others? Whereas at an individual level this question may be answered through a qualitative analysis of individual housing trajectories (Navez-Bouchanine and Dansereau 2002; Florin and Semmoud 2010), quantitative analyses may help identifying more general views for a larger population group. To minimise the risk of overgeneralisation and to provide a more nuanced analysis, the following empirical sections do not analyse single survey questions but combine different sources of evidence.

First and foremost, it was striking that many resettled residents struggled to make an overall judgement of their resettlement to Nouvelle Lahraouiyine. As the quotations at the start of this chapter show, residents often started their attempts to judge the resettlement programme with an appreciation of the house or the general idea of having been provided with "adequate" housing. Subsequently, they raised concerns about various well-known shortcomings of resettlement such as the peripheral location, weakened social networks, or a lack of jobs. This kind of weighing up of pros and cons of resettlement reveals that residents themselves view adequate housing as a comprehensive concept comprising different, inseparable housing functions beyond the shelter function.

Table 6.1 offers a descriptive overview of the stated advantages and disadvantages of living in Nouvelle Lahraouiyine after resettlement, confirming the argument that people's positive associations with Nouvelle Lahraouiyine relate mostly to the material quality of the new houses. This mirrors people's main aspirations back in the *bidonville* when they were looking forward to state-led housing intervention. The first reason for this refers to improved shelter: a considerable number of residents felt less vulnerable due to better-quality roofs and walls that protect them from fires, rain, and extreme temperatures. Second, dwellers pointed to the size of the apartment, which is more spacious than former dwellings. In Nouvelle Lahraouiyine, on average, 1.6 persons share a room, whereas in the shantytown Er-Rhamna the average is 2.3. Third, many inhabitants appreciate that they now live in what they call a "decent" or "respectable" house that, in contrast to the *barraka* (Darjia for "shack"), would allow them to invite friends over without feeling

TABLE 6.1 Stated advantages and disadvantages of life in the resettlement town Nouvelle Lahraouiyine and the number of mentions of each (n=401; multiple mentions possible).

Most frequently stated advantages	*Most frequently stated disadvantages*
Tranquillity (124)	Isolation (199)
Shelter less vulnerable (92)	Bad transport connections (158)
Cleanliness (indoors) (91)	Unsafety (88)
Spacious house (74)	Lack of jobs/clients (79)
Decent/respectable house (65)	Boredom (79)
Beautiful house (37)	Bad infrastructure (39)
Better air quality (26)	No hospitals (35)

ashamed. Moreover, many residents felt that they live in a cleaner housing environment than before. While several women in Er-Rhamna complained that they would not see a difference after cleaning, numerous residents in Nouvelle Lahraouiyine were happy about having a cleaner home and an attractive interior. Beyond the house, a considerable number of residents appreciated classic advantages of a suburban location, such as better air quality and greater tranquillity compared to where they lived before.

While stated advantages of Nouvelle Lahraouiyine most significantly relate to the house, the new town as such – especially its peripheral location and its lack of urban assets – is perceived rather critically by former *bidonville* dwellers (Table 6.1). The feeling of isolation is the most striking disadvantage. More than 90% of the respondents shared strong feelings of social isolation that is largely the consequence of the peripheral location of Nouvelle Lahraouiyine and its limited accessibility. The frequent mentions of "bad transport" are an indicator that the inefficient and unreliable public transport system is likely to feed feelings of marginality and isolation (Beier 2020). However, isolation also refers to an erosion of previous social networks that has weakened community trust (cf. Zaki 2007). Compared to Er-Rhamna, fewer people trust their neighbours, communicating less frequently with them, while even fewer believe that neighbours help each other. This weakened sense of community seems to be at the heart of another major disadvantage, which is a lack of safety. Unlike in the shantytown (cf. Arrif 1999), safety in Nouvelle Lahraouiyine is not guaranteed through intensive neighbourhood interaction and social control. Hence, perceptions of safety in Nouvelle Lahraouiyine were significantly fewer than in Er-Rhamna, where about two-thirds of the residents felt safe.

In addition, residents' perceived marginality refers to various deficiencies of (urban) infrastructure in Nouvelle Lahraouiyine. Most importantly, this includes the lack of adequate health services, limited and more expensive market goods, bad schools, muddy streets, and a limited number of leisure opportunities. Many people mentioned feeling bored and that they would have nothing to do in the new town. Of course, this also reflects the lack of jobs or clients that makes life more difficult for the dwellers in the new neighbourhoods. In most parts of Nouvelle Lahraouiyine, the vacancy rate of shops exceeded 80% and, unlike in Hay Mohammadi, (casual) job opportunities in the new town were scarce. At the same time, the disposable income of resettled residents fell due to higher transport and utilities expenses. While these "missing" urban assets may vary significantly from one household to another, they all refer to a loss of urbanity that seems to be the core problem of the resettlement to Nouvelle Lahraouiyine – similar to other new towns in Morocco (Zaki 2007; Navez-Bouchanine 2012, 170–171; Harroud 2019).

These multiple disadvantages of the new town stand in sharp contrast to residents' generally positive opinion about the new houses, making them feel undecided about the overall outcome of resettlement. These first findings reveal the problem with the narrow, physical definition of housing used by policy makers in the VSB programme. Planners have reduced "adequate housing" to just one element, namely material quality while other relevant dwelling functions were overlooked. This reminds us of what Coelho (2016) calls "shelter poverty", "a slum-centric understanding of urban poverty [...] framing it as a function of housing and services" (113). While not being concerned with the root causes of poverty, large-scale programmes such as the VSB assume that, through the provision of better or rather more "ordinary" shelters and services, slum dwellers can be lifted out of poverty. As such, new housing is understood from an external perspective as an additional, beneficial asset that comes *on top of* existing livelihoods and as an improvement to existing living conditions. This is fundamentally different from the dominant perspective in DCDR projects, where policy makers seem more likely to acknowledge comprehensive livelihood impacts of resettlement (Koenig 2006, 2018). In order to prevent the impoverishment of resettled population groups, Cernea (2003) argues that besides compensation (in the case of the VSB programme this might be the new apartment), resettlement would require concerted public investment in people's development at the new site. This is what many residents of Nouvelle Lahraouiyine demanded from government authorities. "The VSB programme is good, but a lot still needs to be done in Lahraouiyine, especially in terms of creating more jobs", argued a 57-year-old household help. However, there are no indications that public authorities are planning to increase investment in the new town soon, after having achieved their most important objective: the clearance of the shantytown.

Identifying Reasons for (Dis)satisfaction with New Housing

If residents have to weigh increased housing comfort against the deficiencies of the new town, it is interesting to analyse *how* they judge housing quality and *why*. Which determining factors influence people's satisfaction with new housing *to what extent* and how do they differ among different population groups in Nouvelle Lahraouiyine? To start with, it must be noted that besides the majority being undecided about the new housing situation, the data also includes some strong, polarised opinions. For instance, whereas 17% of resettled residents in Nouvelle Lahraouiyine reported being completely dissatisfied, 12% said that they were completely satisfied with the new housing situation. In one case, a 45-year-old woman felt that the situation in Nouvelle Lahraouiyine was worse than in the shantytown, while a 56-year-old woman living just a few metres away from her was convinced of the opposite, i.e., that people were more vulnerable and less safe in Karyan Central. Whereas 24-year-old Saida blamed the authorities of having destroyed a "monument" like Karyan Central, her neighbour was happy not to live in a *bidonville* any longer, having felt that people get sick because of the bad infrastructure.

Thus, indecisiveness about the use value of the new house and the coexistence of strongly opposing opinions highlight the enormous heterogeneity of lives and living conditions in Karyan Central, as well as the huge variation in personal resettlement experiences. These subjectivities are not only often overlooked within housing policy making, but also in research (see Chapter 1). For the case of India, Dupont et al. (2017) highlight that such varied opinions towards resettlement are the norm rather than the exception within heterogeneous communities such as older auto-constructed neighbourhoods: "Those families in the most precarious conditions can improve their situation through resettlement or rehabilitation, whereas the better off are more likely to be impacted negatively by resettlement, and thus are more eager to resist displacement" (Dupont et al. 2017, 201). Other authors have emphasised the relevance of people's long-term housing trajectories in explaining why residents are in favour of or against potential resettlement (Navez-Bouchanine and Dansereau 2002; Beier and Strava 2020).

Individual Factors Influencing (Dis)satisfaction

Following this, individual satisfaction with the housing situation and status prior to the resettlement seems to play a significant role in residents' assessment of the current housing situation after resettlement. However, the level of satisfaction also depends on factors related to the current housing situation. Following my previous arguments, it is necessary to stress both shelter aspects and wider functions of housing that at first glance do not directly relate to the house as such. The most prominent of these factors are social life and access to jobs (see Table 6.1). Table 6.2 presents the results of three ordinary least-square (OLS) multiple regression models explaining residents' stated satisfaction with the general housing situation in Nouvelle Lahraouiyine, measured on a Likert scale, with "1" being fully dissatisfied and "5" fully satisfied. The six independent variables of the model may be seen as proxies for different dwelling functions that constitute adequate housing. Furthermore, they relate to the most frequently mentioned advantages and disadvantages of living in Nouvelle Lahraouiyine (Table 6.1). Independent variables include "satisfaction with the house" and "satisfaction with public services", which are both measured on a five-level Likert scale and which refer to the material quality of shelter. The variable "total transport costs" (numeric) functions as a proxy for the new town's accessibility, as well as some economic housing functions. For example, people that must travel far to reach their workplace have higher transport costs than those working in the new town and are likely to be less satisfied with their housing situation. People's feeling of isolation, measured on a Likert scale from "1" (not feeling isolated at all) to "5" (feeling very isolated), refers to perceptions of social and spatial marginality. The variable "neighbourhood cohesion" is an index measuring residents' perceptions of social life in Nouvelle Lahraouiyine. It is composed of four different dimensions – regular communication with neighbours, trust in neighbours, mutual help amongst neighbours, and mutual respect among residents – all measured on Likert scales reaching from "1" (very low) to "5" (very high). Both variables may be proxies for social dwelling functions. Lastly, the variable "born in Karyan Central" may be read as a proxy of people's feeling of belonging to their former residence and, hence, speaks to the emotional dimensions of housing.

The first model (on the left in Table 6.2) includes only variables related to material quality. In the second model, all other variables are added, except for

TABLE 6.2 Determinants of residents' satisfaction with the general housing situation in Nouvelle Lahraouiyine (results of an OLS regression model).

	(I)		*(II)*		*(III)*		*(IV)*	
	Standard coefficients	**Effect sizes**	**Standard coefficients**	**Effect sizes**	**Standard coefficients**	**Effect sizes**	**Standard coefficients**	**Effect sizes**
Satisfaction with the house	0.423★★★	0.239	0.367★★★	0.206	0.330★★★	0.173	0.328★★★	0.177
Satisfaction with public services	0.283★★★	0.101	0.182★★★	0.052	0.205★★	0.075	0.185★★	0.054
Neighbourhood cohesion			0.281★★★	0.115	0.257★★★	0.098	0.268★★★	0.109
Feeling of isolation			-0.148★★★	0.028	-0.134★★	0.020	-0.174★★★	0.041
Total transport costs			-0.111★	0.024	-0.136★	0.032	-0.131★	0.020
Born in Karyan Central					-0.197★★★	0.020	-0.140★★	0.007
Total household income							*(-0.034)*	*(-0.002)*
Interviewed person (age)							*(0.087)*	*(0.007)*
Interviewed person (sex)							*-0.142★★*	*0.022*
Interviewed person (work)							*0.121★*	*0.015*
★ $p < 0.05$ ★★ $p < 0.01$ ★★★ $p < 0.001$	corr. $R^2 = 0.330$, n = 343		corr. $R^2 = 0.427$, n = 337		corr. $R^2 = 0.438$, n = 245		corr. $R^2 = 0.459$, n = 235	

"born in Karyan Central". Due to data inconsistencies related to this variable, the "n" is significantly lower. Therefore, this variable is only added in the third model. In the fourth model, I added four control variables roughly describing the personal characteristics of the interviewed person. These included sex (female=0/male=1), age bracket, household income bracket, and a dummy variable representing employment or unemployment. These variables further strengthened the model and may help separate programme-related effects of resettlement from personal characteristics.

Table 6.2 shows the standard coefficients β as well as effect sizes (Cohen's f2) for each independent variable based on heteroscedasticity-robust standard errors. Whereas the precise values of the effect sizes should not be overinterpreted, they provide a robust statistical indicator of the extent to which certain dwelling functions matter for resettled people. Model I includes only variables related to material quality, i.e., the shelter functions of the house. Both variables "satisfaction with the house" and "satisfaction with public services" have a medium to strong effect on people's satisfaction with the general housing situation and together account for one-third of its total variance. This seems to confirm the stated long-term desire of *bidonville* dwellers to escape vulnerable and stigmatised housing conditions (Arrif 1999, 302). However, the explanatory power of these shelter functions decreases if one adds independent variables that refer to the other dwelling functions that make up "adequate housing" (models II and III). Moreover, adding them increases the share of variance explained by the model to 43% (model II) and 44% (model III), respectively. This reveals that material quality alone is insufficient to explain people's general satisfaction with their overall housing situation. The significance of all added independent variables referring to social, economic, and emotional dwelling functions confirms that adequate housing signifies more than simply shelter. In models II and III, "satisfaction with the house" still has the strongest positive effect on general satisfaction levels. However, neighbourhood cohesion has a medium positive effect, too, and is even more relevant than "satisfaction with public services", which would also fall under "shelter". High transport costs as well as strong feelings of isolation have a modest negative effect on general satisfaction. The same holds true for people born in Karyan Central. Adding the control variables in model IV increases the share of explained variance to 46% but does not considerably change the weight of the independent variables. The household income and the age category of the interviewed person do not have a significant influence. Males and non-working people tend to perceive the new housing situation more critically than women and people who work. However, most of the variance of the dependent variables is explained by the four housing functions that make up the concept of "adequate housing" – and not by personal characteristics or household income.

Concerning social dwelling functions, the results of the regression analysis indicate that people are likely to be more satisfied with their housing situation if they develop good social relations and if they do not feel isolated. However, in most cases, as shown in Table 6.1, people felt disappointed with the new social situation after resettlement. Many people longed for the intensive social life in the *bidonville* when reflecting on the relatively anonymous and indifferent interpersonal relationships among residents of the new town. If mutual help amongst neighbours was a common practice in the *bidonville*, it has now become a more seldom, but therefore more esteemed, aspect of social life and general well-being.[4]

Concerning emotional dwelling functions, it is also of interest to look at the variable "born in Karyan Central", which has a modest negative effect on general satisfaction. The assumption is that people who were raised in Karyan Central have a higher emotional attachment to the place, being more used to its urban environment and being more familiar with its community. Hence, these people regret having been resettled more often and have greater difficulty adapting to the new town than people who moved to Karyan Central at a later stage. Several residents who resided for a long time in Karyan Central mentioned that residents who arrived relatively recently have been among the first who were willing to move. The latter may have primarily moved to Karyan Central to escape rental accommodation, and acquiring their own property may represent further social advancement to them. Others who moved to Karyan Central from outside the neighbourhood faced difficulties integrating themselves into established community structures and were likely to be happy with the break of social structures. However, it is important to note that a quantitative analysis is limited with regards to explaining emotional housing functions. A proxy referring to the birthplace may only capture a small part of the overall emotional connections to a place, and further qualitative research is necessary to better understand such emotional ties.

Concerning economic dwelling functions, the modest negative effects of the independent variable "total transport costs" shows that people who are forced to spend a significant amount of money on reaching their workplaces are likely to be more disappointed with the new housing situation after resettlement. Thus, the location of the new neighbourhood not only impacts social and emotional dwelling functions though the disruption of social networks and feelings of belonging, but also affects economic dwelling functions. Again, transport costs only capture one part of the overall economic dwelling functions. For example, the (im)possibilities of using the new housing unit for income-generating activities is important to consider as well, but could not be addressed by the existing data.

Group-based Factors Influencing (Dis)satisfaction

The heterogeneity and the sheer number of factors influencing satisfaction with life in Nouvelle Lahraouiyine makes it difficult to say who benefitted most from the resettlement. Single factors alone are unlikely to explain people's (dis)satisfaction with Nouvelle Lahraouiyine. A good example is income. Unlike for other resettlement projects, where people face more affordability issues, households' financial resources cannot explain why people (dis)like resettlement. Due to the third-party scheme, financial risks can no longer be associated with income alone, as they are not borne solely by households. Instead of referring to single variables only, the results from the regression analyses urge us to look at combinations of factors to identify "winners" and "losers" of resettlement. Based on the results of the regression analysis and additional qualitative data from both residents in Er-Rhamna and Nouvelle Lahraouiyine, it is possible to distinguish four population groups that have struggled more than others with resettlement (cf. Beier 2019).

A first group that is disproportionally affected by the negative aspects of displacement to Nouvelle Lahraouiyine are people with a strong sense of belonging to Hay Mohammadi and Karyan Central; this refers not only to people born in Hay Mohammadi. Such a high level of emotional attachment may also be related to the quality and history of the house that people had to vacate (cf. Zaki 2007). People with a large and established family home in Karyan Central often complained about resettlement because of a loss of investment, habitable space, physical housing comfort, and personal memories. Several respondents pointed with pride to their house in the *bidonville* as their own *oeuvre*: "If I am invited elsewhere, I only think about coming back to my home. This house has been my own work!" (54-year-old woman, Er-Rhamna). For others, place attachment was the result of established neighbourhood ties based on mutual trust and help. One young, resettled woman described it as follows: "In Karyan Central, you could leave your doors open. Everyone knew each other and we all took care of each other". Because of the influx of people from other neighbourhoods to Nouvelle Lahraouiyine, the loss of former neighbourhood structures and increased heterogeneity weakened community solidarity. For others, place attachment was heavily related to the character of Hay Mohammadi – its central location, its vibrancy, and its markets. For them, the move to Nouvelle Lahraouiyine meant moving to the "countryside" – away from the diverse opportunities of the "urban". One retired former factory worker, for example, longed for the times when he used to go to the city centre to drink a glass of wine. Back then, it was possible to take a late bus back home – something that, for him, was no longer possible in the new town.

A second group includes residents that were affected by an opaque and unjust resettlement process. Disproportionally often, these were members of larger, multi-generational households that contested the number of plots allocated to them. For example, several people who had married just before the resettlement was announced did not receive their own plots, because they were not counted as a married couple during the census. Another married respondent was not counted because he was in prison during the census. However, also less powerful individuals such as widows, divorced wives, illegitimate children, and victims of internal family conflicts may have been affected. While the former group struggled to get the attribution rights transferred from their former husbands, the latter often used to live in uncounted, small extensions to houses in Karyan Central. They faced difficulties in claiming their place in the household after resettlement. Several people belonging to these groups were forcibly evicted from Karyan Central, could not (yet) move to a new flat, and had to stay with friends or relatives or even became homeless. As they were not living in Nouvelle Lahraouiyine during the data collection period, they were not represented in the survey data and could only be accessed through qualitative methods.

A third group – also related to implementation – suffered from the shortcomings of the third-party approach (Beier 2021). Some third-party investors did not finish constructing the houses or did not construct them in an appropriate way, which forced resettled residents to occupy building shells or to live in inadequately constructed dwellings that carried the risk of collapsing. As mentioned above, this risk was rather randomly distributed among all households depending on a third-party investor.

A last group relates more to economic dwelling functions and includes persons with specific occupational activities that have become less attractive or were less in demand following resettlement. Among them were factory workers earning a minimum wage. The available income of these workers disproportionally decreased because of new transport expenses required to reach their workplaces, which were closer to their former homes. Because of this, several workers gave up their old jobs. Other occupational groups such as day labourers, *bricoleurs* (artisan day labourers), and small-scale craft workers lost their previous income sources through displacement and the demolition of Karyan Central. They had to search for other jobs and most of them were able to secure one. However, a feeling that it has become more complicated and time-consuming to find a reliable income source is dominant among resettled dwellers who have lost their jobs or have changed their occupation. In Hay Mohammadi, if there was a need, social networks allowed one to quickly find work to earn an additional wage. This flexibility has disappeared in the peripheral and less-populated new town.

Towards People-centric Notions of Adequate Housing

One central question was answered in this chapter: What is considered "adequate" housing? Similar to the ideas of Turner (1972) and Navez-Bouchanine and Dansereau (2002), the empirical findings urge us to understand adequate housing in the context of resettlement by seeing it through the eyes of the resettled dweller in relation to a set of subjectively valued housing functions that nevertheless should be viewed against a backdrop of structural constraints and (limited) opportunities for spatial appropriation (see also Harroud 2019). In this regard, the chapter has argued that quantitative research can complement in-depth qualitative analyses in a useful way, providing a more general yet heterogeneous picture of how people of a certain community perceive adequate housing in the context of urban resettlement, despite important limitations, such as the depth of research. The ability to sketch a more general picture of the effects and experiences of housing-related resettlement may help to balance limitations of in-depth analyses of individual cases. As noted by Zaki (2007), some resettled dwellers for example tend to glorify past life in the *bidonville* and, hence, construct a memorial reality that has little in common with their former experiences. Likewise, quantitative data analyses may help to back important claims made in qualitative research – for example, concerning the importance of neighbourhood ties.

The analysis of the resettlement of Karyan Central offers a good opportunity to look at the meaning of "adequate" housing, as questions of affordability have played only a minor role due to the third-party system implemented here. Hence, it offers the chance to look at *adequate* housing without confusing it with *affordable* housing. The empirical results allow for two interrelated statements concerning adequate housing. First, adequate housing is complex and highly subjective and, hence, requires careful empirical analysis. Resettled residents themselves found it difficult to form a definite opinion about whether they were satisfied or not with their new housing situation in the new town, in this case six years after resettlement. Notions of an adequate home are likely to differ between neighbours and even within families. Second, the empirical findings have underlined that "adequate" does not refer to only the physical dimensions of housing related to shelter. Satisfaction with the housing situation after resettlement depends on multiple factors that relate to social, economic, and emotional functions of the house and may only be fully understood by looking at personal life trajectories (Navez-Bouchanine and Dansereau 2002; Dupont et al. 2017; Strong 2018). Certainly, physical housing comfort is significant for dwellers who had been awaiting access to formal property and socially respected houses. However, aspects such as neighbourhood cohesion, an accessible location, job opportunities, and a sense of belonging have a remarkable quantitatively measurable – impact that should not be underestimated by policy makers in urban resettlement. In other words, the data show that adequate housing means much more to people than the material quality of shelter, even if people longed for the latter.

Thus, large-scale housing programmes addressing "inadequate" housing are unlikely to produce "adequate" housing because they are unable to account for demand-side perspectives. In fact, the concept of adequate housing seems to be much more in line with participatory upgrading approaches instead of policies that imply the resettlement of entire communities. As we see in the case of the VSB programme, resettlement may take place without prior sound empirical research. Consequently, the use of a reductionist, one-size-fits-all approach means that housing-related urban resettlement programmes come to define housing quality from an external, supply-side perspective. Being an attractive option to many governments for multiple reasons, such kinds of supply-driven approaches define housing as shelter only, disregarding livelihood impacts of housing projects and thus ignoring nuanced housing demands (Croese, Cirolia, and Graham 2016). These programmes only provide inadequate, short-term solutions to structural housing issues, if at all (Turok 2016, 236). If, over time, housing in Nouvelle Lahraouiyine will further deteriorate and if public authorities will not invest in the infrastructure, accessibility, and economic development of the new town, resettlement is likely to have no or even negative impacts on the fight against urban poverty and exclusion. In this case, it is just a matter of time before renewed claims for adequate housing will start emerging in the "new town".

Notes

1 *Villes Sans Bidonvilles* has frequently been translated into "Cities Without Slums" because of the programme's ideological reference to the homonymous agenda of "Cities Alliance". However, in the Moroccan context and following the official definition of *bidonville* by the

VSB authorities, the more accurate translation is "shantytown" (Ministère de l'Habitat, de l'Urbanisme et de la Politique de la Ville 2012). In Morocco, the term "slum" would incorporate other settlement types that are not targeted by the VSB programme.
2 The French name *Carrières Centrales* is also commonly used.
3 The number of dissatisfied people is likely to be higher if accounting for those people that could not be addressed by the survey, as they were not living in Nouvelle Lahraouiyine during the data collection period. This group includes those who were opposed to (parts of) the programme and who were forcibly evicted from Karyan Central following their refusal to move voluntarily.
4 See Arrif (1999), Zaki (2007), and Beier (2019) for more detailed qualitative analyses of social life in *bidonvilles* and how it changes through resettlement.

References

Arrif, A. 1999. "Les compétences citadins à l'épreuve de l'exclusion: l'exemple du bidonville de Ben M'Sik à Casablanca (Maroc)." In *L'Urbain dans le monde arabe: politiques, instruments et acteurs*, edited by P. Signoles, G. El Kadi, and R. Sidi Boumedine, 297–317. Paris: CNRS Éditions.

Beier, R. 2019. *From the City to the Desert: Analysing Shantytown Resettlement in Casablanca, Morocco From Residents' Perspectives*. Berlin: Logos.

Beier, R. 2020. "The world-class city comes by tramway: Reframing Casablanca's urban peripheries through public transport." *Urban Studies* 57 (9): 1827–1844.

Beier, R. 2021. "Visible and splintered informalities – Reflections on the production of 'formality' in a Moroccan housing programme." *International Journal of Urban and Regional Research* (online first).

Beier, R., and C. Strava. 2020. "Losing or gaining home? Experiences of resettlement from Casablanca's slums." In *The Everyday Life of Urban Inequality: Ethnographic Case Studies of Global Cities*, edited by A. Storey, M. Sheehan, and J. Bodoh-Creed, 3–22. Lanham, MD: Lexington Books.

Bogaert, K. 2011. "The problem of slums: Shifting methods of neoliberal urban government in Morocco." *Development and Change* 42 (3): 709–731.

Bogaert, K. 2018. *Globalized Authoritarianism: Megaprojects, Slums, and Class Relations in Urban Morocco*. Minneapolis: University of Minnesota Press.

Buckley, R.M., A. Kallergis, and L. Wainer. 2016. "The emergence of large-scale housing programs: Beyond a public finance perspective." *Habitat International* 54: 199–209.

Caldeira, T.P.R. 2017. "Peripheral urbanization: Autoconstruction, transversal logics, and politics in cities of the Global South." *Environment and Planning D* 35 (1): 3–20.

Cernea, M.M. 2003. "For a new economics of resettlement: A sociological critique of the compensation principle." *International Social Science Journal* 55 (175): 37–45.

Coelho, K., 2016. "Tenements, ghettos, or neighborhoods? Outcomes of slum clearance interventions in Chennai." *Review of Development & Change* 21 (1): 111–136.

Croese, S., L.R. Cirolia, and N. Graham. 2016. "Towards Habitat III: confronting the disjuncture between global policy and local practice on Africa's 'challenge of slums'." *Habitat International* 53: 237–242.

Dupont, V., D. Jordhus-Lier, E. Braathen, and C. Sutherland. 2017. "Modalities of social mobilisation in substandard settlements." In *The Politics of Slums in the Global South: Urban Informality in Brazil, India, South Africa and Peru*, edited by V. Dupont, D. Jordhus-Lier, C. Sutherland, and E. Braathen, 181–209. Abingdon: Routledge.

Easthope, H., E. Power, D. Rogers, and R. Dufty-Jones. 2020. "Thinking relationally about housing and home." *Housing Studies* 35 (9): 1493–1500.

Florin, B., and N. Semmoud. 2010. "Mobilités résidentielles et territorialisations dans les villes du Maghreb." *Espace populations sociétés* 2010 (2–3): 365–377.

Galster, G. 1987. "Identifying the correlates of dwelling satisfaction: an empirical critique." *Environment and Behavior* 19 (5): 539–568.

Harroud, T. 2019. "D'une marginalité à l'autre: droit à la ville et pratiques de readaptation des 'bidonvillois' dans les nouvelles marges urbaines de Rabat." *Annales de Géographie* 729/730: 14–37.

Heslop, J., C. McFarlane, and E. Ormerod. 2020. "Relational housing across the North–South divide: Learning between Albania, Uganda, and the UK." *Housing Studies* 35 (9): 1607–1627.

Huchzermeyer, M. 2009. "The struggle for in situ upgrading of informal settlements: A reflection on cases in Gauteng." *Development Southern Africa* 26 (1): 59–73.

Iraki, A. 2006. "L'organisation des solidarités dans des territoires en construction: quartiers restructurés au Maroc." *Espaces et sociétés* (127): 63–77.

Jacobs, J.M., and S.J. Smith. 2008. "Living room: Rematerialising home." *Environment and Planning A* 40 (3): 515–519.

Koenig, D. 2006. "Enhancing local development in development-induced displacement resettlement projects." In *Development-induced Displacement: Problems, Policies and People*, edited by C.J. de Wet, 105–140. New York: Berghahn.

Koenig, D. 2018. "Problems endure despite policies: Urban livelihoods after forced displacement." In *Challenging the Prevailing Paradigm of Displacement and Resettlement: Risks, Impoverishment, Legacies, Solutions*, edited by M.M. Cernea and J.K. Maldonado, 75–94. Abingdon: Routledge.

Le Tellier, J. 2009. "Programme Villes Sans Bidonvilles et ingénierie sociale urbaine au Maroc." In *Habitat Social au Maghreb et au Sénégal: Gouvernance Urbaine et Participation en Questions*, edited by J. le Tellier and A. Iraki, 193–212. Paris: l'Harmattan.

Ministère de l'Habitat, de l'Urbanisme et de la Politique de la Ville (MHUPV). 2012. *National Report: Curbing Shanty-Towns: The Moroccan Experience*. Rabat: MHUPV.

Navez-Bouchanine, F. 2003. "Les chemins tortureux de l'expérience démocratique marocaine à travers les bidonvilles." *Espaces et sociétés* 112: 59–82.

Navez-Bouchanine, F. 2012. "Les nouvelles voies de la négociation dans les politiques de résorption des bidonvilles au Maroc: entre recasement et accompagnement social." In *Effets sociaux des politiques urbaines: L'entre-deux des politiques institutionnelles et des dynamiques sociales: Algérie, Maroc, Liban, Mauritanie*, edited by F. Navez-Bouchanine and A. Deboulet, 166–218. Paris: Karthala.

Navez-Bouchanine, F., and F. Dansereau. 2002. "Les stratégies résidentielles dans la ville fragmentée: le cas de la ville marocaine." In *Gestion du développement urbain et stratégies résidentielles des habitants*, edited by F. Dansereau and F. Navez-Bouchanine, 19–65. Paris: l'Harmattan.

Nikuze, A., R. Sliuzas, J. Flacke, and M. van Maarseveen. 2019. "Livelihood impacts of displacement and resettlement on informal households: A case study from Kigali, Rwanda." *Habitat International* 86: 38–47.

Office of the United Nations High Commissioner for Human Rights (OHCHR) and United Nations Human Settlements Programme (UN-Habitat). 2009. *The Right to Adequate Housing: Human Rights Fact Sheet* 21. Geneva: United Nations.

Patel, S., R. Sliuzas, and N. Mathur. 2015. "The risk of impoverishment in urban development-induced displacement and resettlement in Ahmedabad." *Environment and Urbanization* 27 (1): 231–256.

Rachik, A. 2002. *Casablanca: L'urbanisme de l'urgence*. Casablanca: Najah El-Jadida.

Strong, M. 2018. "Influence of memory on post-resettlement place attachment." In *Explorations in Place Attachment*, edited by J. Smith, 19–32. Abingdon: Routledge.

Toutain, O. 2013. "Le programme 'Villes Sans Bidonvilles' au Maroc: un bilan social questionné dans un contexte urbain sous tension." In *Quartiers informels d'un monde arabe en transition: réflexions et perspectives pour l'action urbaine*, edited by P.-A. Barthel and S. Jaglin, 91–108. Paris: Agence Française de Développement.

Turner, J.F.C. 1968. "Housing priorities, settlement patterns, and urban development in modernizing countries." *Journal of the American Institute of Planners* 34 (6): 354–363.

Turner, J.F.C. 1972. "Housing as a verb." In *Freedom to Build: Dweller Control of the Housing Process*, edited by J.F.C. Turner and R. Fichter, 148–175. New York: Macmillan.

Turok, I. 2016. "Housing and the urban premium." *Habitat International* 54 (3): 234–240.

Zaki, L. 2006. "L'action publique au bidonville: l'État entre gestion par le manque, 'éradication' des kariens et accompagnement social des habitants." *L'Année du Maghreb* 2: 303–320.

Zaki, L. 2007. "Après le bidonville: les relogés de Lahjajma (Casablanca): entre déni et nostalgie." In *L'enseignement supérieur dans la mondialisation libérale*, edited by S. Mazzella, 277–294. Tunis: IRMC.

Zaki, L. 2010. "L'électrification temporaire des bidonvilles casablancais: aspects et limites d'une transformation." *Politique africaine* 120: 45–66.

Zaki, L. 2013. "Montée en puissance des mobilisations dans les bidonvilles et transformation de l'action publique au Maroc: de l'ouverture des années 1990 au printemps arabe." In *Quartiers informels d'un monde arabe en transition: réflexions et perspectives pour l'action urbaine*, edited by P.-A. Barthel and S. Jaglin, 37–52. Paris: Agence Française de Développement.

7

RESETTLEMENT AND THE EVERYDAY PRODUCTION OF LIVED SPACE

Urban Informality as a Way of Life in Tehran, Iran

Toktam Ashnaiy and Erhard Berner

Introduction

The public image of informal settlements is invariably negative, be it the favelas of São Paulo, the slums of Mumbai, or the marginal settlements of Tehran. Labels assigned to informal settlements, such as "shantytown", "bidonville", or "encroachment", are linked to perceptions of underdevelopment and human misery. Ever since the end of the Second World War, modernisation as a Eurocentric concept has been advanced as the preferred strategy to facilitate the development of "poor" countries (Escobar 1995, 40; Ziai 2013). To authorities, modernising a country entails confronting its "backwardness" (Escobar 1995, 41), encapsulated in the concept of informality, by rendering the informal formal. Urban modernity is built upon a formal order that urban planners believe cannot coexist with the "disorder" and spatial "unruliness" associated with informality (Kamete 2013). Thus, in mainstream urban development, a formal-informal dichotomy has emerged, closely related to a developed-developing country divide and leading to a sense of alienation among urban dwellers residing in informal settlements. This distinction between formal and informal has historically served as a multifaceted tool for naming, managing, governing, producing, and even critiquing contemporary cities; it has been named a governing technique (McFarlane 2012, McFarlane and Waibel 2016) that allocates to states a particular governance domain and form of intervention. As such, it has been used to design and implement policies of formalisation across the globe that imply the eradication of informality through, amongst others, the eviction of inhabitants of informal settlements, along with their displacement and relocation to social housing (UN-Habitat 2014).

Iran's Mehr Housing Scheme (MHS) is one such resettlement project. Launched in 2007, this project, headed by Iran's Ministry of Roads and Urban Development, was intended to provide mass affordable housing to all low-income groups, prevent

DOI: 10.4324/9781003124559-9

the expansion of existing or the emergence of new informal settlements, and counter an increase in population growth rates in informal settlements (Mehr Housing n.d.). Since 2009, under the MHS, 2.2 million Mehr housing units have been rolled out in approximately 1,000 villages, towns, and cities across the country (MURD News 2019a). Of these, over 1.1 million units had been occupied by applicants by 2019 (MURD News 2019b) indicating that over 50% of the quantitative targets of the project had been met by then. As this research will show, resettled residents scattered across various sites in urban areas viewed this relocation as undesirable, as their needs and aspirations were not completely met. The MHS thus appears to be an instrument for controlling informality in an inherent conflict between the objectives of authorities and planners and the desires of those targeted by the scheme.

We will argue that this conflict stems from mainstream perceptions of urban informality as a blight on the city, to be eradicated through resettlement schemes such as the MHS. We critically discuss these perceptions by applying a post-development approach to detail this conflict and its effects, venturing into the hardly explored, yet significant features of lived space as developed by people residing in informal settlements. A post-development lens challenges the dominant perception of development that emerged from so-called "developed countries" and that is to be adopted by "underdeveloped" countries (Escobar 1995; Ziai 2015). It also criticises development as a concept legitimising organised interventions in the lives of people defined as "less developed" and intrusions in collective affairs according to a generalised standard of improvement. According to this approach, in reality there are numerous ways of living, and it is up to each society to invent its own ways (Escobar 1995; Ziai 2015).

By applying a post-development approach to understanding informality, our research will show that the residents of the Mianabad informal settlement studied here created "people-led homes" for themselves, which differ significantly from the "planned shelters" provided to resettled households under the MHS scheme. We will argue the contrast between these two constructed concepts ("people-led homes" and "planned shelters") represents a conflict between the objectives of authorities to eradicate informality and the desires of those targeted by the scheme to retain informal practices. Findings underline that the production of lived spaces and the way of living in informal settlements should be regarded in their own right and not as processes contributing to "development" in the traditional sense. A paradigm shift towards an alternative approach to informality in urban planning is long overdue.

Our research explores the contrast between the two concepts introduced above by comparing the making of lived spaces at MHS sites and in the Mianabad informal settlement. The first concept of "planned shelter" refers to a prescribed mode of living propagated by authorities through the MHS, embodied in formal houses provided to those resettled to MHS sites. The second is that of "people-led homes" that introduces a way of living based on informal strategies, as practiced in the Mianabad informal settlement. A question arising after comparing these two ways of living is which drivers shaping the lived space in the informal settlement were not taken into account in the resettlement project. This observation points to the necessity of a paradigm shift in urban renewal strategies to include the voices of dwellers of informal settlements with particular views of informality.

As the MHS was a scheme implemented countrywide and following a comprehensive and general instruction not informed by geographical, cultural, or social studies reflecting local dynamics and potential impacts, a critical examination of the MHS based on a document study is presented. For this purpose, secondary data were collected to better understand the conditions and challenges of low-income groups' relocation to MHS sites. We selected articles and reports that provide evaluations and analyses of the MHS in terms of conditions, modalities, and challenges that people encountered after being resettled. These selected articles showcase the perspectives of selected resettled groups. These local and international articles published between 2009 and 2019 presented rich and comprehensive data that could be used to understand how people perceived their relocation to various MHS sites.

On the other hand, to better grasp the concept of informality and the creative construction of lived space in informal settlements, the Mianabad informal settlement was selected as a case study because of its noteworthy transformation from a small, rural village to a significant urban informal settlement over the course of four decades Furthermore, most of its residents have lived in Mianabad for over 20 years, providing us with a good opportunity to record and analyse their experiences of life in this location as it changed. A qualitative research methodology was applied to examine how the studied group of inhabitants of Mianabad understand their lives in informal settlements and seek to shape their lived spaces. Time was spent in Mianabad between 2018 and 2019, and empirical data were collected by means of a series of interviews and focus group discussions with 25 residents of Mianabad who lived in the settlement for at least 20 years, as well as by means of direct observations.

Conceptual Framework

An Enforced Mainstream Urban Development Approach

According to Escobar (1984), development can be viewed as a series of political technologies intended to manage and give shape to the undesired realities of developing countries, including widespread poverty. A mainstream approach to development has stereotyped the Global South as backward and underdeveloped and depicts it as "planet of slums" (Davis 2009) inhabited by a "surplus humanity" (Roy 2011a; Pieterse 2008; Villamizar-Duarte 2015). From such a perspective, urban informality is viewed as a critical development problem of cities in the Global South, and authorities use this perspective to justify repressive intervention projects (Herath 2009) to deal with the supposed "shortcomings" of urban spaces. Therefore, formalisation has been applied as a top-down strategy in a bid to control urban informality.

Engagement with different "shadows" on the edges of urban theory (McFarlane 2008) has led to a "southern turn" in urban studies (Rao 2006) and the inclusion of knowledge produced in and on "southern cities" that has helped in rethinking the geography of authoritative knowledge (Oldfield 2014; Roy 2009). In this regard, a critical perspective of development that views it as "a hegemonic form of representation" (Escobar 1995, 53) is characteristic of the post-development school (Sachs 1992; Rahnema and Bawtree 1997; for a comprehensive discussion, see Ziai 2013). A post-development research approach is characterised by a focus on local culture and knowledge, a critical stance towards established scientific discourses, and the defence and promotion of localised, pluralistic grassroots movements (Ziai 2015). This approach seeks to shift the conceptual framework of discursive analysis to envision the popular resistance of local communities. It intends to critique the logics and devices constructed in the name of "development" in the conventional sense, valuing the knowledge and experiences of local, self-reliant participatory and collective actions as the fundamental sources for alternative social change. Thus, informality can be read differently and in a novel way as representing possibility and autonomous change (Bayat 2000; Robinson 2002, 2006; AlSayyad 2004; Roy 2009, 2012; Pieterse 2008). Moreover, recasting informality can contribute to a paradigm shift in the social sciences toward the inclusion of grounded knowledge that captures lived realities. Empirical research in the Global South is extending ways of thinking about informality, in particular how it can be recognised, studied, expressed, lived, and practiced in particular ways (Bunnell and Harris 2012). Thus, recent research is increasingly built on concrete political and social relations, such as those linked to informality. This might be revealed for example by placing greater emphasis on ethnographic approaches to trace the dynamics of informal and little-known ways of life.

Recasting Urban Informality

In conceptual terms, a number of scholars have put forward new propositions that challenge the conventional formal-informal dichotomy, in particular through their use of a post-development approach in the study of urban dynamics. For instance, Roy (2011b, 233) describes informality as a heuristic device that uncovers the ever-shifting urban relationship between the legal and illegal, legitimate and illegitimate, authorised and unauthorised, and so on, which serves to deconstruct the very basis of state legitimacy and its various instruments: maps, surveys, property, zoning and, most importantly, the law.

AlSayyad (2004) views urban informality as "a way of life" with specific "forms of social action and organisation" that emerges from a specific spatial framework, social structure, and set of attitudes (26). Similarly, such an alternative conceptualisation of informality characterises it as a way of "[struggling] for survival and self-development" (Roy 2012, 5). In the Middle East, subaltern groups have used numerous tactics to challenge the meaning of formal order and state prerogatives (Bayat 2000; AlSayyad 2004; Roy 2012). Appadurai (as cited in Roy

2012) studied the political actions of Mumbai's slum dwellers, similarly showing that informality strategies employed in these forms of negotiation of access to amenities and the protection of their urban way of life can be viewed as a form of "deep democracy". Recent debates on informal urbanism, supplemented by a number of empirical studies highlighting the need for a focus on informality as a way of life, support a paradigm shift away from a conventional concept of informality as a territorial formation or a labour categorisation (Villamizar-Duarte 2015) to an alternative understanding of informality as a form of negotiation that disrupts formal regulations (McFarlane 2012; Roy 2012; Simone 2006).

Academic discussions on informality have attempted to evaluate the making of everyday life and its relevance for a materialist, transformative perception of urban space (Crawford 2004). Dialectics of everyday urbanism have emerged as a fundamental approach to conceiving informality (McFarlane 2012; Dovey 2012). In this regard, the way the residents of informal settlements operate resourcefully is a "practice of everyday life" as conceptualised by Michel de Certeau (1984). It can be acknowledged as a set of commonplace tactics used by the residents of informal settlements to "undo the oppressive grid of power and discipline" (Roy 2012, 5) by developing acts of resistance in the face of a dominant socio-spatial order that is adopted and enforced by planners as lawful strategies (Villamizar-Duarte 2015).

To this end, residents of urban informal settlements are seen as creative co-producers of urban space who seek to change their physical, spatial, and socio-political environment through their everyday practices and their making and remaking of life histories (Hosseinioon 2019). Their everyday practices can reflect their ongoing struggles to reclaim and defend the "right of being" or the "right to the city" (Lefebvre 1996) in a society that excludes them (Villamizar-Duarte 2015; Hosseinioon 2019). To assert this right to the city, ordinary people produce informal settlements through a combination of individual and collective spontaneity, desires and habits, improvised expressions of urban life, and the multi-purpose use of buildings and space (Elian 2015). In addition, everyday life is formed, performed, and disrupted through broader cultural, economic, and political dispositions (McFarlane and Silver 2017).

This is linked to Simone's (as cited in Graham and McFarlane 2015) conceptualisation of infrastructure that is represented as a fluid and dynamic intersection of and between social and material urban worlds. The "social infrastructures" that people put together to sustain life directly refer to people's activities in the city that can facilitate the social interactions (McFarlane and Silver 2017; Simone 2004). Hence, "people as infrastructure" indicates the creation of a social configuration across a range of singular capacities and needs, as well as efforts to achieve maximal outcomes from a minimal set of elements (Simone 2004). They opt for incremental ways in an effort to improve their housing and infrastructure conditions and access, along with managing dynamic reconfigurations and savings in labour and capital (Berner 2000; Silver 2014).

In the light of current studies and taking into account the dynamic complementarities and interrelationships between formal and informal activities, informal settlements cannot be considered marginal and excluded parts of urban spaces. This framing provides a useful conceptual lens for understanding both the continuities and shifts in thought on informal settlements.

The Mehr Housing Scheme as a Large-scale Resettlement Project

The largest of Iran's state-led resettlement programs is the Mehr Housing Scheme (MHS), rolled out nationwide in 2007. Proposed as part of the Fourth Economic, Social, and Cultural Development Plan of the Islamic Republic of Iran (2005–2009), the scheme was envisioned to provide affordable social housing units to six million low-income households across the country (12% of the urban population) (Ajiliyan Momtaz, Rafieyan, and Agha Safari 2018; Etminani-Ghasrodashti, Majedi, and Paydar 2017; Ghafourian and Hesari 2018). Since 2009, under the MHS, 2.2 million Mehr housing units have been rolled out in approximately 1,000 villages, towns, and cities across the country (MURD News 2019a). Of these, over 1.1 million units had been occupied by applicants by 2019 (MURD News 2019b)

The MHS was implemented in many Iranian cities. The national authorities determined specific conditions for applicants who were interested in applying for one of the houses. Four main conditions had to be fulfilled: (1) not owning housing or land at the time of the application, (2) not receiving other government benefits, (3) being married or head of the household, and (4) having lived in the respective city for at least five years. Applicants needed to submit a request for these units by joining the Mehr Housing Cooperative that was in charge of granting or denying applications (Shamsoddini, Safariyan, and Nekooyibakhsh 2018; Zanjani, Golkar, and Mohammadi 2011). The Mehr Housing Cooperative was also responsible for the construction of houses, while the government played a supporting role by granting the housing cooperative free public land and long-term loans for constructing houses. In addition, half of the fees for construction permits and other costs related to preparing land were covered by public subsidies (Ghafourian and Hesari 2018), while 20% of the primary cost was financed through the savings and contributions of applicants (Zanjani, Golkar, and Mohammadi 2011). Applicants were to pay back the loans within 15 years of the units having been delivered to them (Shokouhibidhendi, Sobhani, and Zhand 2018).

One of the most important challenges in providing housing to low-income groups in Iran is the rising price of land. The government consequently waived property costs by allocating public land for housing that would allow applicants to receive houses without paying for the land on which it was situated. Thus, instead of selling property titles to applicants of the Mehr housing units, the government offered them 99-year leasehold contracts (Etminani-Ghasrodashti, Majedi and Paydar 2017; Ajiliyan Momtaz, Rafieyan, and Agha Safari 2018). The policy of discounting the land price from the total cost of housing construction in the MHS was supposed to decrease inequity in access to appropriate housing, help control house prices, prevent the marginalisation of those not able to afford houses, and reduce construction costs to ensure the affordability of legal access to a house for low-income households (Ajiliyan Momtaz, Rafieyan, and Agha Safari 2018; Ghafourian and Hesari 2018, Saeedi Rezvani and Kazemi 2011).

The MHS houses were constructed on a large scale, comprising small apartment units of on average 75 square meters (Ajiliyan Momtaz, Rafieyan, and Agha Safari 2018). The apartment blocks were typically designed as uniform buildings of at least four floors in smaller towns and as high-rise buildings in larger cities, usually constructed in a grid pattern. Poor landscaping, a lack of amenities such as parks, and a lack of services including public transportation were common. Moreover, in order to reduce the tremendous expenses incurred under the scheme, mainly low-value, public land situated at the margins of the city was allocated (Ghafourian & Hesari 2018).

The project has been criticised by academics for not having a convincing motivation for the selection of specific sites and not having been informed by proper feasibility studies (Ajiliyan Momtaz, Rafieyan and Agha Safari 2018). Due to the national and countrywide scale of this project, its execution followed a single and general instruction. For this reason, scholars have been vocal about the uniformity of the works, which seemed to disregard local requirements and regional variations (Shokouhibidhendi, Sobhani, and Zhand 2018; Alaedini and Jamshidinasab 2015). The top-down planning process that disregards the needs and opinions of the potential residents has arguably turned the project into an opportunity for economic exploitation, argue Shamsoddini, Safariyan, and Nekooyibakhsh (2018). Others have argued that the government has regarded this project as a political instrument to legitimise the exercise of its power and make decisions on behalf of its people based on its development-oriented role in the production of housing (Imani Jajarmi and Masoudian 2019).

Planned Shelters and a Prescribed Way of Living

In order to grasp the common features of life in formal houses as viewed by people resettled to MHS sites, we reviewed various scientific studies and articles that detailed such perspectives. The articles provided evaluations and analyses of the MHS in terms of conditions, modalities, and challenges that people encountered after being resettled. We attempted to provide a coherent framework to describe the defining characteristics of this prescribed mode of living and the unintended consequences of resettlement. To conduct a thematic analysis, we generated tiered categories and overall themes by coding the data. These are presented in Table 7.1.

The findings show that those groups relocated to formal houses under the MHS perceive the changes to their way of life as inherently negative, as the sub-categories presented in Table 7.1 show. Factors influencing their negative perceptions include the perceived presence of severe and constant cultural conflicts, a lack of sense of belonging, a loss of sense of home, social displacement, a sense of staying in a "campsite space", distrust in institutions, and disaffiliation. One of the residents' key points is the loss of a sense of home, i.e., the lack of appropriate human and cultural connections to the house and surrounding area. Residents strongly attributed the lack of a sense of belonging to their space to the lack of participation

TABLE 7.1 Themes and categories of perceptions of resettlement, extracted from the reviewed documents (2009–2019).

Overall themes	*Main categories*	*Sub-categories*
Collective culture	Cultural conflicts and struggles	Conflict between lifestyle and apartment design; disregard by urban planners of cultural and social issues; lack of a sense of collectivity; lack of mutual respect and trust.
Social ties	Lack of sense of belonging	Weak social interaction, social control, and social capital; lack of effectiveness of unofficial social control; lack of any kind of participation in social activities.
	Social dis-placement	Displacement and being thrown into an unfamiliar space away from other families; sense of disconnect and poor sense of identity among residents; lack of meaningful and free social interactions; lack of social grouping based on collective cultural values; permanent residency and blood relations.
	Loss of a sense of a home	Lack of appropriate human and cultural connections to the house and surrounding area; prioritisation by planners of economic aspects over the local and cultural aspects of housing provision; dormitorisation; lack of appropriate design based on social, economic, and cultural characteristics; lack of attention to the civic and conceptual aspects of home.
Living and housing space	"Campsite space"	Lack of sense of belonging; sense of temporary shelter; desire to escape; lack of connection to the environment.
	Distrust in institutions	Feeling of being disowned, humiliated, and discriminated against; perceived unbalanced power relations; a feeling of disempowerment; a sense of inferiority to other members of society.
	Disaffiliation	Problems regarding the formation of social networks due to a lack of trust; fewer subjective and objective connec-tions between members of society and subsequent lower participation in social activities; lack of collective identity.

Reviewed documents: Abedini 2018; Ajiliyan Momtaz, Rafieyan, and Agha Safari 2018; Etminani-Ghasrodashti, Majedi, and Paydar 2017; Ghafourian and Hesari 2018; Gholipour, Karimi, and Sadeghi 2019; Imani Jajarmi and Masoudian 2019; Masoudirad, Ebrahimzadeh and Rafieian 2017; Mohammadi, Parvin, and Rastegar 2019; Rafieian, Ajilian and Ahgasa-fari 2016; Shamsoddini, Safariyan, and Nekooyibakhsh 2018.

of the residents in social activities as one dimension of their former way of life. They referred to these new residential areas as "campsite spaces", revealing that they viewed the complexes as makeshift due to the way they were constructed, without a connection to the environment and without the possibility to forge relationships. Therefore, they felt disowned, humiliated, and disempowered, experiencing a lack of urban social relationships that can be understood as subjective and objective connections between the members of society and community. This resulted in an increase in disaffiliation, a decrease in participation in collective practices, and a lack of a collective identity.

Thus, although resettled groups came to own a house comprising four walls and a roof, they lost some features of their former way of life. The concept of planned shelter as put forth under the MHS is built on the strategy of what planners perceive as meeting "basic human needs", affecting the design of the dwellings, which residents considered of inferior quality. The MHS therefore appears to be an instrument for controlling informal settlements that reveals an inherent conflict between the desires of authorities and groups targeted by the scheme. To better understand their preferences for self-produced lived spaces and their dissatisfaction with and resistance to resettlement, we now turn to the Mianabad informal settlement.

Mianabad: From Rural Village to Urban Informal Settlement

This section applies a critical approach to the study of urban planning to discover how the dwellers of the Mianabad informal settlement cope with problems associated with life in an urban locale and invest their energies in the making of everyday life and development of their lived space. We will identify some key differences between the notion of "planned shelter" advocated by planners through the MHS and the lived space produced by residents of Mianabad.

Mianabad used to be a small village situated around 15 kilometres to the south-west of Tehran. Sustained by an agricultural economy and with an initial population numbering 30 in 1955, its population increased considerably from 10,000 to 18,000 residents between 1985 and 1995 following a revolutionary land reform process in 1963 during which agricultural land was rezoned as residential land and opened up for division and purchase. The village gradually turned into an informal settlement as interested persons started migrating to the area and constructing their houses without formal permission. Consequently, the population of Mianabad increased to 26,000 by 2015, the year in which it became an official urban district of the city of Eslamshahr (Statistical Centre of Iran 2016) (Figure 7.1). The municipal boundaries enclosing the settlement ensured that centralised control could be asserted on urban processes, including the informal construction and expansion of the settlement, in a way that was less possible when the settlement did not have strict demarcations.

Negotiating an Urban Way of Life

The way dwellings were constructed in Mianabad and the informal settlement expanded underwent a complete transformation over the past four decades. During the first stage of expansion of the settlement between 1975 and 1995, no strict control was imposed on the informal construction of housing structures by residents, since the settlement was loosely governed by regional authorities. Residents retained links to their places of origin through close families ties and kinship, which accelerated the trend of migration and the construction of shelters that seemed to spring up overnight. Moreover, illegal connections to public services such as electricity and water created acceptable living conditions and opportunities for micro-entrepreneurship to emerge in Mianabad.

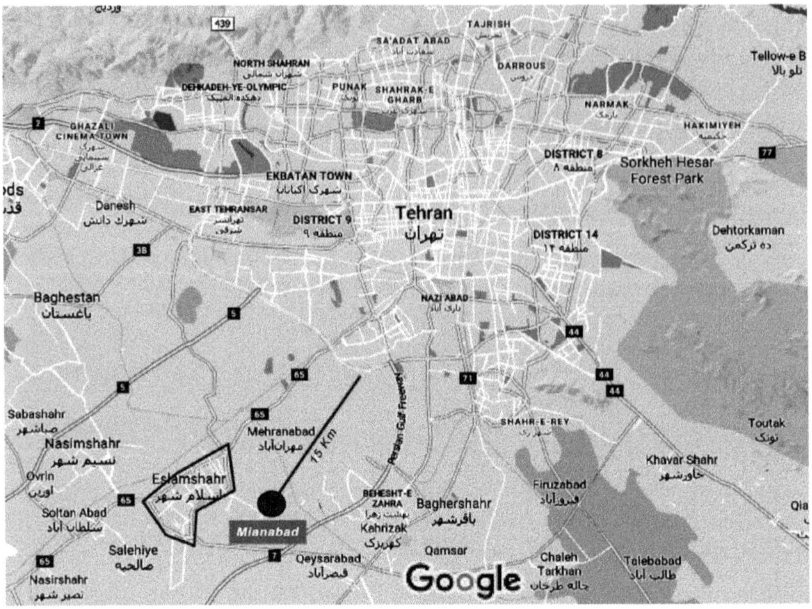

FIGURE 7.1 The Mianabad informal settlement, part of the city of Eslamshahr that lies approximately 15 kilometres to the southwest of Tehran.
Source: Google Maps, retrieved 5 November 2020.

During the second expansion stage (1995–2010), informal structures mushroomed and a large-scale conversion of agricultural land to urban land took place. Mediators providing a connection between people and public organisations were important drivers of informal urbanisation processes at this stage. By facilitating negotiation processes, they provided people with quick access to land. New structures were quickly torn down by authorities, leading to resistance by residents.

Barriers to the conversion of agricultural land into urban land imposed during the second stage of the rural-urban transformation were reinforced during the third stage (2010–2020). Relationships between governmental role players, including local, regional, and national authorities, were strengthened, informal construction activities were strictly controlled by the local authorities, and the mediators gradually started playing a less prominent role. Structures constructed overnight faced a growing risk of immediate demolition by local authorities. As AlSayyad (2004) argued, "if formality operates through the fixing of value, including the mapping of spatial value, then informality operates through the constant negotiability of value" (5). Thus, requesting an official building permit from the municipality was only one of several new negotiation tactics used to retain the informal character of the structures. In this way, houses were at first constructed legally, and informal additions were then made where possible. Residents often used building materials provided for the approved formal building for this purpose.

The above example illustrates that official regulations with regard to spatial transformation were heeded merely for the purpose of enabling flexible negotiation with authorities on the shape Mianabad would eventually come to assume. Residents sought to forge clientelist relations with role players, including the municipality, mediators, the Islamic rural and urban councils, and local organisations, to meet their needs to access infrastructure services. In this way, residents of Mianabad were able to resist a dominant socio-spatial order centred on the promotion of formality. Thus, informality as a "generalised practice" (McFarlane 2012; Simone 2006) can be regarded as an alternative urban order and a different way of organising space in which people access essential services by "negotiating citizenship" (Simone 2006), sharing the benefits of appreciating properties and a thriving economy.

Everyday Practices in Mianabad

Residents of Mianabad seek to create a lived space through an ongoing process of negotiation with local authorities. This section highlights some aspects of reality in this lived space ignored in mainstream approaches to urban planning. A study of people's everyday practices and lived experiences helped identify factors encouraging or inhibiting people's ability to produce space. Inhabitants adopted a variety of tactics to negotiate with municipal authorities about their freedom to shape their daily lives and lived spaces. In conjunction with governance responses, this led to the emergence of complex negotiation processes that have shaped the transformation of Mianabad as it changed from a village into an informal settlement. In the relative absence of a formal infrastructure system, "social infrastructure" within Mianabad is conceptualised as a system that shapes social exchanges, livelihoods, and dynamic relationships between people and things in a complex web of social-material relations.

One of the distinctive features of the process of constantly shaping a lived space in Mianabad is the way inhabitants create social relations and connections by using and transforming public spaces. The evaluation of people's collective behaviour regarding the use of public spaces such as streets and sidewalks indicates the various meanings and usages assigned to such spaces. That outsiders seem reluctant only to enter this space, not to mention their reluctance to sell goods or offer services, has changed it into a communal and more intimate one for residents. For instance, a group of residents of the Amirakram neighbourhood in Mianabad often choose to sit on the sidewalk in front of their houses, which casts it as a semi-private space simply by their carrying out a sofa from one of the houses. Hence, urban space has functions beyond its formal and conventional conceptualisation, such as in this case. Maryam, a member of one of the families gathering on sidewalks, said:

> Our house is too small to accommodate five people. We put a sofa out, in front of the street. We usually go out and talk with our neighbours here in the evening. We can see the pedestrians and children who play on the street.

Some entrepreneurs or vendors similarly turn other public places into semi-private spaces by parking their small handcart or a leased pickup truck in a specific public place. These vendors often regard "their" spots where they sell their wares as specific and reserved, as it helps potential clients to easily find them. Ali, a vendor, explained:

> I have been working here for a long time. All the people know me very well. I am familiar with this street. My cart has its permanent place. This is the place where I can make my life and livelihood.

Even though residents informally occupy public spaces, their encounters with these spaces show that they familiarise them by converting them into intimate spaces. In this regard, some shopkeepers extend their shops to the sidewalk to display and sell their goods and services, drawing passers-by, thereby producing combined spaces (Figure 7.2). Mohsen, a textile retailer, reckoned:

> The open space in front of every store belongs to it. I am most often sitting on my chair placed in front of my store on the sidewalk. Not only can I meet and have a conversation with people and my neighbours, I can also advertise my wares. It is fun and works for me.

Moreover, field observations carried out in 2019 also show that this alteration of public space is shaped day by day through everyday activities and residents' collective and inherent willingness – and desire – to make a place their own. Thus,

FIGURE 7.2 Familiarised spaces in Mianabad.
Source: Photos taken on 25 October 2019 by the authors.

residents are able to "familiarise" urban spaces through transformative everyday practices, making them combined private-public spaces, facilitating social connections and dialogue. Hence, communal spaces become more familiar, intimate, forgiving, liveable, and unaffected.

Residents of Mianabad were able to better manage their living conditions through an incremental and dynamic process (Graham and McFarlane 2015; McFarlane 2012; Berner 2000; Simone 2006). For instance, illegal connections to public services such as water and electricity networks enabled by linking up to their neighbours' connections provide a pragmatic option for incrementally configuring access to infrastructure. This process includes a shifting focus from the development of material infrastructure to the creation of a space for networking, cooperation, and the forging of new relationships. Incremental infrastructure development can be framed not only as a material improvisation but also as a form of social collaboration and cooperation through which residents reproduce living spaces through everyday practices and generate conditions of possibility. For example, changes in the use of residential housing spaces, such as by converting the ground floor of a residential building into a shop, take place incrementally in order to create opportunities and redundancy. Redundancy implies the diversification of livelihoods to mitigate potential crises. Most of these shops serving as an alternative income source are small grocery stores that reduce household insecurity and create income opportunities for mothers of young children and elderly and/or disabled family members (Berner, Gomez and Knorringa 2012). Mobile phone shops, repair service providers, and beauty salons serve the same purpose.

Although such activities create economic opportunities for particular individuals such as shopkeepers, neighbours also benefit indirectly from this. Particularly the proliferation of micro-commercial activities such as small grocery stores contributes to the economic integration of a neighbourhood, which also strengthens social relationships and intensifies face-to-face and everyday interactions. Furthermore, stores may play a role in easing financial burdens by offering savings and credit facilities, inspiring residents' trust in their social networks. Mahmoud, a shopkeeper, explained how this system would typically work:

> After opening a store, our neighbours asked me to open an account for the store in order to deposit a fixed amount of money in it every month. In this way, they can buy their essential goods on credit. They can also ask for a short-term loan. After having done this, our neighbours had more trust in each other and a better relationship.

The process of creating incremental infrastructure and enhancing redundancy resulting from the diversification of livelihood options facilitates plans to live in Mianabad. People who have established long-term residency in Mianabad owing to their ability to make the informal settlement a permanent home desire to provide their children with reasonable living conditions and help them find a job or house after their marriage (Figure 7.3). Hossein, one father we interviewed, explained:

FIGURE 7.3 The incremental addition of an extra floor to a house in Mianabad.
Source: Photos taken on 25 October 2019 by the authors.

> My son got married five months ago, but we did not have enough money to help him rent a house. Therefore, we built a room and bathroom for them on the top floor of our house.

The empirical findings of the study thus reveal two distinctive features of the way of life in Mianabad: a life shaped by strategies of diversity and redundancy. According to Berner, Gomez, and Knorringa (2012), diversification involves the creation of multiple possible adaptation strategies to change, for instance adding one floor to a building, while redundancy implies the diversification of livelihoods such as through the conversion of the ground floor of a residential building into a shop. Consequently, everyday practices are flexibly adapted to change along with growing families and the economic and social environment through the incremental expansion of houses and the upgrading of housing and infrastructure. The conversion of parts of residential buildings into commercial or residential spaces is considered a viable tactic through which people lessen the unfavourable conditions of life in informal settlements.

Although informally constructed houses in Mianabad appear disordered, messy, awkward, and unattractive in comparison to those standardised and well-equipped housing complexes designed and erected under the MHS (Figure 7.4), our findings demonstrate that the perceived well-being of residents living in the informal settlement is significantly higher. Mehr housing sites as "planned shelters" restrict social and economic activities by preventing the incremental development and multi-purpose use of buildings and space desired by the studied urban populations. Buildings offer appropriate *shelter* in physical terms, while in Mianabad a living space is perceived as a "people-led *home*". Indeed, it is referred to as a living space that people produce themselves through processes of negotiation by drawing on social infrastructure and through increased diversity and redundancy of livelihood sources. This informal way of constructing and maintaining urban spaces is centred on meeting people's needs, strengthening their capacity for adaptation, and achieving self-devised solutions.

FIGURE 7.4 Mehr housing complexes near Tehran (left); housing of an informal nature in Mianabad (right).
Source: Photos taken on 25 October 2019 by the authors.

Conclusion

The MHS is a government-led housing scheme employing a formalisation strategy to counter informality in the housing sector and targeting low-income households who often cannot afford to erect or own formal houses. A critical evaluation of this project and the underlying mainstream formality-informality dichotomy that drives strategies to counter informality in Iran and elsewhere reveals stark differences between the way of life propagated through formalisation strategies and the one created by residents of informal settlements. This observation fills an empirical gap in understandings of informality by showing how it is practiced in urban spaces in ways that fulfil a specific function.

The findings show that those groups relocated to formal houses under the MHS perceive the changes to their way of life as inherently negative, citing severe and constant cultural conflicts, a lack of sense of belonging, a loss of sense of home, social displacement, a sense of staying in a "campsite space", distrust in institutions, and disaffiliation. In contrast, the examination of the everyday practices rooted in life in Mianabad shows a dynamic and vibrant community invested in their living space and with strong social ties. Activities such as the setting up of reciprocal support systems, the promotion and strengthening of social and intimate relationships among community members, involvement in collective activities, the making of decisions on improving their neighbourhood, and the encouragement of civic and voluntary participation in social and economic affairs were commonplace in Mianabad, showing how people's agency in shaping their lived space is asserted. In contrast, the government's formalisation strategy provides no room for agency to be asserted in a way that can shape lived space.

Furthermore, analysing the negotiated and lived experiences of residents of Mianabad by applying a post-development lens reveals some crucial advantages of understanding informality as a way of life. The research shows that, over time, residents of a place as the main actors producing lived spaces build social consensus stemming from processes of social learning, while the transparency of intra-group relations shaping the organisation of the material world is strengthened, revealing the inner consciousness of dwellers based on the recognition and adaptation of their way of life in line with the restrictions and possibilities of a space. This means reclaiming a space-centred collective identity linked to a sense of belonging and social commitment not only to a common race, religion, or ethnicity binding dwellers, but also to the community itself as a group of people living in proximity to one another and sharing a space. Consequently, socially constructed, lived spaces open opportunities for residents in informal settlements to cope with social displacement. Coping is made possible by their ability to participate in the production of a space and the exertion of their citizenship. A sense of community therefore also provides residents with a sense of a safe, comfortable, and liveable home. Therefore, social bonds leading to a sense of community are forged from relationships and local organisations in order to counter poverty and shortages.

A comparison between the notions of a "planned shelter" embodied by Mehr housing units and "people-led homes" in an informal settlement like Mianabad does not paint a positive picture of people's living conditions in the former. The houses under the MHS follow a standardised design that does not take into account the social, environmental, economic, and cultural dynamics shaping the acceptance of houses by inhabitants. The most vital aspect of differences between the way of life in planned shelters and in people-led homes lies in people's agency that is neglected and dismissed by planners. The resulting standardised dwellings offer little space for (re-)constructing lived spaces in a way that facilitates the emergence and consolidation of social networks, and for this reason they are negatively perceived by beneficiaries. Moreover, residents of the Mehr housing complex have become even more vulnerable as they have lost the supportive and collective way of life enabled in spaces they are able to shape themselves, as well as the incremental process of production, a common and space-centred identity, social and human capital, and, finally, their dynamic spatial life.

Urban planners following a mainstream approach in the modernisation of cities have neglected the blurriness of boundaries that are constantly being negotiated and readjusted, and a paradigm shift towards a people-centric approach to urban planning is long overdue. The challenge of enforcing a conceptual shift in urban planning and policy and mobilising authorities to deviate from mainstream approaches is formidable. A strategy to meet this challenge is beyond the scope of this chapter, but it may start from Roy's (2009) suggestion to craft "new geographies of theory" (819–820) and to "locate the production of theory and policy in the cities of the developing world" (Roy 2005, 149). The inclusion of valuable and distinctive experiences of urban informality in the Global South into the study of urban development would generate productive frameworks to recalibrate urban theory itself and the geographies of authoritative knowledge.

References

Abedini, A. 2018. "The assessments and prioritize [sic] of challenges Mehr housing in relation to low-income families in Iran. Case study: city of Urmia." *Journal of Sustainable City* 1 (1): 41–56.

Ajiliyan Momtaz, S., Rafieyan, M., and Agha Safari, A. 2018. "Study of individual components of residential satisfaction in low-income housing projects (case study: Ghorghi Mehr Housing)." *Geography and Territorial Spatial Arrangement* 8 (29): 215–228.

Alaedini, P., and Jamshidinasab, M. 2015. "Mehr Housing and new communities' right to the city: a case study of the Parand Project." *Journal of Community Development (Rural and Urban Communities)* 7 (2): 241–258.

AlSayyad, N. 2004. "Urban informality as a 'new' way of life." In *Urban Informality: Transnational Perspectives from the Middle East, Latin America, and South Asia*, edited by A. Roy and N. AlSayyad, 7–30. Lanham: Lexington Books.

Bayat, A. 2000. "From 'dangerous classes' to 'quiet rebels'." *International Sociology* 15 (3): 533–557.

Berner, E. 2000. "Poverty alleviation and the eviction of the poorest: towards urban land reform in the Philippines." *International Journal of Urban and Regional Research* 24 (3): 554–566.

Berner, E., Georgina, G., and Knorringa, P. 2012. "'Helping a large number of people become a little less poor': the logic of survival entrepreneurs." *European Journal of Development Research* 24: 382–396.

Bunnell, T., and Harris, A. 2012. "Re-viewing informality: perspectives from urban Asia." *International Development Planning Review* 34 (4): 339–347.

Crawford, M. 2004. "Everyday urbanism." In *Everyday Urbanism: Margaret Crawford vs. Michael Speaks*, edited by R. Mehrotra, 16–33. Michigan Debates on Urbanism, Vol. 1. Ann Arbor, MI: University of Michigan.

Davis, M. 2009. *Planet of Slums*. London: Verso.

De Certeau, M. 1984. *The Practice of Everyday Life*. Translated by S. Rendall. Berkeley, CA: University of California Press.

Dovey, K. 2012. "Informal urbanism and complex adaptive assemblage." *International Development Planning Review* 43 (3): 371–389.

Elian, T. 2015. "The city as collaborative field. Tackling informal spatial practices in Bucharest." *sITA – studies in History and Theory of Architecture* 3: 183–195.

Escobar, A. 1984. "Discourse and power in development: Michel Foucault and the relevance of his work to the Third World." *Alternatives* X 85: 377–400.

Escobar, A. 1995. *Encountering Development: The Making and Unmaking of the Third World*. Princeton: Princeton University Press.

Etminani-Ghasrodashti, P., Majedi, H., and Paydar, M. 2017. "Assessment of residential satisfaction in Mehr Housing Scheme: a case study of Sadra New Town, Iran." *Housing, Theory and Society* 34 (3): 323–342.

Ghafourian, M., and Hesari, E. 2018. "Evaluating the model of causal relations between Ssense of place and residential satisfaction in Iranian public housing (the case of Mehr Housing in Pardis, Tehran)." *Social Indicators Research* 139 (2): 695–721.

Gholipour, S., Karimi, J., and Sadeghi, G. 2019. "Government-funded residential apartments and informal settlements." *Research Journal on Social Work* 3 (10): 73–106.

Google Maps. n.d. Accessed 5 November 2020. https://www.google.com/maps/dir///@35.653702,51.3956409,11z/data=!4m2!4m1!3e0

Graham, S., and McFarlane, C. 2015. *Infrastructural Lives: Urban Infrastructure in Context*. London: Routledge.

Herath, D. 2009. "The discourse of development: has it reached maturity?" *Third World Quarterly* 30 (8): 1449–1464.

Hosseinioon, S. 2019. "Urban resilience and informality: effects of formalisation in Golestan, Iran." In *Urban Resilience for Risk and Adaptation Governance, Theory and Practice*, edited by G. Brunetta, O. Caldarice, N. Tollin, M. Rosas-Casals, J. Morató, 111–127. New York: Springer.
Imani Jajarmi, H., and Masoudian, M. 2019. "The Mehr Housing Project and the reproduction of social inequality (living experiences in Sadra)." *Quarterly of Social Studies and Research in Iran* 8 (1): 200–222.
Kamete, A.Y. 2013. "On handling urban informality in southern Africa." *Geografiska Annaler: Series B, Human Geography* 95 (1): 17–31.
Lefebvre, H. 1996. "The right to the city." In *Writings on Cities*, edited by E. Kofman, and E. Lebas, 147–159. Oxford: Blackwell.
Masoudirad, M., Ebrahimzadeh, I., and Rafieian, M. 2017. "Assessment of Mehr Housing Policy according to sustainability indicators case study: Khorramabad City." *Geography and Environmental Planning* 28 (2): 1–20.
McFarlane, C., and Silver, J. 2017. "Navigating the city: dialectics of everyday urbanism." *Royal Geographical Society* (Institute of British Geographers) 42: 458–471.
McFarlane, C., and Waibel, M. 2016. "Introduction: the informal-formal divide in context." In *Urban Informalities: Reflections on the Formal and Informal*, edited by C. McFarlane and M. Waibel, 1–13. London: Routledge.
McFarlane, C. 2012. "Rethinking informality: politics, crisis, and the city." *Planning Theory & Practice* 13 (1): 89–108.
McFarlane, C. 2008. "Urban shadows: materiality, the 'southern city' and urban theory." *Geography Compass* 2 (2): 340–358.
Mehr Housing. n.d. "*Mehr Housing*." Accessed 15 June, 2019. http://mehr.mrud.ir
Mohammadi, F., Parvin, S., and Rastegar, Y. 2019. "Challenges of social policy in the field of housing and its effect on the formation of social anomalies (case study on Prand Mehr Housing)." *Social Development and Welfare Planning* 9 (36): 141–174.
MURD News. 2019a. "A report of the Ministry of Roads and Urban Development of Iran." *MURD*, February 26, 2019. Accessed 10 March, 2020. https://www.mrud.ir/news-view/ArticleId/17231
MURD News. 2019b. "A report of the Ministry of Roads and Urban Development of Iran." *MURD*, June 18, 2019. Accessed 20 August, 2019. https://www.mrud.ir/news-view/ArticleId/19197
Oldfield, S. 2014. "Critical urbanism." In *The Routledge Handbook on Cities of the Global South*, edited by S. Parnell and S. Oldfield, 7–9. London: Routledge.
Pieterse, E. 2008. *City Futures Confronting the Crisis of Urban Development*. London: Zed Books.
Rafieian, M., Ajilian, S., and Ahgasafari, A. 2016. "Principles, dimensions and variables concerning the residential satisfaction in Mehr housing project (the case study of Mehregan town)." *Journal of Urban Studies* 5 (18): 27–36.
Rahnema, M., and Bawtree, V. 1997. *The Post-Development Reader*. London: Zed Books.
Rao, V. 2006. "Slum as theory: the South/Asian city and globalization." *International Journal of Urban and Regional Research* 30 (1): 225–232.
Robinson, J. 2006. *Ordinary Cities : Between Modernity and Development*. London: Routledge.
Robinson, J. 2002. "Global and world cities: A view from off the map." *International Journal of Urban and Regional Research* 26 (3): 531–554.
Roy, A. 2012. "Urban informality: the production of space and practice of planning." In *The Oxford Handbook of Urban Planning*, edited by R. Crane and R. Weber, 1–17. Oxford: Oxford University.
Roy, A. 2011a. "Postcolonial urbanism: speed, hysteria, mass dreams." In *Worlding Cities: Asian Experiments and the Art of Being Global*, edited by A. Roy and A. Ong, 307–335. London: John Wiley & Sons.

Roy, A. 2011b. "Slumdog cities: rethinking subaltern urbanism." *International Journal of Urban and Regional Research* 35 (2): 223–238.

Roy, A. 2009. "The 21st-century metropolis: new geographies of theory." *Regional Studies Association* 43 (6): 819–830.

Roy, A. 2005. "Urban informality: toward an epistemology of planning." *Journal of the American Planning Association* 71 (2): 147–158.

Sachs, W. 1992. *The Development Dictionary: A Guide to Knowledge as Power.* London: Zed Books.

Saeedi Rezvani, N., and Kazemi, D. 2011. "Recognition within the framework of infill development in criticizing the current policies towards housing development (Maskan-e-Mehr) (Case Study: Natanz City)." *Human Geography Research* 43 (75): 113–132.

Shamsoddini, A., Safariyan, E., and Nekooyibakhsh, M.R. 2018. "Challenges and performance of Mehr Housing from citizens' viewpoint (case study: Pardis Town – Kazerun)." *Human Geography Research Journal* 50 (3): 609–625.

Shokouhibidhendi, M.S., Sobhani, A., and Zhand, S. 2018. "A critique on the urban and architectural processes regarding Mehr Housing Program, in comparison to the endemic architecture and urban planning measures and values: the case study of Khameer Seaport." *Journal of Iran University of Science & Technology* 6 (3): 91–116.

Silver, J. 2014. "Incremental infrastructures: material improvisation and social collaboration across post-colonial Accra." *Urban Geography* 35 (6): 788–804.

Simone, A. 2006. "Pirate towns: reworking social and symbolic infrastructures in Johannesburg and Douala." *Urban Studies* 43 (2): 357–370.

Simone, A. 2004. "People as infrastructure: intersecting fragments in Johannesburg." *Public Culture* 16 (3): 407–429.

Statistical Centre of Iran. 2016. "*Household population*". Accessed 15 September, 2019. http s://www.amar.org.ir

United Nations Human Settlements Programme. 2014. *A Practical Guide to Designing, Planning and Implementing Citywide Slum Upgrading Programmes.* Kenya: United Nations Human Settlements Programme.

Villamizar-Duarte, N. 2015. "*Theorizing informality as a lens to rethink planning theory and practice in Bogota, Colombia.*" Paper presented at RC21 Conference,Urbino, August 27–29, 2015.

Zanjani, H., Golkar, Z., and Mohammadi, H. 2011. "A study on the social aspect of Mehr Cooperative Housing Project: a case study of Karaj Township." *Cooperation and Agriculture* 22 (7): 89–117.

Ziai, A. 2013. "The discourse of 'development' and why the concept should be abandoned." *Development in Practice* 23 (1): 123–136.

Ziai, A. 2015. "Post-development: premature burials and haunting ghosts." *Development and Change* 46 (4): 833–854.

PART 3

Long-term Perspectives

PART 3

Long-term Perspectives

8

THE PRODUCTION OF (RE)SETTLEMENTS IN MAPUTO, MOZAMBIQUE

Hovering Between Habitats and Inhabited Spaces

Sílvia Jorge and Vanessa Melo

Introduction

In the current global context of rapid urbanisation and climate change, resettlements linked to the adaptation and modernisation of cities to meet new urban challenges and embody new imaginaries have also gained prominence in Southern Africa, including in Mozambique. These urban transformations assume specific scales and contours that are better understood by taking into account: 1) the characteristics of each urban context, marked by the self-production of the space and increasing backlogs at various levels in the provision of housing, infrastructure, basic facilities, and commerce and services to urban residents; 2) market-driven logics; and 3) dominant governmental policies and practices that shape urban spaces. In Maputo, capital of Mozambique, urban space is expected to be organised in a way that both addresses the needs of the majority of the city's inhabitants who face resource constraints and responds to the consequences of climate change, which for the city includes an increased risk of flooding. At the same time, viewed from a Lefebvrian perspective ([1974] 1991), urban space also tends to be transformed into and conceived as a product, usually linked to new aspirations and ways of understanding the city that are increasingly becoming associated with significant investments in urban renewal projects, such as infrastructure megaprojects, allegedly "in the public interest" or to promote development (Melo and Jenkins, 2021; Jorge 2020).

Focusing on Maputo, the article aims to deepen existing knowledge of urban resettlements for more inclusive resettlement policies and practices that are able to minimise the usually negative impacts of resettlement processes by acknowledging the powers and rationalities installed in the current neoliberal context. More than simply the creation of new and isolated habitats, resettlement can be understood as part of the wider process of the production of urban space and as an open process, changeable over time and susceptible to appropriation by its inhabitants, individually

DOI: 10.4324/9781003124559-11

or collectively, and of subsequent upgrades initiated by different agents. Following the Lefebvrian understanding of space as a social product ([1974] 1991) and the notions of habitat and inhabiting explored by this and other authors, we ask the following question: (How) can resettlement habitats become inhabited settlements? We argue that this outcome depends on a complex set of factors related to the ways of inhabiting the different spaces that form the city and the perceptions of these, the features of the habitat provided and developed over time, as well as the motivations and processes associated with resettlement interventions.

In the scope of the collective research project "Africa Habitat: From the Sustainability of Habitat to the Quality of Inhabit of the Urban margins of Luanda and Maputo" (2018–2021),[1] the article draws on previous empirical research conducted by the authors between 2011 and 2013 (Melo 2015; Jorge 2017) but also on further follow-up empirical research undertaken between 2017 and 2019. We engaged with resettled residents of two new housing sites through direct observation, surveys, and in-depth interviews, as well as with agents involved in the interventions and residents from neighbouring expansion areas and places of origin.

In a dialogue between theory and practice, and from a broader perspective to a local focus, we start with a brief contextualisation of the production and perception of Maputo's urban space that underlies the notion of inhabiting and then shift our focus to the resettlements developed from the current neoliberal governance regime and the habitats that were produced. This was followed by a critical analysis of socio-spatial transformations and levels of appropriation in two resettlements, namely Matendene and Chiango: the former a settlement for those displaced by the floods of 2000 and the other to an infrastructure megaproject rolled out in 2013. Since different types of relocation tend to be studied separately (Wilmsen and Webber 2015), we analyse these two resettlements with different causes alongside each other to help bridge this analytical divide.

The Production and Perceptions of Maputo as City

The act of inhabiting is not restricted to the quality of a habitat, encompassing more than simply a sound housing policy, urban planning, and architecture (Paquot 2005). As such, besides the physical and conceptual dimensions of space, it also relates to its lived and symbolic spheres, embodying the dimensions of Lefebvre's ([1974] 1991) understanding of the production of space.[2] Inhabiting is linked to the notion of appropriation, a process through which a group or an individual values a space (or an object), accordingly investing their affective energy in it (Sá 2019). This implies a close relationship between urban space and everyday life that is established over time both at an individual-familiar level personalised in the house or at an individual-social level expressed on the street, in the neighbourhood, and in the city (Sá 2019). Such a "lived experience" of space is related to "the diversity of ways of living, urban types, patterns, cultural models, and values associated with the modalities and modulations of everyday life" (Lefebvre ([1970] 2003, 81). The extent to which residents actively inhabit a space is thus fundamental for understanding how urban resettlement processes can facilitate the inhabiting of settlements that stretches beyond relocation.

Following the rapid urbanisation process observed in the Global South in which market-driven logics promote great and lasting socio-spatial inequalities within the current competition for mobile capital, as discussed in the introductory chapter of this book, Maputo has also experienced a jump in resettlement interventions. These interventions have been taking place mainly since the 1990s following a shift away from the socialist ideology adopted after the country's independence in 1975 and the introduction and consolidation of the neoliberal paradigm in the country that extended opportunities for private capital to shape urban spaces according to their interests (Brenner and Theodore 2005; Harvey 2005; Jorge 2020).[3] Although the socialist legacy of state-owned land remains in place under the 1997 Land Law,[4] this legal instrument introduced the right of urban residents to occupy and use land through the *Direito de Uso e Aproveitamento da Terra* ("Right to Use and Enjoy Land" – DUAT) and the possession of a DUAT title, which tends to support real estate dynamics (Melo 2015; Jorge 2017). Furthermore, the growth of resettlement interventions in Maputo occurs in a city still marked by its colonial origins and rapidly expanding since the 1970s, due to both internal rural-urban migration and natural population growth (Lopes, Amado, and Muanamoha 2007). Maputo is composed of different spaces produced and consolidated over time, as presented below, and is inhabited by residents with different ways of living and perceptions of their city, increasingly affected by resettlement interventions that both transform existing urban spaces and produce others (Figure 8.1).

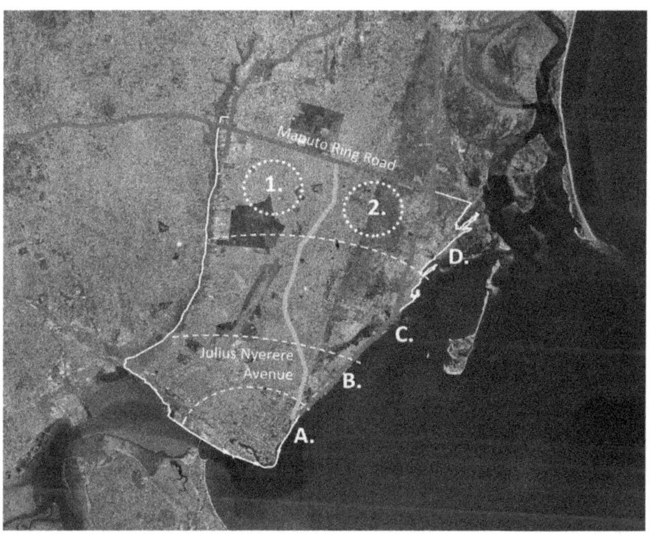

FIGURE 8.1 Schematic overview of Maputo and the location of Matendene and Chiango.

Note: A. Maputo city centre; B. pericentral areas; D. mid-peripheral areas; further away peripheries; 1. Matendene; 2. Chiango.

Source: Own work using satellite imagery from Google Earth © 2018 DigitalGlobe.

The city centre, with its orthogonal layout dating from the colonial period, nowadays tends to be inhabited by more affluent groups. This urban core is marked by a concentration of high-rise buildings and areas with more expensive houses, as well as sites of formal employment, commerce, services, and social and leisure facilities. As in other African cities, the city centre carries a Western urban imagery that represents development, modernity, and condignity usually linked to the market-driven logics of space production (Viegas and Jorge 2019). As different city residents underlined, this central area embodies the notion of the city ("we convinced ourselves that that is the city because of its cement, asphalt roads, high-rise buildings") and is seen as an "order space" ("organisation is needed in a city"). These perceptions reflect official strategies, policies, and planning that also contribute to notions of formal order, aesthetics, and urban efficiency (Melo and Jenkins 2019; Watson 2009).

The surrounding peripheral areas, generally classified as slums or informal settlements known as *bairros* (neighbourhoods) in Maputo, sprawl around the city centre. Housing around 70% of the city's one million residents (UN-Habitat 2010, 16),[5] the areas comprise a diverse set of urban spaces, with different processes of occupation, different physical characteristics, and different habitat conditions. The pericentral neighbourhoods closest to the city centre have been occupied since the colonial period mainly by the autochthonous population, who managed to settle there by themselves, through what we call processes of self-production of space, according to their necessities, resources, and capacities, following customary practices, and conforming to a dense and organic neighbourhood layout.[6]

The benefits of living close to the city centre were clearly stated by residents, local leaders and activists in interviews. These include: 1) a greater sense of urbanity ("[it is] a bridge from the peri-urban area to the urban"); 2) a gradual upgrade of the area ("it was full of reeds from end to end, but now it is full of houses of cement blocks, with little streets and wider roads as well"); 3) the availability of local and informal commercial services, which many families depend upon ("when I go to the market, I bathe, I do everything. [...] If you don't have money for *chapa* [in the further away areas], you don't sell [goods] and as such you die of starvation");[7] 4) the employment opportunities ("since it is close to the city, [residents] come in search of jobs"); and 5) increased mobility ("we can walk without catching a *chapa*").

Beyond the city centre and its pericentral areas, Maputo expanded and became more densely populated after the country's independence in 1975 and during the Mozambican Civil War (1977–1992) – locally known as the "Sixteen-Year War" – mainly as a result of migration from rural areas and forced displacement due to the war (Lopes, Amado, and Muanamoha 2007). To make space for newcomers, plots were subdivided, land not suitable for construction was used for housing, and roads and spaces reserved for social and basic infrastructure were occupied (Raposo and Salvador 2007; Vivet 2012). However, some areas were also officially demarcated for occupation – especially under the Basic Urbanisation Programme – and upgraded for the purpose of occupation. With the end of the war in 1992 and a booming real estate market, these new areas also started to receive those who left rented flats in inner Maputo in exchange for a plot on the outlying areas where they could build their own house (Lopes, Amado, and Muanamoha 2007).

These areas still benefit from their relative proximity to the city centre to which a thriving local informal market adds. However, urban problems are also concentrated in these areas, as in the pericentral ones, including overburdened infrastructure and drainage and sanitary issues – some due to the occupation of environmentally sensitive areas – and overcrowding, which has persisted despite several much-needed upgrades. Especially the pericentral self-produced areas tend to be regarded as those that contradict official intervention processes and are usually viewed as unfit for living and undesired, as observed in other African cities (see for example Tibaijuka 2005; Huchzermeyer 2011; Melo 2015; Jorge 2017). Municipal council officials tend to depict these places as disorderly: "It is dense in an unorganised way" where "each one builds a house as they see fit". An ex-official described the area as "a little chaotic", while an academic noted problems such as "when it rains, it really rains – everything is flooded". Following this negative image, these areas tend to be perceived as provisional and objects of future market-driven renewal interventions enabling the expansion of the city centre. "The municipality is becoming inclined towards progressive and immediate modernisation", one urban planning scholar stated, while another guessed that "what will happen is that investors will start to remove everything".

Although the self-production of urban space has persisted, the remaining northern areas of the city have started to become more occupied since the shift to neoliberal urban governance that has led to the promotion of resettlement in these further-away areas, as detailed below. These areas used to have transportation issues and lacked other urban services and facilities, as noted by a technical expert ("to live far away means transportation costs; people do not earn [enough] for this") and an official of the Maputo Municipal Council ("it is just an orthogonal layout – houses and nothing else"). Nevertheless, some local economic dynamics can already be observed: "There are many people making money in these peripheries," an ex-official of the Maputo Municipal Council stated. Some upgrading initiatives, including road infrastructure megaprojects and real-estate housing developments (Morange et al. 2012; Vivet 2015; Melo 2015), have also contributed to local perceptions similar to those of the city centre. "The neighbourhood starts to have a different image, to have another status", the Secretary of the Zimpeto Neighbourhood Committee stated, while a resident remarked that "here in the suburbs, we are building our city".

The areas beyond the city centre continue to reflect a symbiosis between rural and urban practices assumed over time (Raposo and Salvador 2007). In the most peripheral areas, some rural attributes tended to be regarded positively, as several residents noted: "There is not that kind of coexistence one finds in a city"; "it is quieter"; "the environment [here] is better for one's health than in the city". Others associated the areas with greater freedom: "A person can do what he wants, have a vegetable garden. Even if the house is small, he can extend it"; "it is our passion to live outside the city". At the same time, urban attributes such as electricity and water supply and an organised space are appreciated: "the area is well demarcated"; "it is an organised space".

Resettlement in Maputo in a Neoliberal Era

The Mozambican government's adherence to structural adjustment programmes with the support of the World Bank and the International Monetary Fund starting in mid-1980s marked the beginning of the neoliberal era in the country. The progressive commodification and financialisation of urban space that resulted generated new ways of thinking of and producing the city in many of the cases associated with resettlement interventions. Based on the expropriation of land "in the public interest", without adequate regard of pre-existing occupied areas, and affecting especially the most vulnerable social groups (Jorge 2015), these interventions usually involved partnerships between different agents, including government institutions, (inter)national agencies, and investors (financial institutions or others) and have been underpinned by different rationales.

On the one hand, resettlements in Maputo aim to improve the living conditions of urban dwellers, usually being regarded as contributing to development in general and related to attempts to address backlogs in housing, infrastructure, and services provision, among others, as in other similar urban contexts (Cernea 1994; Terminski 2015).[8] As Noorloos and Kloosterboer (2018) observe, these processes are usually framed as "urgent" and "inevitable" and the consequent relocations as a "necessary evil" (1225). Some of these are also associated with market-driven logics of urban space (re)production, attractive to investors and local elites, as in other African cities (see for example Watson 2014; Wilmsen and Webber 2015; Viegas 2015; Melo 2015; Jorge 2017; Noorloos and Kloosterboer 2018; Nikuze et al. 2019). These logics are underpinned by the central role of the urban in profit formation and distribution, with space as a key product of capital accumulation (Lefebvre [1974] 1991; Harvey 1989, 2001). Strategic areas are gradually made available for lucrative interventions through a process of "creative destruction" for "accumulation by dispossession", as described by Harvey (2005).

In Maputo, the first of these major resettlements followed the upgrading of the EN4 highway in the mid-1990s, fostering the expansion of the Maputo Development Corridor running from Maputo to Witbank in South Africa and the emergence of real estate projects directed especially at higher-income groups (Jenkins 2012).[9] This intervention was followed by other major investments in the (re)construction of access roads triggering significant resettlements – namely Julius Nyerere Avenue (one of our case studies), the Maputo Ring Road, and the bridge between Maputo and Katembe – that were already previewed in the Urban Structural Plan of Maputo Municipality of 2008.[10] Besides the improvement of accessibility, these interventions also promoted new real estate opportunities: the acquisition and sale of plots and construction works in the surrounding areas grew, and new gated communities and other housing projects mushroomed, again mainly directed at higher-income groups.

On the other hand, resettlement can also be associated with growing climate change hazards. Resettlement in Maputo has been promoted especially in light of the city's exposure to floods. This situation has been aggravated by urban expansion in environmentally sensitive areas, leading to the progressive destruction of natural ecosystems such as mangroves and thereby leaving the areas more vulnerable to floods and erosion (Beja da Costa and Jorge 2019). According to USAID (2002), the floods of 2000 alone – one of the worst flooding events ever recorded in Mozambique – led to the resettlement of around 500,000 people across the country, with great international mobilisation, in particular of non-governmental organisations. In Maputo, this was the case of the paradigmatic resettlement in the Magoanine C neighbourhood (the second case study), in Matendene.

These reasons for resettlement, which are also influenced by different perceptions of urban space, are often connected to each other: interventions to improve the living conditions of urban dwellers can be associated with assisting communities affected by floods; both of these can go hand in hand with interventions developed within market-driven logics that justify the clearance of certain urban areas. However, these movements are part of a wider process of urban space production, which links existing and new, central and peripheral, valued and undervalued, and physical, representative, and symbolic spaces in a dynamic and continuous urban transformation process that involves various agents, including people on the move. In line with Butcher (as quoted in Mills-Tettey 1989), these long processes do not end with relocation, but continue both at the origin and destination.

While resettlements may range from makeshift camps with no basic infrastructure to complete new towns (Mills-Tettey 1989), concerns with physical aspects, including the provision of parcelled out land, the (self-)construction of housing, infrastructure, and social facilities, tend to prevail. Under state (and market) governance rationalities, resettlements tend to be conceived as habitats, a concept used as a synonym for the physical space where social, familiar, and individual life is organised (Paquot 2005). The prime focus on habitat especially under the modernist movement underpinned a rationalised, standardised, and quantitative production of space as an object in an assembly chain (Sá 2019), but this has proven insufficient by itself to recover or improve the quality of life in resettlements (Cernea 1994; Adam, Owen, and Kemp 2015; DeMoss-Norman 2015). For Lefebvre ([1970] 2003), this production of space represses fundamental inhabiting dimensions such as the diversity, cultural, and symbolic aspects of a space and different values and rhythms of everyday life. In resettlements, inhabiting evokes the need for the affected population to be actively involved in all stages of the process,[11] but also the ability to exert their agency in the remaking of a given resettlement space through the best use of available and highly circumscribed resources, networks, and capacities that need to be supported (Hammar 2014; Arnall 2015; Arnall, Hilson, and McKinnon 2019).

A habitat and the settlements within it are related to the Lefebvrian notion of abstract space ([1974] 1991) – a space of power and domination, represented by governments and (inter)national institutions, passed to technical experts and officials and conceived in laws, strategies, policies, and plans through which the homogenising rationality of the state is reflected in space. Abstract space is influential throughout the relocation process and in the new space produced, considering the state's desire for modernisation through the reorganisation of space and of control by making people more legible (de Wet 2012). Wilmsen and Webber (2015), highlights that resettlement is also an attempt to bring into the domain of the capitalist market those who remain outside it or in the way of its development. This dominant system influences how affected lives or livelihoods are assessed and envisioned, assets (including land) are valued, and land property and titling are framed. Other logics of living, meaning, conceiving, and thus of producing space are neglected in the process.

Regulatory instruments used to frame and guide relocations are forged, some of them aimed at the prevention of negative impacts, of which the World Bank policy on resettlement of 1980 stands out.[12] In Mozambique, settlements started to be legally framed by a new legislative package under World Bank influence mainly after the mid-2000s. The Territorial Planning Law[13] of 2007 and its related regulation of 2008[14] focus especially on the expropriation of land "in the public interest", which is commonly associated with positive urban development and justified according to this objective. Expropriation can be declared within the collective interests previewed in planning instruments, such as the acquisition of areas for "the implementation of economic and social infrastructures with great positive social impact" or "situations of emergency, originated by the occurrence or possibility of disasters or natural calamities".[15] This process implies the attribution of a "just indemnity", in cash or in kind, and compensation for the disruption of social cohesion and the loss of tangible and intangible assets.[16] However, the situations that can lead to expropriation and claims of being in the "public interest" can be diverse and mired in ambiguities and contradictions (Wilmsen and Webber 2015; Jorge 2017). In Mozambique, where land is owned by a sometimes authoritarian and undemocratic state (Cahen 2013; Pereira and Nhanale 2014), the "public interest" may become subordinated to the economic interests of (inter)national investors.

However, these legal directives are not oriented towards urban contexts, where free space is rare, and the national regulation omits the "Principle of Avoiding and Minimising Resettlements" (Oliveira 2018). This principle is only recognised in the Resettlement Policy Framework of the Municipal Council of Maputo of 2010, also supported by the World Bank, which indicates that resettlement should be kept to a minimum and linked to a "sustainable development program" that provides resources to benefit and improve the quality of life of the affected population on the long term.

Two years later, the scale and prominence of resettlement in Maputo, but also in the north of the country due to the discovery and exploitation of natural resources, led to the publication of the Regulation on the Resettlement Process Resulting from Economic Activities[17] that establishes: 1) the right to the same or a higher income level and a better living standard following resettlement and the transportation of belongings to the new place of residence; 2) the right to information about the resettlement and to participation in public audiences; and 3) the elaboration of a resettlement plan that contemplates the attribution of a regularised plot with a specific housing typology, access roads, water supply, sanitation, electricity, and different social facilities. However, these guidelines are not always applied in practice, as is shown below.

Two Cases, Two Realities: Matendene and Chiango

The processes of resettlement to Matendene and Chiango that we analyse in this part reveal several similarities and differences, which illustrate the particularities of the resettlement processes in Maputo, taking into account the characteristics and perceptions of the city, as discussed above. The two resettlement cases studied were motivated by two different events. The floods of 2000 prompted resettlement to Matendene, while the resettlement to Chiango was related to the reconstruction of Julius Nyerere Avenue between 2011 and 2016 under the current legal framework described above (Figure 8.1). Matendene, a mainly rural place about 19 kilometres from the city centre, received the affected families from different pericentral and peripheral neighbourhoods. Families from the Polana Caniço pericentral neighbourhood where Julius Nyerere Avenue was constructed were sited at a similar distance from the city centre in Chiango, in an environmentally sensitive coastal area and on small, unproductive farms in the middle of already parcelled out and occupied land where vacant spaces could still be found (Figures 8.2 and 8.3).

FIGURE 8.2 Matendene: urban configuration of the places of origin and of resettlement.
Note: A. example of a pericentral neighbourhood of origin; B. example of a mid-peripheral neighbourhood of origin; C. part of the resettlement area of Matendene.
Source: Own work using satellite imagery from Google Earth © 2018 DigitalGlobe.

FIGURE 8.3 Chiango: urban configuration of the places of origin and of resettlement.
Note: A. Part of the Polana Caniço neighbourhood affected by the reconstruction of Julius Nyerere Avenue; B. Different resettlement areas in Chiango: i. small unproductive farm in the middle of parcelled out and occupied land, ii. environmentally sensitive area.
Source: Own work using satellite imagery from Google Earth © 2018 DigitalGlobe.

After the Floods: Resettling in Matendene

In an emergency situation following the 2000 floods, around 2,500 families were resettled in Matendene through a process coordinated by the Maputo Municipal Council. An organising committee, with some autonomy and its own technical office, was created "to allow for a greater acceleration of the processes [and to avoid taking] thirty steps to do one thing", a Matendene administrator noted. This committee was responsible for several aspects related to the construction of the new habitat, such as the plots' demarcation into parcels of 15 by 30 metres and for the allocation of areas for the standardised construction of low-cost housing. "This was very important, because this allowed the neighbourhood to develop according to certain rules, and today it has an ordered and a homogeneous configuration", one technician remarked. Mirroring the layout of the city centre, the houses were constructed along an orthogonal grid to allow for the easy management of the area, an official explained (Figure 8.2). Families were first housed in tents, but were moved to plots as these were being parcelled out by the municipality, and kits of construction materials (wooden beams, reeds, and zinc plates) were provided so that residents could build the houses themselves after clearing the existing vegetation from the plots (Figure 8.4).[18]

The resettlement process included local governments, various donors, multilateral agencies, and non-governmental organisations, but also the beneficiaries themselves. In the beginning of the resettlement process, a first meeting with local entities and institutions was led by the municipal council, and an awareness campaign to raise funds launched. The participating agents were then progressively involved in, for example, the organisation of the site, the parcelling out of plots, their delimitation and cleaning, the installation of water supply and sanitation systems, and the design and construction of some of the 560 low-cost houses. There was an attempt to keep those with the same origin together based on the previous identification of the families, since it would ease the adaptation process. As the Matendene administrator observed, "the solidarity between families was also our bet. [...] We didn't want to waste [this solidarity]".

In this sense, residents mentioned positive aspects of the resettlement process, for example the dialogue between the municipal council and relocated families and their ability to participate in the resettlement process and negotiate for certain conditions. "There was a strong process of negotiating the space", a technician noted. At the same time, tensions and conflicts also emerged: "It doesn't mean we didn't make some mistakes. [...] No process is clean", the Matendene administrator quipped. Complaints were related especially to the occupation of land previously used by other families, the limited number of houses provided, and irregularities or corruption, such plots being provided to households who were not affected by the floods. However, those involved tended to see these as understandable difficulties in an emergency situation and given the lack of resources. One resident for example stated that "only the fact of changing from one area to another is complicated", adding that "it is easy to say that this or that could have been done, but it was not easy".

FIGURE 8.4 The development of the resettlement site in Matendene.
Note: A. Matendene in the first years of the occupation; B. Matendene in 2011.
Source: A. © Melo, 2011 (photograph of a picture from 2001/2003 by ONG AMDU); B. © Melo, 2011.

After a Road Megaproject: Resettling in Chiango

The resettlement in Chiango followed the expropriation of the land affected by the new layout of Julius Nyerere Avenue "in the public interest" (Figure 8.3). Financed by the World Bank and the city's municipal council, this megaproject was executed by two Portuguese construction companies and resulted in the resettlement of at least 116 families (Jorge 2017). The resettlement process was led by the municipal council and followed initial public hearings. However, it was not as timeously planned as it could have been, and it contradicted the legal resettlement framework in terms of the limited participation of affected families who failed to receive information in a timely manner. As one resident noted, "nobody will be harmed. [...] Registration brigades have passed, but they didn't do what they promised". Many residents were informed of the place to which they would be relocated, of demolitions to make way for the avenue, and of the relocation day only some weeks before and others on the day of the events, aggravating the negative impacts of the irregular and unequal participation during the process. One resident exclaimed that "they evaluated [the situation], provided a plot, and said they would build there, but that you had to leave here because [the area will become] a road" and that "they don't give you the right to say what you want".

The families whose houses were entirely demolished received monetary compensation based on the combined value of the built-up area that was expropriated and its construction materials. The loss of other tangible and intangible assets, as well as the rupture of social cohesion, were not considered, which devalued the notion of inhabiting the resettlement. As questioned and observed by a resettled resident, "this is all my effort, isn't it? But their compensation is little". In Chiango, the habitat provided by a municipal department, with the cooperation of district and local government actors (the neighbourhood secretary and block heads), was restricted to overgrown plots of 15 by 30 metres without houses or basic infrastructure (Figure 8.3). "We had to clear the grass to be able to sleep there", one resident remarked, while another complained of having to work hard to clear the plot. Arriving in Chiango was experienced as a disordered and violent process. When the new residents complained about a number of issues, they mentioned that "the government came with its strength" and "threatened to beat [and] intimidate us".

The absence of baseline research on the existing situation and its specificities, support mechanisms for the resettled families, and subsequent investments did not help to attenuate the negative impacts of resettlement, creating a feeling of mistrust and abandonment in relation to the state. "Frelimo dropped us here", one resident quipped, "we are crying".[19] The process promoted the loss of the previous networks of solidarity and social relations in the Polana Caniço neighbourhood from which families were dislocated: private space gained more importance, streets and other collective spaces lacked the dynamic life of the previous inhabited place, and families were dispersed and neighbourhood ties weakened. A resident explained that "couples divorced – the men didn't want to come here; they preferred to get a girlfriend there and now the wives are suffering here", reiterating that "each [area] has its own specific problems, but they didn't pay attention".

From Occupation to Inhabiting

In Matendene, several factors contributed to the appropriation of space by new residents since the first stage of the resettlement process and, consequently, to the gradual inhabiting of the space. The participatory process promoted not only access to information, but also an early sense of community and a feeling of security of tenure, although plots were conferred only upon registration as residents of the neighbourhood and without a legal title of DUAT. At the same time, according to a technical expert involved in the relocation of families, the presence of local leaders among the affected families, some of which remained in Matendene with similar functions, helped in this regard. The trauma resulting from the floods also helped them see the space as a place to inhabit, as a technical expert remarked: "People had gone through such hardship [that] they wouldn't want to go back".

The continuous presence of public entities and other agents also contributed to this scenario. This could be seen in, for example, the gradual implementation and upgrading of water and electricity supply networks, the improvement of access to infrastructure and the provision of social facilities, and the gradual arrival of some services and commerce. As underlined by the Matendene administrator, "in the first days it was a very hard battle, [but] over time we saw some progress". Even so, in some cases, access to certain urban benefits such as basic infrastructure, transport, and employment opportunities was still lacking by 2013, especially among those residents with fewer resources. One of them complained that "what we really miss is water [because some families still collect it in cans]" and requested "employment for young people and more services, such as a hospital and transportation" because "the city is far".

At the same time, Matendene was gradually woven into the overall urban fabric of the city. In accordance with the resources available to each family, houses self-constructed with conventional materials gradually replaced the initial makeshift structures, while everyday practices were slowly reshaped (Figure 8.4). In this sense, the majority of the residents interviewed mentioned that they liked the neighbourhood and preferred to remain there. As one resident quipped, "I love [being here] – nobody will make me move out". This preference is associated with several local characteristics already mentioned by residents, such as 1) a sense of rurality ("we can have a vegetable garden [and] my wife can make something to eat from it"); 2) greater freedom ("I like to live at ease, to be free"); 3) the organisation of the space ("here, it is organised by the government itself"); and 4) problems at the places of origin ("how can I like a place that does not have [proper] conditions?") (Figure 8.2).[20] A study conducted years after the resettlement, in 2013, indicated that the majority of the surveyed families remained in the area and only about 4% were newcomers, regardless of being in an area where houses were supplied or self-constructed (Melo 2015, 2017).

On the other hand, in Chiango, the resettlement initially presented some advantages in comparison to Matendene, since plots in the former were accompanied by a DUAT title that enhanced the feeling of security of tenure. In addition, the areas demarcated for housing were more accessible and closer to educational and health facilities, which already served the population who lived in the neighbourhood. Proximity to transportation networks was seen as advantageous, as one resident expressed: "The government did well in placing me near a transport stop, so I can go get bread in the city". There are similarities to Matendene with regards to the dimensions of plots and rural attributes as areas on the city periphery were also appreciated (Figure 8.3). However, attempts to reproduce the original houses that had been torn down led to worsening habitability given the small compensation for relocation and the fluctuating prices of construction materials (Figure 8.5). Some families were also unable to access electricity and water supply networks for a long period and had to secure access by themselves. One resident complained that "[since] the municipality doesn't enter here, the water and all of that is up to you. [...] There is no public electricity and water supply and private water is expensive". Because the plots were assigned in an environmentally sensitive area, the habitat conditions were negatively perceived: "When it rains, the area gets flooded; there are many mosquitoes and ants", another resident complained.

All these aspects hampered the adaptation of resettled families to the new space and their appropriation of the space in a way that would allow it to become an inhabited settlement. The violence of the resettlement and the limited conditions of the provided habitat thus hindered the emergence of an inhabited resettlement despite the process and the space showing potential to facilitate this. The problem "is the conditions that the government didn't provide; it's not worth it here", one resident expressed. In such an unfavourable habitat, some families sold the assigned plot, sometimes to enable the acquisition of another or the construction of a house in a more favourable location. Others returned to a place closer to the city centre

FIGURE 8.5 Chiango at the start of the occupation.
Note: A. Provisional occupations and first permanent constructions; B. First appropriations of the space.
Source: A. © Jorge, 2013; B. © Melo, 2013.

or to the neighbourhood of origin, where some rented a house. A survey performed five years after this resettlement indicated that newcomers occupied around 30% of the plots surveyed and that 80% of these had bought the plot from resettled families (see also Vivet 2015; Melo 2017; Melo and Jenkins forthcoming).

Nevertheless, in the neoliberal context, the departure from the resettlement space is also influenced by market-driven logics, marked by the growing commodification of urban space defining the place of each citizen in the city according to his/her economic resources. These forces are experienced less strongly in Matendene despite the development of the area due to its relative distance to main access roads. In turn, Chiango's proximity to the Maputo Ring Road, constructed in the meantime, has increased the value of property in the area and exposed it to this increasing market pressure. Moreover, since resettlements are conceived and implemented within the dominant system, the individual titles of land occupation also increase the value of the plots and facilitate market transactions. Although the future of the families who sell their space is unknown, these transactions do not necessarily represent a socio-economic benefit, rather constituting a survival strategy that keeps eroding a sense of community as found at the places from which resettled families were displaced.

Conclusion: Reconstructing Inhabited Space through the Reconstruction of Lives

A resettlement implies the start of a new life in a new place and in some instances may represent an opportunity to improve habitat conditions and restore newly inhabited spaces. At the same time, resettlements also imply violent situations, as they are associated with different sorts of individual and social ruptures that require the creation of adequate conditions for the remaking over time of livelihoods, ways of life and everyday rhythms, relationships with and in the new neighbourhood, and the consequent emergence of space-appropriation processes. In this regard, the notions of habitat and inhabiting here explored are intrinsic to a hypothetical good practice of resettlement not limited to guaranteeing certain physical conditions, but understood as a long and complex process of the reconstruction of tangible and intangible assets over time, as well as social ties – a difficult feat.

The two cases presented here, resettlement to Matendene and Chiango, reveal some of the aspects influential in the recreation of an inhabited space. On the one hand, Matendene and Chiango present similarities in habitat characteristics. Both sites are located on the periphery of a city, namely Maputo, with some disadvantages related to the distance to the city centre and persisting insufficient urban benefits. However, residents recognised a number of positive characteristics when it comes to rural and urban attributes of these new habitats. On the other hand, the families affected by both resettlements also came from denser pericentral and peripheral neighbourhoods with several urban problems that tend to underpin negative perceptions of the city that can overshadow perceived benefits such as greater proximity to the city centre and a dynamic informal economy. In both case studies, the quality of the habitat provided or that which could be constructed, including housing, infrastructure, and other basic social facilities, were important in the resettlement process outcomes. However, while in Matendene the resettlement tended to be regarded more as an opportunity for improving living and housing conditions and the restitution of an inhabited space was gradually promoted, violence related to how the process was conducted and the hard impacts this had on the lives of those affected by it marked the resettlement process in Chiango.

The primary factors driving these two resettlements have also influenced their outcomes. In Matendene, the floods were an external danger that could be "overcome" through resettlement, while in Chiango, resettlement resulted from the expropriation of land "in the public interest", which legitimised the Julius Nyerere Avenue megaproject and facilitated ambiguities and conflicts of interpretation. Besides contributing to an increase in external debt and social and environmental impacts, these interventions do not always benefit the majority of the population and are often associated with market-driven real-estate developments that conceal different intentions, powers, and rationalities, often colliding with the needs of those with fewer resources (Nova and Mosca 2018). As such, this kind of resettlement is often equated with a mechanism to "get people out of the way", perpetuating situations of urban exclusion and inequality (Levenson 2019).

Both cases also show that the compensation principle restricted to habitat characteristics, which ignores the disruption of the social cohesion present in former neighbourhoods and the loss of intangible assets, is manifestly insufficient to guarantee the maintenance or improvement of living and housing conditions. At the same time, accountability and effective cooperation between the agents involved and the affected families, as well as the improvement over time of the resettlement area, proved to be particularly important in the resettlement process. In Matendene, although some families had been given houses in addition to a plot, the majority received only a kit of basic materials and had to construct their own houses. Nevertheless, the participatory process and continuous upgrades created a feeling of community and a sense of security and belonging, among other intangible and social aspects, which reinforced the (re)construction of an inhabited space in parallel with the improvement of habitat conditions.

In Chiango, on the other hand, the limited monetary compensation relocated households received hampered the reconstruction of the houses and the ability to access basic services or basic infrastructure so that, at times, basic housing conditions could not be met. However, the mismanagement of the resettlement process as to the promotion of participation, supply of adequate information, and provision of support mechanisms was determinant in the increased vulnerability of affected families, as was the occupation of environmentally vulnerable spaces, which reinforced the unsustainability of this violent process. It undermined the achievement of a minimum level of acceptable habitat conditions and the remaking of the inhabiting dimension. The different agents involved in each case, the resettlement to Matendene with an important presence of international organisations, and the resettlement to Chiango mainly conducted by national institutions, may have also influenced these outcomes. However, further research would have to be carried out in this regard.

Moreover, the Chiango case study shows the shortcomings of the notion of abstract space as a space of power and domination with regard to the construction of both habitats and inhabited resettlements, since the current legal package associated with the resettlement represented a set of seemingly good intentions that were not translated into practice and were insufficient to guarantee the effective maintenance and improvement of living conditions of the resettled families. On the one hand, these situations are similar to other resettlements in Mozambique partly due to the lack of government capacity to supervise the implementation of resettlement processes (Jossias and Cunguara 2017; Ploeg and Vanclay 2018). On the other hand, it follows the global tendency (Cernea 1994; Cook 1994; de Wet 2012; Terminski 2015; Adam, Owen, and Kemp 2015; De Moss-Norman 2015; Wilmsen and Webber 2015; Levenson 2019; Nikuze et al. 2019) of resettlements failing to improve, or even to recover, the living standards of the affected population due to aspects such as 1) poor implementation of anticipated measures, for example, the promotion of participation and the prevention of risks already identified, and 2) policies' content, such as insufficient emphasis on resettlement as development process and the inadequacy of the compensation model.

Finally, besides the quality of the habitat, the resettlement motivations and process, and the changes introduced over time, the market-driven logics in place are equally influential in the consequent development of these areas into inhabited settlements, as observed especially in Chiango, where these forces are more evident. As such, if the improvement of the quality of life and housing is achieved, enabling the recreation of the inhabiting dimension, as in Matendene, it may end up benefiting not the resettled families, but those who can afterwards purchase a place in these locations, as in Chiango.

Notes

1 This project (http://africahabitat.gestual.fa.ulisboa.pt/) by the *Grupo de Estudos Socio-Territoriais, Urbanos e de Ação Local* (Group of Socio-Territorial, Urban and Local Action Studies – Gestual) of Research Centre for Architecture, Urbanism and Design (CIAUD) at the University of Lisbon is coordinated by Isabel Raposo and financed by *Fundação para a Ciência e Tecnologia* (the Portuguese national funding agency for science, research, and technology) and the Aga Khan Development Network (Ref. FCT-AKDN/333121392/2018).

2 Lefebvre's three dimensions of space production are: "spatial practice", concerning the material sphere of social activity and interaction; "representations of space", related to the conceptualisations of space; and "spaces of representation", associated with directly lived experiences, images, and symbols ([1974] 1991). For a more detailed reflection, see Schmid (2008).

3 During the first years of independence, the socialist ideology constrained the advances of market-driven logics in the country (see for example Raposo et al. 2012).

4 Law no. 19/1997, 7 October 1997.

5 Although, according to the Census of 2017, Maputo has 1,080,277 residents, Greater Maputo, that includes the municipalities of Matola and Boane as well as the District of Marracuene, has around 2.5 million inhabitants.

6 According to Morais (2001), the existence of these areas has been contemplated in legislation at least since 1912 and due to its growing expansion, in the 1930s, the municipality forbade the construction of buildings of a permanent nature.

7 *Chapa* in the local vernacular refers to the most common form of public transportation in a small van.

8 Terminski (2015) identifies eight causes of development-induced displacements and resettlements, of which urbanisation, re-urbanisation, transformation of urban space, and

population redistribution schemes in urban areas have been considered to have become more prominent in recent years.

9 This intervention was promoted by the National Roads Administration and the construction company CMC.

10 More information about the impacts of the construction of Maputo Ring Road and the bridge can be found, respectively, in the documentaries "Women, Resettlement and Development" produced in 2014 by *Centro Terra Viva* – https://www.youtube.com/watch?v=b_o7ueyHYS4 and "My House Was Here" realised by Chico Carneiro in 2018. The Maputo Ring Road and the bridge were both financed and constructed by Chinese entities in partnership with Mozambican central and local government institutions.

11 Scudder (as quoted in Nikuze et al. 2019) identifies four stages of relocation: 1) planning, 2) transition, 3) potential adaptation and development, and 4) incorporation (when resettled families start feeling at home).

12 This policy was revised in 1990, becoming Operational Directive (OD) 4.30, and in 2001 becoming Operational Policy (OP) 4.12.

13 Law no. 19/2007, 18 July 2007.

14 Decree no. 23/2008, 1 July 2008.

15 Decree no. 23/2008, Article 68.

16 Law no. 19/2007, Article 20, no. 3.

17 Decree no. 31/2012, 8 August 2012.

18 This situation influenced the naming of this area, since Matendene in a local dialect means "a place with tents".

19 Frelimo has been Mozambique's ruling party since independence.

20 For more information on these appropriation processes, see Melo (2017).

References

Adam, A.B., J. Owen, and D. Kemp. 2015. "Households, livelihoods and mining-induced displacements and resettlement." *The Extractive Industries and Society* 2: 581–589.

Arnall, A. 2015. "Resilience as transformative capacity: exploring the quadripartite cycle of structuration in a Mozambican resettlement programme." *Geoforum* 66: 26–36.

Arnall, A., C. Hilson, and C. McKinnon. 2019. "Climate displacement and resettlement: the importance of claims-making 'from below'." *Climate Policy* 19 (6): 665–671.

Beja da Costa, A., and S. Jorge. 2019. "Uma paisagem em mutação: o caso do Bairro dos Pescadores em Maputo, Moçambique." *Finisterra* 54 (112): 145–162.

Brenner, N., and N. Theodore. 2005. "Neoliberalism and the urban condition." *City* 9 (1): 101–107.

Cahen, M. 2013. "Moçambique só há partidos de direita." *Plural, Revista do Programa de Pós-Graduação em Sociologia da USP* 20 (25): 155–174.

Cernea, M. 1994. "African population resettlement in a global context." In *Involuntary resettlement in Africa*, edited by C. Cook, 14–31. Washington: World Bank.

Cook, C. 1994. *Involuntary resettlement in Africa*. Washington: World Bank.

De Moss-Norman, T. 2015. "From informal settlements to formality: a resettlement group's adaptation to a newly planned community in Port Elizabeth, South Africa." *Economic Anthropology* 2: 224–240.

de Wet, C. 2012. "The application of international resettlement policy in African villagization projects." *Human Organization* 71 (4): 395–406.

Hammar, A. 2014. "Displacement economies in Africa: paradoxes of crisis and creativity." In *Displacement economies in Africa: Paradoxes of crisis and creativity*, edited by A. Hammar, 3–32. London: Zed Press.

Harvey, D. 1989. *The urban experience*. Baltimore: John Hopkins University Press.

Harvey, D. 2001. *Spaces of capital: towards a critical geography*. New York: Routledge.

Harvey, D. 2005. *Spaces of neoliberalization: towards a theory of uneven geographical development*. Munich: Franz Steiner Verlag.

Huchzermeyer, M. 2011. *Cities with 'slums': from informal settlements eradication to a right to the city in Africa*. Claremont: UCT Press.

Jenkins, P. 2012. *Understanding 'home space' in the African city: context report*. Copenhagen: The Royal Danish Academy of Fine Arts.

Jorge, S. 2017. *Lugares interditos. O caso dos bairros pericentrais autoproduzidos de Maputo*. PhD diss., Lisbon School of Architecture, University of Lisbon.

Jorge, S. 2015. "The re-emergence of urban renewal in Maputo: importance and scale of the phenomenon in the neoliberal context." In *Urban Planning in Lusophone African Countries*, edited by C. Silva, 203–213. Farnham: Ashgate.

Jorge, S. 2020. "The financialization of the margins of Maputo, Mozambique", *Housing Policy Debate* 30 (4): 606–622.

Jossias, G., and C. Cunguara. 2017. *Análise da situação dos reassentamentos: Município de Maputo*. Maputo: Centro de Aprendizagem e Capacitação da Sociedade Civil.

Lefebvre, H. [1974] 1991. *The production of space*. Oxford: Blackwell.

Lefebvre, H. [1970] 2003. *The urban revolution*. London: University of Minnesota Press.

Levenson, Z. 2019. "'Such elements do not belong in an ordered society': managing rural-urban resettlement in democratic South Africa." *Journal of Agrarian Change* 19: 427–446.

Lopes, C., F. Amado, and R. Muananoha. 2007. "Dinâmicas populacionais em Luanda e Maputo." In *Subúrbios Luanda e Maputo*, edited by J. Oppenheimer and I. Raposo, 37–64. Lisbon: Edições Colibri.

Melo, V. 2015. *A produção recente de periferias urbanas africanas. Discursos, práticas e configuração espacial: Maputo versus Luanda and Maputo*. PhD diss., Lisbon School of Architecture, University of Lisbon.

Melo, V. 2017. "Top-down low-cost housing supply since mid-1990s in Maputo: bottom-up responses and spatial consequences." *Transformations Journal* 93: 41–67.

Melo, V., and P. Jenkins. 2019. "Between normative product-oriented and alternative process-oriented urban planning praxis: how can these jointly impact on the rapid development of metropolitan Maputo, Mozambique?" *International Planning Studies* 26 (1): 81–99.

Melo, V., and P. Jenkins. 2021. "Peri-urban expansion in the Maputo city region: land demarcations and middle-class advances." *Journal of Southern African Studies* 47 (4).

Mills-Tettey, R. 1989. "African resettlement housing: a revisit to the Volta and Kainji Schemes." *Habitat International* 13 (4): 71–81.

Morais, J. 2001. *Maputo: património da estrutura e forma urbana topologia do Lugar*. Lisbon: Livros Horizonte.

Morange, M., F. Folio, E. Peyroux, and J. Vivet. 2012. "The spread of a transnational model: 'gated communities' in three Southern African cities (Cape Town, Maputo and Windhoek)." *International Journal of Urban and Regional Research* 36 (5): 890–914.

Nikuze, A., R. Sliuzas, J. Flacke, and M. Maarseveen. 2019. "Livelihood impacts of displacement and resettlement on informal households – a case study from Kigali, Rwanda." *Habitat International* 86: 38–47.

Noorloos, F., and M. Kloosterboer. 2018. "Africa's new cities: the contested future of urbanisation." *Urban Studies* 55 (6): 1223–1241.

Nova, Y., and J. Mosca. 2018. "Quanto custa a ponta da Catembe?" *Destaque Rural* 38. Accessed 1 December, 2020. https://omrmz.org/omrweb/wp-content/uploads/DESTAQUE-RURAL-N%C2%BA-38-1.pdf

Oliveira, M. 2018. *Alternatives to involuntary resettlement: making an argument for in-situ multi-story social housing in Maputo*. Master's diss., University of the Witwatersrand.

Paquot, T. 2005. "Habitat, habitation, habiter. Ce que parler veut dire …." *CNAF I Informations Sociales* 123: 48–54.

Pereira, J., and E. Nhanale. 2014. *As eleições gerais de 2014 em Moçambique: análise de questões fundamentais*. Johannesburg: Open Society.

Ploeg, L., and F. Vanclay. 2018. "Challenges in implementing the corporate responsibility to respect human rights in the context of project-induced displacement and resettlement." *Resources Policy* 55: 210–222.

Raposo, I., and C. Salvador. 2007. "Há diferença: ali é cidade, aqui é subúrbio: urbanidade dos bairros, tipos e estratégias de habitação em Luanda e Maputo." In *Subúrbios Luanda e Maputo*, edited by J. Oppenheimer and I. Raposo, 105–138. Lisbon: Edições Colibri.

Raposo, I., S. Jorge, S. Viegas, and V. Melo. 2012. "Luanda e Maputo: inflexões suburbanísticas da cidade socialista à cidade-metrópole neoliberal." *urbe. Revista Brasileira de Gestão Urbana* 4 (2): 189–205.

Sá, T. 2019. "Houses for whom? Between the habitat and the inhabiting, on Henri Lefebvre's quest". *Proceedings of the II Congreso Internacional Cultura Y Ciudad*. Granada, 23–25 January.

Schmid, C. 2008. "Henri Lefebvre's theory of the production of space: towards a three-dimensional dialectic." In *Space, Difference, Everyday Life: Reading Henri Lefebvre*, edited by K. Goonewardena, S. Kipfer, R. Milgrom, and C. Schmid, 27–45. New York: Routledge.

Terminski, B. 2015. *Development-induced displacement and resettlement: causes, consequences, and socio-legal context*. Stuttgart: ibidem-Verlag.

Tibaijuka, A. 2005. Report of the fact-finding mission to Zimbabwe to assess the scope and impact of Operation Murambatsvina. Geneva: United Nations. Accessed 14 January, 2021. https://reliefweb.int/sites/reliefweb.int/files/resources/A3EAD4A3C643D7318525704600592184-habitat-zwe-18jul.pdf

UN-Habitat. 2010. *Mozambique cities profile. Maputo, Nacala and Manica*. Nairobi: UN-Habitat Regional and Technical Cooperation Division.

USAID. 2002. Moçambique, Cheias de 1999–2000. Avaliação de impacto: actividade de Doação para o reassentamento da população. Accessed 14 January, 2021. https://sarpn.org/documents/d0000811/P907-Mozambique_floods_1999-2000_USAID_072002_P.pdf

Viegas, S. 2015. *Luanda, cidade (im)previsível? Governação e transformação urbana e habitacional: paradigmas de intervenção e resistências no novo milénio*. PhD diss., Lisbon School of Architecture, University of Lisbon.

Viegas, S., and S. Jorge. 2019. "The role of the urban grid in Luanda and Maputo's current transformation: between the idealised city and the pre-existing self-produced spaces." *Architext, Journal of the School of Architecture at Ariel University* 7: 114–121.

Vivet, J. 2012. *Déplacés de guerre dans la ville: la citadinisation des deslocados à Maputo (Mozambique)*. Paris: Karthala.

Vivet, J. 2015. "Déplacés de guerre et dynamiques territoriales postconflit au Mozambique." *Hérodote* 158: 160–181.

Watson, V. 2009. "'The planned city sweeps the poor away…': urban planning and the 21st century urbanization." *Progress in Planning* 71: 151–193.

Watson, V. 2014. "African urban fantasies: dreams or nightmares?" *Environment and Urbanization* 26 (1): 215–231.

Wilmsen, B., and M. Webber. 2015. "What can we learn from the practice of development-forced displacement and resettlement for organised resettlement in response to climate change?" *Geoforum* 58: 76–85.

9

EXPERIENCING THE POLITICS OF RESETTLEMENT IN LALIBELA (ETHIOPIA) THROUGH TIME

From Displacement to the Impossible Rebuilding of Ordinary Lives

Marie Bridonneau

> I keep returning thinking that you will follow me. But you stay there, my land, Adi Shadey. So that you don't see me sad and thin, I have lost my mirror, Adi Shadey.
>
> *K., 78 years old*

Introduction

In the spring of 2020, below Unity Park in Addis Ababa,[1] landscaping and gardening work was well under way on the hillsides that will eventually come to form a place in the city centre where the inhabitants of the Ethiopian capital can catch a breath and unwind. Less than ten years ago, the same slopes were densely populated, harbouring mainly small, informally constructed mud houses with tin roofs that facilitated a mixture of residential, artisanal, and commercial activities. These houses were torn down to finally make way for a planned public space and its inhabitants vanished from the slopes, pushed out of the city centre in a bid to modernise the zone.

Displacement and Resettlement in Ethiopian Cities

This rapid urban transformation is not an unusual sight: almost every major infrastructure and urban development project observed since the early 2000s in Ethiopia has been associated with population displacement (Gebre Yntiso 2008; Elias Yitbarek Alemayehu 2008; Abebe and Hesselberg 2013; Gebre 2014; Kloosterboer 2019; Weldeghebrael 2020). In 2021, Ethiopian cities are still facing an endless cycle of destruction for reconstruction and renewal. Megaprojects in Addis Ababa are touted by the government as representing an ultra-modern urban future in the making, while those same projects are criticised for envisioning cities where the

DOI: 10.4324/9781003124559-12

poorest are always excluded, driven further to the peripheries and invisibilised (Terrefe 2020).[2] In the city, urban renewal combines the destruction of old neighbourhoods with infrastructure projects and the modernisation of buildings in the city centre, as well as the large-scale construction of collective housing units called "condominiums" on the outskirts of the city, ever more numerous and ever further away from the city centre (Duroyaume 2015; Bridonneau 2018). As sites promoting access to individual ownership of housing as well as the resettlement of displaced city dwellers from the central "slums", these so-called condominiums are a major tool in the reorganisation of the urban system and the city's socio-political transformation (Ejigu 2012; Planel and Bridonneau 2017).

Forced displacement, dislocation, or resettlement logically occupy a central place in the study of the Ethiopian city (Gebre Yntiso 2008; Abebe and Hesselberg 2013; Bridonneau 2014; Spire et al. 2017), with growing attention paid to some emerging forms of resistance to these. These phenomena are a major area of study for researchers, echoing a well-studied Ethiopian phenomenon, the *sefera*, or act of resettlement, which occurs in a great variety of spatial and temporal contexts ever since the end of the imperial period in the 1950s with an unprecedented upsurge in the 1980s under the Derg regime (Dessalegn Rahmato 2003; Pankhurst 1992; Pankurst and Piguet 2009).[3] *Sefera* remained "a mode of government" (Labzaé 2019: 122) during the era of rule of the Ethiopian People's Revolutionary Democratic Front (EPRDF), even though narratives have changed, with resettlement first described as "forced" and then as "voluntary" displacements, for instance.[4] Resettlement has recently been endorsed for helping young Ethiopians gain access to land ownership (Pankhurst 2009) but also as enabler of development projects such as urban renewal projects.

Urban Studies in Ethiopia: From Addis Ababa to the Emerging Heritage Town of Lalibela

The understanding of urban dynamics in Ethiopia tends to focus on Addis Ababa; several major works regard aspects such as the social and political dynamics of the capital (Di Nunzio 2019), the shortcomings of its urban public policies (Rode et al. 2020; Terrefe 2020), and the workings of land and real estate investment (Goodfellow 2017). Such research clearly shows the power that administrative and political authorities have to relocate and regulate city dwellers (Di Nunzio 2014; Planel and Bridonneau 2017), as well as the continuation of political practices in the city despite the government's announcement of an era of political reform (Terrefe 2020). These state-driven development projects applied to the city continue to marginalise and exclude some categories of people, especially as seen through the eyes of young urban dwellers (Mains 2012a, Di Nunzio 2019). Less often, scholars have looked at secondary cities in Ethiopia, drawing similar conclusions (Mains 2012b; Mains and Kinfu 2017; Appelhans 2016). Apart from few exceptions, small cities and towns have been seen as places structuring and framing the rural environment and thus have not really been studied as urban spaces. However, such small cities and towns have their own dynamics that require scholarly attention, especially since they are elementary places of urbanisation. As will be shown, as the site of heritage rock-hewn churches declared a UNESCO World Heritage Site in 1978 and a high place of pilgrimage for Ethiopian Orthodox Christians, Lalibela is much more than merely a town, representing the deep religious beliefs of numerous Ethiopians and a major touristic attraction in the country. Lalibela is situated in the Amhara National Regional State (ANRS) in northern Ethiopia. The historic and religious site is nestled in a small town whose population has tripled in the last decade, counting some 60,000 residents in 2020. Urban dynamics in Lalibela are at once those of an ordinary small Ethiopian highlands town and of a heritage site in which land pressures are extremely high.

Resettlement in Lalibela: 10 Years' Research

Lalibela forms the central focus of this study. Here, resettlement was driven by a concern shared by multiple actors to keep the area around the churches pristine. Between 2009 and 2014, about 5,000 people had been resettled to urban peripheries some kilometres away from the historic site, and by 2019, acceptance of the resettlement had made way to dissatisfaction and despair. This chapter shows that resettlement, while also a public policy inscribed within the neoliberal logic that dominates urban policies in the Global South (Cernea and Maldonado 2018; Rogers and Wilmsen 2019), is first and foremost a public resource to manage people through the reorganisation of space. This chapter aims to show that resettlement in Lalibela is a program with a long history that ranges from the construction of the legitimacy of resettlement to its durable effects in both urban memories and the rebuilding of daily lives. Resettlement involves numerous actors situated across different scales. Its roots lie in practices of displacement and resettlement that are modernised, normalised, and even moralised, change over time, and have long-lasting social impacts. The forms of resistance that can emerge from the implementation of the World Bank project leading to resettlement are here illuminated: often silent and invisible, people do replay their relation to the state and even defy it.

This research spans a decade. Data collection took place over three rounds between 2009 and 2019, with the first study undertaken between July 2009 and August 2011 as part of a doctoral thesis, the second in August 2014, and the final study in December 2019. Nearly 200 interviews with resettled inhabitants were conducted. Respondents were selected at random for semi-structured interviews among residents to be resettled from the churches' compound and then, inhabitants of the resettlement site. Interview frameworks were designed in such a way that the day-to-day routines and practices in the relocation area could be analysed, but also to capture perceptions and memories of daily life both before and after resettlement; these include views and memories of occupation status and access to housing, activities, neighbourhood relations and life in community-based associations, and practices related to the churches. These interviews were combined with

neighbourhoods enclosed within the walls. While the neighbourhood appeared shabby, the group of inhabitants to be displaced was socially heterogeneous, structured by neighbourhood associations such as funerary aid associations called *edir*, and all of these inhabitants wished to live in the Lalibela city centre and close to its churches.

Experiencing Constraints from Tough to Soft

In May 2009, the inhabitants of *kebele* houses who until then had lived in the Mikael Gebbi neighbourhood (see Figure 9.2) were re-installed in new social housing units situated in what was then the outskirts of Lalibela, near a recent urbanised area called Worke Dingay, three kilometres away from the city centre (see Figure 9.2). This event marked the start of resettlement in Lalibela. In early 2010, property owners in Mikael Gebbi were told to raze their houses by the local authorities to clear the area. As compensation for demolishing their homes and this forced eviction, they received parcels of land five kilometres away, in a not-yet urbanised area locally called Kurakur (see Figure 9.2), as well as a cash payment based on the lost property. We were told of compensations ranging from 2,000 ETB to 400,000 ETB[12] and plots of land from 150 m^2 to much greater parcels for the wealthiest.

In February 2010, an elderly, childless widow was destroying the walls of her old property. She told us that she had already built a house in the resettlement zone and that she was trying to recuperate building materials so as to construct latrines on the new land. She wondered how she was going to transport these materials to the resettlement zone. She also noted that the *kebele* authorities had given them a week's notice to break down their homes; after that, bulldozers would be brought in to demolish them. Several weeks later, the municipal authorities came in to destroy the last remaining homes. The resettlement thus saw the authorities, and especially the *kebele* as "the principal incarnation of the state and the meeting place between the state and those it administers" (Labzaé 2019: 10) had mobilised tactics such as inducing panic and hurry or threatening inhabitants with demolition.

A 30-year-old female who, until she was resettled, was selling local beer at her home, as well as onions and potatoes in the market, recounted:

> We were the first to leave our homes because we have nothing. We have no money, we are poor. […] The mayor and the head of the Culture and Tourism office forced us to leave. […] At the time, we were not ready. They came with the *kebele* [managers]. They told us to leave, and we lost our things because we had to hurry. Glasses and photograph frames were broken.
>
> *(interview, October 2010)*

The *kebele* representatives are well acquainted with the inhabitants they manage administratively and politically on a day-to-day basis: their presence makes sense to any resident. The attendance of both the mayor and the head of the Lalibela Culture and Tourism office signified, however, how this resettlement project was inscribed within a broader urban, heritage, and tourism program. The *kebele houses* tenants were displaced in a hurried and brutal manner, but as tenants of social housing units, they were offered new housing by the authorities, a practice also common in resettlement programs in Ethiopian cities.

The inhabitants of Mikael Gebbi – social housing and private housing tenants, as well as private owners – were all displaced before the World Bank validated the Resettlement Action Plan (RAP) in September 2011. In June 2010, under the authority of the Ministry of Culture and Tourism, the consultant presented the RAP framework, specifying that

> [...] the Lalibela Town Administration with the support from the Amhara National Regional State Administration has conducted the relocation of about 98 households from the churches' compound. As this intervention is initiated independently by the town administration, the resettlement activity is neither informed nor guided by the Resettlement Policy Framework and of course not by a RAP either.
>
> *(Wub Consult 2011)*

M. is in his forties and an inhabitant of the Adi Shadey neighbourhood – the oldest and most populous of the neighbourhoods enclosed within the churches' compound (see Figure 9.2). He rented a *kebele* house and headed the Adi Shadey *edir* before he was relocated. After many years as a soldier, he returned to Lalibela and found work as a security guard for a hotel. As an association leader, he was regularly invited to meetings concerning heritage conservation. When the ESTDP team started organising meetings in August 2010 with neighbourhood residents, M. was elected by his community to represent them and to convey their grievances as the Resettlement Action Plan was being prepared. M. described an information meeting for the inhabitants of Adi Shadey:

> A committee came from Addis Ababa and Bahir Dar [the capital city of the Amhara Regional State]. During the meeting, the committee members promised that they would pick a [reinstallation] area that we wanted. Two of the committee members were white. They showed us the plan. [...] But the Town Administration forced us to leave. [...] The two foreigners went to see the Prime Minister and wrote up a report for him. We waited for them. They are from the World Bank. The mayor refused our idea. He wanted to take the World Bank's money and distribute it himself. We from the neighbourhood did not agree and wanted the foreigners to disburse money to inhabitants. We wanted land next to the bus station, but the mayor wanted to give that land to investors.
>
> *(interview, October 2010)*

M. presented the World Bank's role in a very positive light – he viewed it as a foreign institution that is able to deal directly with the highest Ethiopian authorities. He also pointed to the multi-scalar nature of the Ethiopian state and its government, distinguishing between regional and federal authorities that cooperate with the World Bank, on the one hand, and the local authorities, embodied by the mayor, on the other, who work against the affected people's interests. The rushed rollout of the first stages of resettlement in Lalibela shows two faces of a single program: on the one hand, it was a measure implemented by Ethiopian authorities as anywhere else in the country when constrained displacement was needed to impose its developmental model; on the other, it was another way to displace people, a "softer" constraint (Spire and Pilo, see Chapter 3) in the World Bank's toolbox to impose its rules and norms.

Criticising the State through the Compensation System

In 2010, the intervention of the international donor and the expert and consultants of the ESTDP came to blur the representation of power at a time when the management structures of the Ethiopian state were less openly questioned (Lefort 2010) than they would be a decade later (Labzaé 2020). By August 2014, the resettlement of Lalibela was almost entirely completed. Almost all of the tin-roofed houses enclosed within the churches' compound were razed. The ESTDP continued to operate in the area, constructing ablution facilities and other kind of facilities such as shaded areas for tourists. Some inhabitants refused to leave and tried to renegotiate their compensation or the position of the parcel picked for them by the resettlement committee piloted by the Lalibela Town Administration. Having faced the ESTDP's actions for a period of four years, these unyielding inhabitants concentrated their claims on the compensation given to the resettled, which they considered to have been unfairly attributed, and on the reinstallation parcels (either their size or positioning). These inhabitants, most of them urban homeowners, did not hesitate to contest the legitimacy of the local authorities or the wider resettlement project. While there were very few such individuals in relation to the total resettled population, they nonetheless posed an important question about how the relationship of a community with the state could replay within a multi-actor and multi-scale project anchored in a local space for multiple years.

If nearly all of the inhabitants interviewed considered the compensation given to be insufficient (too low given the loss incurred or insufficient to cover the costs of a new house), those who refused to be resettled considered the very system of compensation as unjust. The principle of compensation is at the heart of the World Bank's thinking about resettlement. Compensation is indispensable, but it is nearly always insufficient and, in most cases, contested and criticised due to unequal access to it, corruption, or a lack of transparency (Cernea 2003). In the Chifrigoch neighbourhood, next to the emblematic Saint George church, 65-year-old A. W. related:

> They promised us [...] that the compensations would be transparent for everyone. [...] But the compensation is not fair. [...] [The consultant] is spreading butter with his tongue [he is lying]. Those who decided and worked

> on the compensations, we found out, are the same people who now decide on appeals. That is not normal.
>
> *(interview, March 2014)*

A.G., the owner of the first private hotel in Lalibela, also stated:

> We were asked to pick certain individuals to establish committees to inspect our property and evaluate the compensation offered. The committee members did not count rooms; they did not look closely at the ceilings. They only saw the walls and the roof. They did not even measure the plot. For three years they hid everything from us. They did not tell us anything. At the end of three years, they wrote the compensation figures on a sheet of paper. Then the government told us, "we are going to raze the homes". I am waiting for them. Now they say that we are members of the opposition. We are not, but that is what they say. They are organising new committees to look into the complaints. But some of the members of these new committees belonged to the first committees. The ESTDP works with politicians. They are not independent.
>
> *(interview, March 2014)*

By working closely with the demands of the World Bank's committees and consultations, the local authorities modified their place in the program, but also their relationship to the city dwellers, who openly criticised how local authorities had operated. A. G. explained: "The government ordered us to leave in the name of heritage. [...] They promised that we would have double the value of what we have, that our houses would be of an international standard". H., a young, 24-year-old female who owns a restaurant near Adi Shadey, also refused to leave her home until the court renders its decision few months later:

> At first, they said that an agreement between the government and the inhabitants had been reached, that there should be no use of force. They said that no decision could come from on high, that they do not control our lives. Because they said that, and because we do not agree with the compensation, we will not quit our houses.
>
> *(interview, August 2014)*

J., who is 70 years old, remained where she was:

> They have hurt me a lot. The land down there really is the worst, the worst place, and that hurts even more. I am crying. Why are they doing this to me? I am really old. My family living in Dessie asked me to join them. But I want to die here, near the churches of Lalibela. I keep hoping that the municipality will change the position of my plot. But the manager told me, "we have already given you land, I don't want to see you again", and then pushed me away.
>
> *(interview, August 2014)*

FIGURE 9.3 Kurakur, the resettlement area in 2019.
Source: Author's own.

modest and cheap housing. At the end of 2019, the resettlement mainly housed young families who had bought plots from resettled persons so as to build their own houses, renters seeking out cheap rents or civil servants seeking to be close to their place of work, and, finally, the resettled who managed to build a house and have remained there.

The neighbourhood also has 30 houses constructed through the Peter Bachmann Foundation. For several decades, this foundation has aided inhabitants of Lalibela, especially among the poorest. In the heart of the resettlement area, these units house displaced individuals from different neighbourhoods from Lalibela, not just those who had lived close to the churches. In front of one of these houses, several women have gathered for a charity drive organised to help one of them who at that time was in great difficulty. Y. states:

> I don't know my age, maybe 50 or 60 years. I used to live in a house of corrugated iron in the World Vision.[14] Our houses were destroyed to build a road and for the new Bureau of Agriculture. That was five or six years ago. All three of us are handicapped. Here, now, we have our own *carta* [land title]. Before, next to the hospital, I had a container to sell small consumer goods. When I arrived here, I fell and lost my business. There is nothing here. It is for the rich. It is not a place to live in, but to work. […] The poverty here is the worst thing. But we can always sell the house. I have to pay 16,000 ETB for the lease. I have to pay 18,000 ETB in four years. I took out a loan from the ACSI [Amhara Credit and Savings Institute] for 30,000 ETB. […] I used that loan to pay my medical costs and to survive when I couldn't work, when I was recovering from my injuries.
>
> *(interview, December 2019)*

The level of indebtedness is an indicator of the long-term difficulties for resettled people. For the majority of them, the compensation they received was not sufficient to finance the construction of a new house. Some of them immediately ceded their plot, often to a young family seeking land to settle. Many of them got into debt, either with their family or the regional microcredit agency, the Amhara Credit and Savings Institute (ACSI). Sixty-year-old D. no longer works: "At Adi Shadey, we had a *kebele* house. They gave us a plot of land but no cash payment. We borrowed 15,000 ETB from the ACSI. We also borrowed from our family. The family living in Beta Anbessa [a village near Lalibela] gave us wood". The rate of indebtedness of the resettled population remained very high. The difficulty of paying back loans to microcredit agencies led a number of inhabitants to resell part or all of their land or house. In these cases, resettlement unleashed a tangible risk of "impoverishment" (Cernea 2003: 15).

Furthermore, the geography of Lalibela has changed greatly since the start of resettlement in 2009. On top of lands attributed to reinstalled inhabitants, new peripheral neighbourhoods have been developed in line with the urban master plan and through land distribution. If these outskirts were enhanced through improved urban services such as water and electricity, the development of motorised transport networks (*bajaj*, collective taxis), and improved public facilities (schools, health centres), downtown Lalibela remains associated with the churches and the market, especially by those inhabitants displaced from the churches' compound. Almost all of the women who worked as small vendors in the market or from their homes had lost their source of income. In the resettlement area, commercial activity was concentrated along the asphalted road, behind which almost all of the activity was residential. As has also been observed in the peripheral neighbourhoods of Addis Ababa, the women relegated to the periphery were forced to put a stop to their professional activities, leading them to focus on domestic work (Planel and Bridonneau, 2017). This was partly due to transportation problems but also the fact that in the central neighbourhoods residential buildings and small trade were easily mixed together.

Whether they were resettled in Kurakur or whether they arrived there because the rents were cheap or because they had a chance to purchase property, the resettlement area was never their first choice – they reside in the neighbourhood as a result of a largely constrained displacement from either central neighbourhoods or the surrounding countryside. The story of M., 37 years old, with four children, reveals the limited possibilities of resettled persons: "We built this house with my ex-husband. The plot was then divided after our divorce. We cut the house in two". A wall separates the tiny house in two and a fence separates the plot in two so that husband and wife, now divorced, each live on their half of an 80-square-metre plot.

The deconstruction of social life through resettlement, and its impossible reconstruction, is anchored in several spatial dimensions of the resettlement area. First of all is the materiality of space and the "compound" effect. Unlike the old neighbourhoods of Lalibela whose plots seem to have no defined boundaries, with houses opening onto the street and no walls, the resettlement zone, like every other recent urban form in a rural or proto-urban area in Ethiopia, is characterised by a rectilinear plot plan. As soon as a property owner has the

Fasil Giorghis and D. Gérard. 2007. *The city and its architectural heritage Addis Ababa 1886–1941*. Addis Ababa: Shama Books.

Gebre, H.A. 2014. "The impact of urban redevelopment-induced relocation on relocatees' livelihood asset and activity in Addis Ababa: the case of people relocated Arat Kilo area." *Asian Journal of Humanities and Social Studies* 2 (1): 43–50.

Gebre Yntiso. 2008. "Urban development and displacement in Addis Ababa: the impact of resettlement projects on low-income households." *Eastern African Social Science Review*, 24 (2): 53–77.

Goodfellow, T. 2017. "Urban fortunes and skeleton cityscapes: real estate and late urbanization in Kigali and Addis Ababa." *International Journal of Urban and Regional Research*, 41 (5): 786–803.

Kloosterboer, M.H. 2019. "*The 'new' Addis Ababa: shantytown or global city? An assessment of large-scale inner-city renewal, redevelopment and displacement for the construction of a 'new' Addis Ababa*". PhD diss., University of Glasgow.

Labzaé, M. 2019. "*La terre est au gouvernement: droits fonciers, encadrement bureaucratique et conflictualité politique dans deux périphéries éthiopiennes*". PhD diss., Université Paris 1.

Lefort, R. 2010. "Powers – mengist – and peasants in rural Ethiopia: the post-2005 interlude." *The Journal of Modern African Studies* 48 (3): 435–460.

Mains, D. 2012a. "Blackouts and progress: privatization, infrastructure, and a developmentalist state in Jimma, Ethiopia." *Cultural Anthropology* 27 (1): 3–27.

Mains, D. 2012b. *Hope is cut: youth, unemployment, and the future in urban Ethiopia*. Philadelphia: Temple University Press.

Mains D., and E. Kinfu. 2017. "Governing three-wheeled motorcycle taxis in urban Ethiopia: states, markets, and moral discourses of infrastructure." *American Ethnologist* 44 (2): 263–274.

Pankhurst, A. 1992. *Resettlement and famine in Ethiopia: the villagers' experience*. Manchester: Manchester University Press.

Pankhurst, A. 2009. Revisiting resettlement under two regimes in Ethiopia – the 2000s programme reviewed in the light of the 1980s experience. In *Moving People in Ethiopia-development, displacement & the state*, edited by A. Pankhurst and F. Piguet, 138–179. Woodbridge: James Currey.

Pankhurst, A., and F. Piguet, eds. 2009. *Moving people in Ethiopia –development, displacement & the state*. Woodbridge: James Currey.

Planel, S., and M. Bridonneau. 2017. "(Re)making politics in a new urban Ethiopia: an empirical reading of the right to the city in Addis Ababa's condominiums." *Journal of Eastern African Studies*, 11 (1): 24–45.

Rode, P., B. Terrefe, and N.F. Cruz. 2020. "Cities and the governance of transport infrastructure interfaces: Ethiopia's new rail systems." *Transport Policy* 91: 76–94.

Rogers, S., and B. Wilmsen. 2019. "Towards a critical geography of resettlement." *Progress in Human Geography*, 44 (2): 256–275.

Spire, A., Bridonneau, M., and Philifert, P. 2017. "Droit à la ville et replacement dans les contextes autoritaires d'Addis-Abeba (Éthiopie) et de Lomé (Togo)." *Métropoles* 21.

Terrefe, B. 2020. "Urban layers of political rupture: the 'new' politics of Addis Ababa's megaprojects." *Journal of Eastern African Studies*, 14 (3): 375–395.

Weldeghebrael, E. H. 2020. "The framing of inner-city slum redevelopment by an aspiring developmental state: The case of Addis Ababa, Ethiopia". *Cities*. https://doi.org/10.1016/j.cities.2020.102807

World Bank. 2001. *Operational Policy 4.12. – Involuntary Resettlement*. Washington: World Bank.

World Bank. 2009. *Project Appraisal Document on a Proposed Credit in the Amount of SDR 23.6 Million to the Federal Democratic Republic of Ethiopia for an Ethiopia Sustainable Tourism Development Project.* Washington: World Bank.

Wub Consult. 2011. *Resettlement Action Plan for Lalibela Town – Ethiopian Sustainable Tourism Development Project.* Addis Ababa: Wub Consult.

PART 4

Outlook

involved the establishment of temporary relocation areas in order to de-densify informal settlements. This resonates with the pre-COVID-19 cases of urban displacement presented through narratives of lived experiences in this book. With the continued urgency for these parameters to be met, the conclusion to this chapter provides pointers for future research.

Home and Un-homing in the Poorly Mediated Tension Between Economies, Cities, and Housing

Cities are sites of continual change. The introduction to this book refers to "rapid and fundamental urban transformation" and points to processes of destruction and production or creation within this (Beier et al., in this book). McFarlane (2011: 652) emphasises a political dimension in this dialectic when speaking of a "dis-assembly and reassembly through unequal relations of power and resource". Cities continually adjust to different forms and intensities of productivity and exchange, commodification and accumulation, governed by powerful actors and politically defined parameters, which may be more or less transparent, and which in turn may be resisted and contested (McFarlane, 2011; Bogaert, 2018 citing Massey, 2010).

Cities express a grounded and spatial dimension of the contemporary political economy set out above. In cities of the global South, and depending on their histories also regions of the global North, the "unequal relations of power and resources" (McFarlane, 2011:652) are mapped onto historical dispossession (Potts, 2020). Few states have mediated this inequality effectively. In the new millennium, urban governance, in which actors beyond the state exert considerable influence in their own interest, allows the urban economy to continually relegate the majority of the urban population to spatial and economic margins (Brenner, 2004; Devas, 2004). In these margins, dwelling is modest and often insecure, with uncertainty and threats of disruption shaping everyday life. Livelihoods are meagre, profits are low, and many enterprises are survivalist, only weakly tied into capitalism's perpetual pursuit of growth and therefore of little interest to it. In contrast, powerful actors in cities embed what they deem suitable localities of varying scale into wider national, international (or cross-national), and global economic networks, flows, and ambitions, committing urban space to their expanding pursuits. The rise of financial actors and the associated process of profit making through financial flows to drive growth in the finance sector is captured in the term financialisation (Aalbers, 2008).

Capitalist pursuits and their interests in particular urban locations may result in rapid change in housing systems, as Fernandez and Aalbers (2016) show. These authors reveal a growing trend for housing to be at the centre of the financialisation process and therefore "central to the real-world political economy" (Fernandez and Aalbers, 2016:83). Housing policies, both in the global North and where they exist in the global South, aim to facilitate, or are tied into quests for profit extraction and absorption of excess capital. The construction industry, urban land and its clearance for profitable development, and debt-dependent homeownership models play a key role in this dynamic (Fernandez and Aalbers, 2016; Bogaert, 2018; Rolnik, 2019; Sengupta, 2019). Therefore, a common theme in the chapters of this book is that urban resettlement emanating from housing policy implementation results in displacement from areas of economic potential to peripheral locations and places new economic burdens on the relocated households. In response to or anticipation of resistance from those affected by relocation, citizen buy-in for such policies may be achieved through forms of governmentality, which manipulate individual and collective subjectivities (Bogaert, 2018; Hernández Bertone, de la Vega, and Ciuffolini, in this book).

Against this charged backdrop, cities are host to the most intimate aspects of human life, which are lived out in what is commonly called housing. Housing refers to the physical dwelling units, their production, and their physical arrangement in urban space. Deficits and inadequacies, cost, production processes, financing, and tenure, as well as questions of land that housing occupies, are typically subjects of housing policies. A qualified right to adequate housing enshrined through constitutional provisions or through ratification of international law to which I return below, underpins housing policy in most countries and obliges respective governments to use their available resources towards its progressive realisation. Housing takes up the largest portion of urban space in cities, even where the majority of the housing units are makeshift, sub-standard in size, and/or stacked into tenements or apartment buildings. In an effort to push back against neoliberal directives for cities to facilitate and maximise growth in the urban economy, the United Nations (UN), through the New Urban Agenda adopted in 2016, promotes the realisation of the universal right to adequate housing as part of a city's "social function" (Habitat III, 2016, para 13). The New Urban Agenda also promotes "sustainable urban development programmes with housing and people's needs at the centre" (Habitat III, 2016, para 112).

For people's needs to be taken seriously, the physical shell of housing has to fulfil complex roles of dwelling and home. Beier et al. (in this book) introduce the subjective nature of dwelling by spelling out material or physical, economic, social, and emotional functions that it needs to perform. Dwelling is a highly philosophised concept. Influential though controversial 20th-century German philosopher Martin Heidegger's translators chose this term for the German verb "wohnen", which Heidegger (1954/1971) found inseparable from the continual activity of building. Linguistically Heidegger (1954/1971) explains roots of the term "neighbour" as someone building nearby and understands building of one's dwelling as central to human being. Heidegger (1954/1971) connects "wohnen" with "gewohnt", which means familiar or habitual. This suggests that the verb "inhabit" (which shares roots with "habitual") may have equally applied in the translation. Translators of French philosopher and sociologist Henri Lefebvre (1968/1996) chose the term "inhabit" for Lefebvre's emphasis of occupants' creative involvement in housing. Lefebvre drew on Heidegger, but for Lefebvre the town or city more than the home "expressed and symbolised a person's being and consciousness" (Kofman and Lebas, 1996:7–8). In more recent conceptions, the term not hold in court, where evidence was presented to the contrary (CLP, 2020; Times Live, 2020). In some cases, the informal settlement communities had secured orders against the state in response to pre-COVID-19 eviction attempts (CLP, 2020). Informal settlement demolitions and evictions took place in Durban, Cape Town, East London, and Johannesburg, the eviction scenario followed by court condemnation repeating itself in different municipal administrations (New Frame, 2020; Phillips, 2020; Xolo, 2020). Households resorting to new occupation of land during the officially declared state of disaster cited unhindered evictions by private landlords, these resulting in their ejection from the private rental market. Human rights organisations responded with calls for a more appropriate interpretation of the lockdown regulations, namely one that prohibited eviction from any residential dwelling, even if erected without authorisation during the state of disaster (CLP, 2020; SERI, 2020a, 2020b).

The second state initiative of un-homing in South Africa arose out of a simplified assumption that unit density in informal settlements correlates with an increased spread of COVID-19. High level advisors of the Minister of Human Settlements had recommended an emergency undertaking to de-densify informal settlements through the rapid establishment of temporary relocation areas for which budgets were to be repurposed (DHS, 2020a). Experts and NGOs, which the Ministry and national Department of Human Settlements involved in a new online COVID-19 Sector Engagement Platform, warned that this costly approach would remove vulnerable households from their social networks. They further pointed to far more life-threatening consequences of food insecurity in informal settlements resulting from the lockdown measures and recommended alternative *in situ* interventions (Afesis Corplan et al., 2020; Huchzermeyer, 2020; Visagie et al. 2020). The discussion over urban density and the pandemic received extensive coverage in the media (Daily Maverkick, 2020; Clark, 2020).

The COVID-19-and-density debate has not been conclusive. Kang et al. (2020) review various studies conducted in the global North, which found no relation between urban density and COVID-19. For the African continent, such a correlation has also not been established (Cullinan, 2020). In September 2020, medical scientists in South Africa reassessed early assumptions that the disease would result in high death rates in tightly populated, low-income areas such as informal settlements (Harding, 2020). New hypotheses emerged suggesting that high population densities in such areas may instead have provided protection (Harding, 2020). However, the high death rates in informal settlements in India and Brazil, the January 2021 surge in cases across Africa, and the emergence of a more rapidly spreading strain of the virus in South Africa in December 2020 added complexity to any attempt to provide explanations and predictions (Harding, 2020; Reuters, 2020).

Reasons why the South African Ministry of Human Settlements, Water, and Sanitation dismissed expert and NGO objections and proceeded with its contested de-densification plan (interchangeably referring to it as decongestion, decanting, and also re-blocking) has not been fully revealed. As implementation unfolded, the Ministry performed regular public relations events and broadcasted messages of a caring state (MHSWS 2020). However, suspicions of corruption led to an Auditor General probe, which found the procurement and implementation process lacking on many fronts (Daniel, 2020; PMG, 2020). This was amidst damming corruption findings on the procurement of COVID-19 personal protective equipment (Businesstech, 2020). In April 2020, the initial de-densification plan involved a total of 7,017 temporary housing units across the country (DHS, 2020b). A month later, the figure planned for the Gauteng Province alone had risen to over 22,000 units, targeting 15 of the province's 775 informal settlements (Gauteng Province Human Settlements, 2020:2). At a fixed price of R64,000 per unit, the cost of this endeavour justified the Auditor General's probe (PMG, 2020).

Deliberate Un-homing During the Pandemic: Temporary Relocation and Home Intrusion

Un-homing has taken complex forms under the COVID-19 lockdown measures. Evictions, even if not carried out illegally as in the case of South Africa, remain a future reality under moratoria, therefore reducing a sense of security and home, violating the temporal facet of home, and inhibiting home-making activities. Removals to temporary relocation areas, as carried out in South Africa, involve literal uprooting from a geographical location and from social relations, and suspension in time, captured in the British term "decanting" (Ferreri, 2020), and associated with the experience of "displacement anxiety" (Watt, 2018). Home-making in temporary relocation areas is limited by controls, restrictions and uncertainty and is overshadowed by the nullification of previous home-making. Added to this is the stress of multiple moves (Watt, 2018; Ferreri, 2020).

The unsuitability of temporary relocation as a COVID-19 response is evident from the poor track record of implementation of this policy tool. Terms such as "decanting area" in the case of Kenyan informal settlement redevelopment (Huchzermeyer, 2011), "holding camps" in the case of the Zimbabwean government's "handling of informality" (Kamete, 2017:78) or "transit camps" (or more recently "temporary relocation areas" or TRAs) in South Africa display a utilitarian approach that has no basis in human need. Kamete (2017:84) refers to "warehousing", when reporting of overcrowding, poor living conditions, surveillance, repression, and curtailment of rights, in addition to the uncertainty about bureaucratic decisions over the future of those residing in Zimbabwe's temporary relocation areas. Kamete (2017) therefore frames these as "spaces of exception". Similarly, Dupont and Gowda (in this book) point to poor conditions, legal precariousness, uncertainty, and surveillance that shape everyday life in a transit camp in Delhi, also invoking the notion of a state of exception. Surveillance and control, as well as seemingly indefinite occupation as the promised permanent housing retreats from the horizon of hope, are recurring themes in the literature on Cape Town's temporary relocation areas (Chance, 2015; Levenson, 2017). As Cirolia (2014) shows, this is an inadequately conceived and executed component of South African housing policy.

New Frame. 2020. "Brutal evictions worsen South Africa's urban crisis. Editorial." *New Frame*, 10 July, 2020. Accessed 10 July, 2020. https://www.newframe.com/brutal-evictions-worsen-south-africas-urban-crisis/

Nzeadibe, C., Ejike-Alieji, A., Mbaegbu, C., Onyishi, C., Ezeibe, C., Ajaero, C., Mbah, P., and Onyebueke, V. 2020. "Why African cities should have engaged non-state actors in the fight against COVID-19." *The Conversation*, 29 October, 2020. Accessed 5 November, 2020. https://theconversation.com/why-african-cities-should-have-engaged-non-state-actors-in-the-fight-against-covid-19-147926

OHCHR. 1991, *ESCR General Comment No. 4: The Right to Adequate Housing*. Geneva: Office of the High Commissioner for Human Rights.

OHCHR. 1997. *ESCR General Comment No. 7: The Right to Adequate Housing (Art. 11.1.): Forced Evictions*. Geneva: Office of the High Commissioner for Human Rights.

Hickey, S., and Mitlin, D. (eds.) 2009. *Rights-Based Approaches to Development: Exploring the Potentials and Pitfalls*. Sterling VA: Kumarian Press.

Pettersson, H., Manley, B., and Hernandez, S. 2021. "Tracking coronavirus' global spread." *CNN Health*, Last updated January 17, 2021. Accessed 17 January, 2021. https://edition.cnn.com/interactive/2020/health/coronavirus-maps-and-cases/

Phillips, J. 2020. "Redefining the meaning of 'home' could help solve South Africa's unlawful eviction crisis." *Daily Maverick*, 3 September, 2020.

Phillips, T., Costa. W., and Nuño, A. 2020. "'Just unimaginable': Latin America's Covid crisis lurches from bad to worse." *The Guardian*, 10 December, 2020. Accessed 17 January, 2021. https://www.theguardian.com/world/2020/dec/10/latin-america-covid-crisis-heads-from-bad-to-worse

PMG. 2020. *Department of Human Settlements on Temporary Residential Areas: follow-up meeting with Minister*. Parliamentary Monitoring Group (PMG), Meeting Report, 6 October, 2020.

Potts, D. 2020. *Broken Cities: Inside the Housing Crisis*. London: Zed Books.

Rapoport, A. 1990. "Systems of activities and systems of settings." In *Domestic Architecture and the Use of Space*, edited by S. Kent, 9–20. Cambridge: Cambridge University Press.

Reuters. 2020. "South Africa identifies new coronavirus strain causing surge in cases." *Reuters*, 18 December, 2020. Accessed 17 January, 2021. https://www.reuters.com/article/us-health-coronavirus-safrica/south-africa-identifies-new-coronavirus-strain-causing-surge-in-cases-idUSKBN28S2HH

Reuters. 2021. "China imposes lockdown as Covid-19 cases surge." *Business Day*, 15 January, 2021. Accessed 17 January, 2021. https://www.businesslive.co.za/bd/world/asia/2021-01-15-china-imposes-lockdown-as-covid-19-cases-surge/

Rolnik, R. 2019. *Urban Warfare: Housing under the Empire of Finance*. London: Verso.

Sengupta, U. 2019. "The State-led housing development in Brazil and India: A machinery for enabling strategy?" *International Journal of Housing Policy* 19 (4): 509–535.

SERI. 2020a. *Protecting Housing and Home in South Africa*. Information Sheet. Socio-Economic Rights Institute of South Africa, Johannesburg. Accessed 6 November, 2020. http://seri-sa.org/images/SERI_Protecting_housing_and_home_in_SA_FINAL.pdf

SERI. 2020b. *SERI challenges Sisulu to Stop Demolitions of Homes Across the Country*. Press release. Socio-Economic Rights Institute of South Africa, Johannseburg. Accessed 6 November, 2020. http://seri-sa.org/images/SERI_Press_statement_Sisulu_response_Final.pdf

Sharif, M., and Rajagopal, B. 2020. "Opinion: Housing must be at the heart of the COVID-19 response and recovery." *Devex*, 30 October, 2020. Accessed 6 November, 2020. https://www.devex.com/news/opinion-housing-must-be-at-the-heart-of-the-covid-19-response-and-recovery-98448

Tsunga, A., Mazarura, T., and Heywood, M. 2021. "Covid-19 second wave ravages southern Africa." *Daily Maverick*, 10 January, 2020. Accessed 10 January, 2020. https://

www.dailymaverick.co.za/article/2021-01-10-covid-19-second-wave-ravages-southern-africa/

UN. 1976a. *International Covenant on Civil and Political Rights*. New York: UN.

UN. 1976b. *International Covenant on Economic, Social and Cultural Rights*. New York: UN.

UN. 2020a. *COVID-19 Guidance Note: Prohibition on Evictions*. Special Rapporteur on the Right to Adequate Housing, Leilani Farha, 8 April, 2020. New York: UN Human Rights Special Rapporteurs.

UN. 2020b. *COVID-19 Guidance Note: Protecting Renters and Mortgage Payers*. Special Rapporteur on the Right to Adequate Housing, Leilani Farha, 28 April, 2020. New York: UN Human Rights Special Rapporteurs.

UN. 2020c. *COVID-19 Guidance Note: Protecting Residents of Informal Settlements*. Special Rapporteur on the Right to Adequate Housing, Leilani Farha, 28 April, 2020. New York: UN Human Rights Special Rapporteurs.

Vaughan, A. 2020. "Coronavirus: second wave hits Asia as global cases continue to soar." *NewScientist*, 27 July, 2020. Accessed 17 January, 2021. https://www.newscientist.com/article/2249982-coronavirus-second-wave-hits-asia-as-global-cases-continue-to-soar/

Visagie, J., Misselhorn, M., Scheba, A., and Turok, I. 2020. "Reconfiguring dense informal settlements is in the policy spotlight – and rightly so." *Daily Maverick*, 17 July, 2020. Accessed 18 July, 2020. https://www.dailymaverick.co.za/article/2020-07-17-reconfiguring-dense-informal-settlements-is-in-the-policy-spotlight-and-rightly-so/

Watt, P. 2018. "'This pain of moving, moving, moving:' Evictions, displacement and logics of expulsion in London." *L'Année sociologique* 68 (1): 67–100.

WHO. 2020. *Timeline of WHO's Response to COVID-19*. Geneva: World Health Organization. Accessed 3 November, 2020. https://www.who.int/news/item/29-06-2020-covidtimeline

Woodhall-Melnik, J., Hamilton-Wright, S., Daoud, N., Matheson, F., Dunn, J., and O'Campo, P. 2017. "Establishing stability: exploring the meaning of 'home' for women who have experienced intimate partner violence." *Journal of Housing and the Built Environment* 32: 253–268.

Xolo, N. 2020. "Merciless evictions continue in Durban." *New Frame*, 8 April, 2020. Accessed 8 April, 2020. https://www.newframe.com/merciless-evictions-continue-in-ethekwini/

Zuboff, S. 2019. *The Age of Surveillance Capitalism: The Fight for a Human Future at the New Frontier of Power*. New York: Public Affairs.

Taylor & Francis Group
an informa business
Taylor & Francis eBooks
www.taylorfrancis.com
A single destination for eBooks from Taylor & Francis with increased functionality and an improved user experience to meet the needs of our customers.
90,000+ eBooks of award-winning academic content in Humanities, Social Science, Science, Technology, Engineering, and Medical written by a global network of editors and authors.
TAYLOR & FRANCIS EBOOKS OFFERS:
A streamlined experience for our library customers
A single point of discovery for all of our eBook content
Improved search and discovery of content at both book and chapter level
REQUEST A FREE TRIAL
support@taylorfrancis.com
Routledge
Taylor & Francis Group
CRC Press
Taylor & Francis Group